D1580521

United We Serve

United We Serve

*National Service and the
Future of Citizenship*

E.J. DIONNE JR.
KAYLA MELTZER DROGOSZ
ROBERT E. LITAN

Editors

BROOKINGS INSTITUTION PRESS
Washington, D.C.

Copyright © 2003

THE BROOKINGS INSTITUTION

1775 Massachusetts Avenue, N.W., Washington, D.C. 20036
www.brookings.edu

All rights reserved

Library of Congress Cataloging-in-Publication data

United we serve : national service and the future of citizenship / E.J.
Dionne, Jr., Kayla Meltzer Drogosz, and Robert E. Litan, editors.
  p. cm.
Includes bibliographical references and index.
  ISBN 0-8157-1866-7 (cloth : alk. paper) —
  ISBN 0-8157-1865-9 (pbk. : alk. paper)
  1. National service—United States. I. Dionne, E. J. II. Drogosz,
Kayla Meltzer. III. Litan, Robert E., 1950–
  HD4870.U6U6 2003
  323.6´0973—dc21   2003007543

9 8 7 6 5 4 3 2 1

The paper used in this publication meets the minimum requirements of the
American National Standard for Information Sciences—Permanence
of Paper for Printed Library Materials: ANSI Z39.48-1992.

Typeset in Adobe Garamond

Composition by Cynthia Stock
Silver Spring, Maryland

Printed by R. R. Donnelley
Harrisonburg, Virginia

*We dedicate this book to members of our families
who served in the United States Armed Forces:*

James J. Boyle (Army)

Emile J. Cote (Army)

Eugene J. Dionne (Army)

Ulric A. Dionne (Army)

Francizek Bronislaw Drogosz syn Francizek i Amelia (Army)

Arthur C. Galipeau (Army)

David Litan (Army Air Corps)

Irving J. Meltzer ben Yosef v'Gitel (Army Air Corps)

Sidney H. Meltzer ben Yitzchak v'Delphine (Navy)

Lester H. Meltzer ben Yosef v'Celia (Army Air Corps)

Richard A. Morgan (Army)

Lucie-Anne Dionne Thomas (Navy)

Andrew Arnold Thomas (Navy)

Contents

PART TWO
POLITICS OF THE SERVICE DEBATE

PART THREE
UNIVERSAL SERVICE?

Foreword

NATIONAL SERVICE IS part of the credo of Brookings. The Institution is founded on the principle that independent, nonpartisan research can produce ideas that will serve the nation. It is therefore appropriate that E. J. Dionne and his colleagues would collaborate on this book. While it contains a diversity of views and resonates with an often vigorous debate, it lives up to its title: *United We Serve.* There is an overarching theme that America cannot fulfill its potential as a nation of service simply through the will of dedicated individuals. We also need policies—at all levels of government and in the private and not-for-profit sectors as well—that encourage service, strengthen the institutions that promote it, and bolster a sense of civic pride that generates civic energy.

National service is not a passing fad or a feel-good throwaway slogan for a politician's Fourth of July oration. As the book's subtitle, *National Service and the Future of Citizenship,* suggests, service is essential to democratic citizenship. Free societies do not prosper, and do not remain free, unless citizens voluntarily and enthusiastically devote themselves to advancing the common good, through public work and public achievement. Individual freedom is a project that depends on the vitality of that most American of concepts: community. Political freedom depends upon the right of citizens and groups to assert their interests, but to do so with a decent respect for the best interests of the republic as a whole, notably its prosperity and security (two subjects much on all our minds these days)

and also its covenant to protect the freedom of the individual and the pluralism of society. Freedom of all kinds, including economic freedom,
depends on mutual trust and accountability that are possible only when
individuals consciously regard it as part of their civic duty to think about
more than themselves. The impulse for service arises not only out of a
philanthropic instinct, though that is certainly part of it, but also out of
self-interest of the most enlightened kind.

The service movement has its roots in our founding documents. As
the introduction to this book notes, the founders of our nation pledged
not only service but also their lives, their fortunes, and their sacred honor.
They understood that no community can flourish as a walled city on a
hill. Paradoxically, service protects the city not by building walls but by
breaking them down. Civic life is dependent on small associations that
enable citizens to cultivate democratic virtues and develop avenues for
public participation. One reason that Alexis de Tocqueville's classic,
Democracy in America, has never gone out of fashion is that it captured
what makes our democracy tick and prosper.

In its latest form, the service movement took root in the 1980s, motivated by impulses from across the political spectrum. Conservatives critical of government understood that public tasks still needed doing and
emphasized the important role of the voluntary sector, while progressives
who respected government's role understood that democratic government
could succeed only when strong networks independent of the state enlist
citizens in public work.

United We Serve looks at the movement from several angles, ranging
from the practical to the philosophical; from the perspective of both government policy and community activism; from the standpoints of social
science and religion; as a unifying concept and as a controversial, even
polarizing idea. The book demonstrates that service is not necessarily a
cost-free goal or an anodyne notion. Nor is any one position the monop-
oly of either major political party. Senator John McCain, initially a skeptic of national service, now a supporter, won a wide following among the
young by urging them to aspire to things "beyond their own self-interest."
And far from being a partisan initiative, service learning, popular in public and private schools, has been linked with a heightened sense of civic
engagement and personal responsibility.

That is also why the editors have included the debate over compulsory service between Brookings's Robert Litan, the director of our Economic Studies program, and Bruce Chapman, a long-time foe of the draft, as well as Representative Charles Rangel's now famous *New York Times* op-ed article calling for a restoration of the draft, along with the powerful reaction it drew from former defense secretary Caspar Weinberger, former navy secretary John Lehman, and former army secretary Louis Caldera. The story of the development of a national service policy is well told by Harris Wofford, who headed the Corporation for National Service under President Clinton, and by President Bush's top lieutenants in the service cause, John Bridgeland, Stephen Goldsmith, and Leslie Lenkowsky. Senator John McCain, Will Marshall, and Marc Magee explore lines for future developments in the national government's approach to service.

No book on service at this stage in our history could ignore the impact of the September 11 attacks on the civic mood of the nation. Therefore these pages include reflections on that event from some of the nation's leading social scientists and civic thinkers. Robert Putnam, internationally known for his book on civic participation and the shortages thereof, *Bowling Alone*, argues in these pages that by the end of 2001, "Americans were more united, readier for collective sacrifice, and more attuned to public purpose than we have been for several decades."

But how long can such a mood last? Theda Skocpol, another leading scholar on civic participation, is skeptical that even this powerful event could "suddenly remake the institutional face of American civic democracy."

Whether the new patriotic impulses are mere ripples or a tide that will eventually ebb—or whether, as the editors and many of the authors assembled here hope, they reflect a capacious sense of national purpose—will depend, of course, on policy, on leadership, and on the responses of individual Americans. The service movement in all its manifestations—from those that preceded the birth of the nation to those that have been apparent since September 11—has been built on the individual decisions of millions of Americans who devoted all or a part of their lives to the commonweal. In that spirit, *United We Serve* includes testimony from men and women who served the nation in public capacities: Daniel Blumenthal in VISTA, Louis Caldera in the army, Charles Cobb in the civil rights movement, Robert Haas in the Peace Corps, Alan Khazei as the founder of City

Year—one of the nation's most celebrated service programs—and Brookings economist Alice Rivlin in the executive branch. Cobb's essay makes a powerful and much overlooked point: that the civil rights movement "is best understood as a movement of community organizing rather than one of protest." Service was linked to power as "civil rights organizing produced a politically literate network of people who challenged and changed the status quo." Yes, service is about change, and as Jane Eisner argues, it often leads—and should—to "a commitment to address the social problems that have created the need for service in the first place."

While the service impulse has many sources, from protest to patriotism, its roots are often religious, as the essays here by Jean Bethke Elshtain, Robert Wuthnow, and Steven Waldman make clear with eloquence—and careful research.

I am required by custom to remind readers that the views expressed in this book are those of the authors alone and should not be attributed to the trustees, officers, or employees of the Brookings Institution. But, to return to the point I made at the outset, I can qualify that boilerplate disclaimer in the case of this book. *United We Serve* is reflective not just of what Brookings stands for but of the way we go about our business on Massachusetts Avenue in the nation's capital. It is an outgrowth of the sense of community—and national service—with which the Institution is deeply imbued. The idea for the project arose from the interaction of several Brookings scholars who discovered each other's shared passion for the topic. E.J. had written about the service movement for nearly a decade and published *Community Works: The Revival of Civil Society in America,* about the importance of America's voluntary sector. Kayla Meltzer Drogosz came at the subject from her interest in the public obligations of religion, and first broached the idea of a larger project on national service. Bob Litan developed an interest in service during research on social cohesion in Israel, eventually published in *Sticking Together: The Israeli Experiment in Pluralism.*

Encouraged and aided by Brenda Szittya, the editor of the *Brookings Review,* the three edited an issue of the *Review* on national service, which grew into this book. As they worked, E.J., Kayla, and Bob discovered how many of their colleagues wanted to chip in. This volume thus includes Alice Rivlin's powerful essay on "recreational government bash-ing" and Paul Light's typically community-minded and hardheaded analysis of what makes voluntary organizations work. When he heard about the book, Steve Hess came to the editors with his warm and mov-ing open letter to his sons, penned some two decades ago, but as relevant now as it was then.

Our hope in publishing this book is that, like Steve's letter, many of the other essays offered here will have resonance and relevance for a long time to come since the idea that they have in common is both funda-mentally and enduringly American.

Strobe Talbott
President

Washington, D.C.
May 2003

Acknowledgments

THIS VOLUME WAS inspired by the millions of Americans who serve others. Its editors are especially mindful of the men and women in the armed forces and in the uniformed services at home who protect our country every day. And this book would not exist absent the work of the thousands of our fellow citizens who have built the service movement into one of the most vital forces in American public life.

United We Serve might thus be seen as a modest effort to be of service to the service movement. We have tried here to link theory and practice, current affairs and history, policy and politics, the scholarly and the practical—though we like to think these last two are not as much in conflict as many might think. The book's orientation toward service is plainly positive, but we have included critical perspectives here. No idea worthy of respect should be immune from criticism. No cause will prosper absent a constant reexamination of its methods, ideas, and purposes. Yet for all that, we are not at all cynical about service. On the contrary, this book makes no sense apart from our shared belief that a citizenry inspired by the call to public service is essential to the health of a democracy.

Most of the essays here were written expressly for this project. A few op-ed articles were printed first elsewhere. Several of these essays are substantial adaptations, revisions or extensions of lectures, articles, or other earlier work. In some cases, authors were kind enough to synthesize several pieces that had appeared earlier into new essays. At the end of these acknowledgments, we offer our thanks to the publications and institutions that allowed our reprinting, revising, and extending.

Our first debt is most obvious: to the men and women who worked so hard to produce the essays here. Each of them lives their commitment to service through pen and practice, and all responded with enthusiasm to the idea of this collection.

As editor of the *Brookings Review*, Brenda Szittya encouraged us to guest edit the Fall 2002 issue of the magazine, which got this project off the ground and provided the first home for a large number of these essays. She is a wise and gifted editor who demonstrates daily that enthusiasm, realism, and a sense of humor are complementary virtues.

Brookings president Strobe Talbott has consistently encouraged our explorations. He poured through the draft of this manuscript, and his advice greatly improved the text. We thank him also for his generous foreword. But most of all, we thank him for embodying the spirit of public service not only in what he says but also in what he does.

Carol Graham, director of the Governance Studies program, has brought to the study of political economy extraordinary insights about the relationship between human happiness and material prosperity. Happiness encourages productivity: it is a lesson she applies constantly in her exceptional generosity to her colleagues. It is a generosity of the intellect and also of the spirit. The sum of human happiness inside Brookings—we could prove this with elaborate mathematical models if we had to—is so much higher because of Carol.

The same could be said of Christina Counselman, a joyful, warm, and brilliant presence. Her magic includes making problems disappear. Her intelligence and focus keep problems from appearing in the first place. And her laughter makes the problems that do turn up seem, somehow, not so important. This book could not have happened without her.

Sandip Sukhtankar was immensely thoughtful and resourceful in drawing together facts and arguments in the debate over compulsory service. We are deeply grateful.

Carol's predecessors, Tom Mann and Paul Light, are model leaders, colleagues, and friends. Our heartfelt thanks also go to Susan Stewart and Elizabeth McAlpine.

We are also grateful for the assistance that the Pew Forum on Religion and Public Life provided us so that the sixth section of the book, "Serving God and Country," could see the light of day. We are particularly indebted to Missy Daniel who helped us edit two of the chapters. With her depth of experience and breadth of knowledge—particularly in the area of religion and its public purposes—she helped fit these chapters into the particular (and compressed) framework of this book, and did so with elegance.

The Brookings Institution Press has been enthusiastic from beginning to end. Bob Faherty, vice president and director of the press, is one of the great publishers to work with because he is a model of service—to the community and to those with whom he works. Janet Walker and Starr Belsky are superb copy editors, and they sped this book to publication by their generous willingness to edit articles as they came in and to accommodate our last-minute additions. Susan Woollen is as great a designer as she is a human being. She took particular care in helping us develop our cover, and Susan, along with her artists Maria Sese Paul and Christopher Paul of Sese-Paul Design, did magnificent work.

Dionne and Litan offer special thanks here to Kayla Drogosz for finding the inspiration for the cover and title through her interest in popular artistic expressions of hope and civic spiritedness. They also thank Kayla for doing so much of the heavy lifting that enhanced the book's contribution to scholarship about citizenship.

Becky Clark of Brookings Press is a marvel at getting books into the right hands, and Nicole Pagano works with such intelligence and energy on behalf of all Brookings authors. Renuka Deonarain and Puja Telikicherla were extremely helpful with the permissions process. Emily Horne provided valuable assistance during the final stages of assembling the manuscript.

We would also like to thank Marshall Wittman, Eli Segal, Harris Wofford, Leslie Lenkowsky, Steve Goldsmith, Alan Khazei, Michael Brown, Vanessa Kirsch, Chuck Supple, Will Marshall, Robert Sherman, Steve Macedo, William Galston, and William Schambra for a superb education on service and civic engagement. Thanks also to Bob Putnam and all the participants in the Saguaro Seminar at Harvard University.

Drogosz wishes to offer special thanks to Steven Ascheim, Margaret Bates, Paul Mendes-Flohr, Kenneth Jeruchim, Ira Katznelson, Paul and Selma Klingenstein, Eugene Lewis, Mike Michaelson, Elliot L. H. Ratzman, George Steiner, Fred Strobel, Michael Walzer, Ken Weinstein, Cornel West, and above all her mother, Gloria Gitel Meltzer Drogosz, who continues to inspire her in countless ways.

We could burden an overly long list with elaborate thanks to our families. Our service to our readers—and to our families—will be to skip that part, except to say: we are very blessed.

For permission to reprint, expand upon, or revise pieces that were published previously, we thank the following organizations and individuals:

Thanks to Harold Meyerson, editor-at-large of the *American Prospect,* for arranging permission to expand Robert Putnam's article "Bowling Together," from vol. 13, no. 3, published February 11, 2002.

Theda Skocpol draws heavily on an article previously published in the September 2002 issue of *PS: Political Science & Politics*, reprinted with the permission of Cambridge University Press. And thanks to Joe Heller, editorial cartoonist, for the illustration included in Theda's chapter.

Charles Moskos's chapter is adapted from the Spring 2002 issue of the *Public Interest* and the Summer 2001 edition of *Parameters.* Adam Wolfson, editor of the *Public Interest,* graciously helped us with permissions.

Senator McCain's article draws from work previously published in the *Responsive Community,* vol. 12, issue 2, Spring 2002, and the *Washington Monthly,* October 2001. Thanks to Washington Monthly Publishing and to Amitai Etzioni, editor of the *Responsive Community* and founder of the Communitarian Network. We also thank Amitai for his years of dedication to the cause of community.

Mark Shields's column ran in the *Washington Post* on October 15, 2002. It is reprinted here by permission of the author and Creators Syndicate. Thanks to them, and also to the *New York Times* for allowing us to include Representative Charles Rangel's op-ed from December 31, 2002. Thanks to Dow Jones and Company—and to Paul Gigot and William McGurn of the *Wall Street Journal* for helping expedite matters—for allowing us to reprint Caspar Weinberger's commentary, which appeared January 10, 2003. Thanks to the *Washington Post* for allowing us to reprint

John Lehman's article, which ran January 26, 2003. We are also grateful that Messrs. Rangel, Weinberger, and Lehman all agreed to allow us to reprint their pieces, and did so on very short notice.

Our gratitude to the Times Mirror Company and the *Los Angeles Times* for permission to adapt the op-ed by Louis Caldera published January 13, 2003. This provided a powerful supplement to an article he had already written for us.

Alice Rivlin's essay is adapted from her remarks on receiving the Elliot Richardson Prize on May 28, 2002. Jean Bethke Elshtain's contribution draws from her chapter in Diane Ravitch and Joseph P. Viteritti's *Making Good Citizens*, published by Yale University Press in 2001—we thank the press for its permission—and also from remarks she made on September 10, 2002, at the First Presbyterian Church of New York City. The event, "Remembering September 11," was cosponsored by the church, Auburn Theological Seminary, and the Pew Forum on Religion and Public Life.

We would also like to thank Ohio University student Bryan Randolph for sharing his thoughts on his post–September 11 volunteering experience, and Mason Anderson, staff writer for the American Red Cross, for her interview and for helping us tell his story.

Robert Wuthnow's chapter draws from a much longer article published by the Brookings Institution Press in the collection *Civic Engagement in American Democracy*, edited by Theda Skocpol and Morris Fiorina.

Thanks, finally, to Dr. Robert Avery, chair of the Department of Communications at the University of Utah, for granting permission to reprint an adaptation of Michael Schudson's 2001 B. Aubrey Fisher Memorial Lecture delivered at the University of Utah.

E.J. DIONNE JR.
KAYLA MELTZER DROGOSZ
ROBERT E. LITAN

1

United We Serve?
The Promise of National Service

E.J. DIONNE JR. AND
KAYLA MELTZER DROGOSZ

AMERICANS ARE ALWAYS for national service—except when we are not. Our public rhetoric has always laid heavy stress on the obligations of citizenship. "With rights come responsibilities." It is a statement that rolls off the tongues of politicians. "Ask not what your country can do for you. Ask what you can do for your country." John F. Kennedy's words are so embedded in our civic catechism that the mere mention of the word *service* automatically calls them forth. On Veterans Day and Memorial Day, we rightly extol the valor of those "without whose sacrifices we would not enjoy our freedom." Bill Clinton praised the idea of service. George W. Bush now does the same. It is one of the few issues on which our last two presidents agree.

Yet how firm is our belief in service? There is no prospect anytime soon that we will return to a military draft. The number of politicians who support compulsory national service—the case for it is made powerfully here by Robert Litan—is small. Representative Charles Rangel, in his important and now famous op-ed article reprinted in these pages, succeeded in creating the most serious debate on renewing the draft since its repeal in 1973. But most of the American military remains skeptical of a renewal of the draft, a view reflected here by former defense secretary Caspar Weinberger.

It is true that the service idea took an important new institutional form when President Clinton succeeded in pushing his AmeriCorps program through Congress. Clinton talks of it to this day (and in these pages) as one of his proudest achievements. But it is worth remembering that at the time and for years afterward, there were many who denounced the idea as "paid volunteerism."[1] Former representative Dick Armey, the outspoken Texas Republican who became one of AmeriCorps' leading critics, described it as "a welfare program for aspiring yuppies" that would displace "private charity with government-managed, well-paid social activism, based on the elitist assumption that community service is not now taking place."[2]

And many Americans doubt the basic premise that they or their fellow citizens actually "owe" anything to a country whose main business they see as preserving individual liberty, personal as well as economic. In a free society, liberty is the right of all, worthy and unworthy alike.

Finally, Americans differ widely over which kinds of national service are genuinely valuable. Many who honor military service are skeptical of voluntarism that might look like, in Armey's terms, "social activism." Supporters of work among the poor are often dubious of military service. Most Americans honor both forms of devotion to country, and we have included here moving testimonials to the varieties of civic dedication. But in our public arguments, the skeptical voices are often the loudest.

Our divisions about the meaning of service are rooted deeply in our history. At the founding of our nation, liberal and civic republican ideas jostled for dominance. The liberals—they might now be called libertarians—viewed personal freedom as the heart of the American experiment. The civic republicans valued freedom, too, but they stressed that self-rule demanded a great deal from citizens. The liberals stressed rights. The civic republicans stressed obligations to a common good and, as the philosopher Michael Sandel has put it, "a concern for the whole, a moral bond with the community whose fate is at stake."[3] In our time, the clash between these older traditions lives on in the intellectual wars between libertarians and communitarians. When it comes to national service, the libertarians lean toward skepticism, the communitarians toward a warm embrace.

Yes, we have changed since September 11, 2001. Respect for service soared as the nation forged a new and stronger sense of solidarity in the face of deadly enemies. What has been said so often still bears repeating: our view of heroes underwent a remarkable—and sudden—change. The new heroes are public servants—police, firefighters, rescue workers, postal workers whose lives were threatened, our men and women in uniform—not the CEOs, high-tech wizards, rock stars, or sports figures who dominated the culture of the 1990s. At a time when citizens focus on urgent national needs, those who serve their country naturally rise in public esteem. In the face of an attack that imperiled rich and poor, powerful and powerless alike, it was natural that, in Sandel's words, "a concern for the whole" and "a moral bond with the community whose fate is at stake" became more than abstract concepts. Robert Putnam, a true pioneer in research on civic engagement, captures the post–September 11 moment in his essay here. He writes that because of the attacks on the World Trade Center and the Pentagon—and the courage shown by those on the plane that went down over Pennsylvania—"we have a more capacious sense of 'we' than we have had in the adult experience of most Americans now alive."

"The images of shared suffering that followed the terrorist attacks on New York and Washington," Putnam argues, "suggested a powerful idea of cross-class, cross-ethnic solidarity. Americans also confronted a clear foreign enemy, an experience that both drew us closer to one another and provided an obvious rationale for public action."

Accordingly, the politics of national service were also transformed. Even before the attacks of September 11, President Bush had signaled a warmer view of service than many in his party. In choosing two Republican supporters of the idea—former mayor Steve Goldsmith of Indianapolis and Leslie Lenkowsky—to head his administration's service effort, Bush made clear he intended to take it seriously. After September 11, service became a stronger theme in the president's rhetoric. In his 2002 State of the Union message, he called on Americans to give two years of service to the nation over their lifetimes and announced the creation of the USA Freedom Corps. It was a patriotic, post–September 11 gloss on the old Clinton ideas—and the ideas of John Kennedy, Lyndon Johnson, and his father, the first President Bush, who offered the nation a thousand points of light.

There is also a new acknowledgment across the political divide that government support for volunteers can provide essential help for valuable institutions that we too often take for granted. It is easy for politicians to talk about the urgency of strengthening "civil society." But through AmeriCorps and other programs, the government has found a practical (and not particularly costly) way to make the talk real. Paradoxically, as Steven Waldman points out here, AmeriCorps, a Democratic initiative, fit neatly with the Republicans' emphasis on faith-based programs. Democrats accepted the need to strengthen programs outside of government; Republicans accepted that voluntary programs could use government's help. This interplay between government and independent communal action may be especially important in the United States where intricate links have always existed—long before the term *faith-based organizations* was invented—between the religious and civic spheres. By way of underscoring this vital American difference—and bowing to Tocqueville, as all books of this sort must—we have included a separate section on religion and service, with essays by Waldman, Jean Bethke Elshtain, and Robert Wuthnow, who rank among America's most important explorers of the terrain where religion and public life meet.

That national service has become a bipartisan goal is an important achievement. It is reflected in the White House's Citizen Service Act and in bills cosponsored by, among others, Senators John McCain and Evan Bayh, described well in these pages by McCain himself, and also by Will Marshall and Marc Magee. These legislative ideas mirrored the spirit of the moment. As Magee and Steven Nider of the Progressive Policy Institute have reported, in the first nine months after September 11, applications for AmeriCorps jumped 50 percent, those for the Peace Corps doubled, and those for Teach for America tripled.[4] Yes, a difficult private economy certainly pushed more young Americans toward such public endeavors. Nonetheless, their choices point to the continued power of the service idea.

But what is the connection between the ideas of service and citizenship?

Citizenship and Service

Citizenship cannot be reduced to service. And the good works of faith communities, the private sector, or "communities of character," as the president has called them, cannot replace the responsibilities of government. Service can become a form of cheap grace, a generalized call on citizens to do kind things as an alternative to a genuine summons for national sacrifice or a fair apportionment of burdens among the more and less powerful, the more and less wealthy. But when service is seen as a bridge to genuine political and civic responsibility, it can strengthen democratic government and foster the republican virtues.

Lenkowsky made this connection when he urged attendees at a Corporation for National and Community Service conference to turn "civic outrage into civic engagement" by increasing the reach and effectiveness of volunteer programs.[5] No one can dispute visionaries like Harris Wofford and Alan Khazei, who have shown how AmeriCorps, VISTA, the Senior Corps, and the Peace Corps have transformed communities. But Paul Light questions whether this transformation is sustainable. Can episodic volunteerism build the capacity and effectiveness of public and nonprofit organizations? And to what extent can we separate respect for service through volunteerism from a genuine respect for those who make public service a way of life—in the military, in the local uniformed services, in the schools and the hospitals, and (dare one even use the word) in the bureaucracies? As Alice Rivlin notes, recreational government bashing "saves us from facing up to how hard it is to make public policy in a free market economy." Will the new respect for service make government bashing less satisfying as a hobby? It is possible, but we are not holding our breath.

Underlying the debate over national service is an argument over whether service is necessary or merely "nice." If service is just a nice thing to do, it is easy to understand why critics, well represented in these pages by Bruce Chapman and Tod Lindberg, express such strong reservations about government-led service programs. But service has the potential to be far more than something nice. As Marshall and Magee argue, the service idea could be a departure comparable to breakthroughs in earlier eras toward a stronger sense of citizenship. "Like settlement houses and night school, which helped America absorb waves of immigration," they write, "national service opens new paths of upward mobility for young Americans and the people they serve. And, like the G.I. bill, national service should be seen as a long-term investment in the education, skills and ingenuity of our people."

And what if service is—as Bob Litan, Harris Wofford, Carmen Sirianni, and Charles Cobb suggest in different ways—a means to strengthen the ties that bind us as a nation? What if it creates bridges across groups in our society that have little to do with each other on any given day—a point implicit in Charles Rangel's argument for the draft and explicit in Steve Hess's realistic yet poignant open letter to his sons on the value of military service? What if service, as the New Left's Port Huron Statement put it forty years ago, can mean "bringing people out of isolation and into community"? What if it fosters civic and political participation in a society that seems not to hold the arts of public life in the highest esteem? In sum, what if service is not simply a good in itself, but a means to many ends?

Still, it must be admitted that this plurality of ends can be a problem as well as an advantage. Michael Lind, in his icon-smashing essay, is right when he says that "within the small but vocal community of national service enthusiasts, there is far more agreement on the policy of national service than on its purpose." Lind, along with several authors, suggests that the post–September 11 environment may have created a genuinely compelling argument for citizen service: the need to expand the nation's capacity to prepare for and respond to domestic emergencies, notably those caused by terrorism.

Service and a New Generation

However one conceives of service, surely one of its ends—or at least one of the ends that wins the broadest assent—is the urgency of finding new ways to engage young Americans in public life in the wake of a significant period of estrangement. As Peter Hart and Mario Brossard argue here, the evidence of many surveys suggests that young Americans are deeply engaged in civic activity. In his 2000 campaign, Senator John McCain—initially a skeptic of national service, now a strong supporter—won a wide following among the young by urging them to aspire to things "beyond your own self-interest." Service learning, increasingly popular in our public schools, has been linked with a heightened sense of civic responsibility and personal effectiveness. If the new generation connected its impulses to service with a workable politics, it could become one of the great reforming generations in our nation's history.

And service could become a pathway to a stronger sense of citizenship. As Jane Eisner argues, service "must produce more than individual fulfillment for those involved and temporary assistance for communities in need." It should, she says, "lead to an appetite for substantive change, a commitment to address the social problems that have created the need for service in the first place." Eisner suggests that as a nation, we should celebrate the First Vote cast by young people with the same fanfare that greets other moments of passage to adult responsibility. The goal would be to encourage a new generation to make the connection "between service to the community and participation in the very process that governs community life."

A focus on service and the links it forges between rights and responsibilities of citizenship could also offer new ways out of old political impasses. For example, Andrew Stern, the president of the Service Employees International Union, suggests that a two-year commitment to national service could become a pathway for undocumented workers to legalize their status and for legal immigrants to speed their passage to citizenship. And former felons now denied voting rights might "earn credits toward restoration of full citizenship" through service.

Jeff Swartz, the CEO of Timberland, offers practical proposals for business at a moment when the public demand for responsible corporate behavior is rising. He suggests that obligations to shareholders, to employees, and to the community are linked. One reason his company has been on *Fortune* magazine's list of the 100 "Best Companies to Work For" is its program of service sabbaticals through which employees can spend up to six months working at existing or start-up nonprofits. Their purpose is not simply to do "good works" but also to build the capacity of the organizations that promote social change.

At its best, service is not make-work but what Harry Boyte and Nancy Kari have called "public work." It is work that "is visible, open to inspection, whose significance is widely recognized" and can be carried out by "a mix of people whose interests, backgrounds, and resources may be quite different."[6] Service as public work is the essence of the democratic project.

It solves common problems and creates common things. Public work entails not altruism, or not only altruism, but enlightened self-interest— a desire to build a society in which the serving citizen wants to live. And as Boyte tells us in his essay here, service alone cannot build a stronger sense of citizenship. Citizenship, he reminds us, is meaningless unless citizens have power—real power, not illusory power—to achieve their goals and change their communities and their nation. Boyte writes from the organizing tradition that also inspired Charles Cobb, who notes that "community organizers do not lead. Instead, they cultivate leadership."

Skepticism, Realism, and Hope

It is thus possible to be skeptical about the new call to service, and it is absolutely necessary to be realistic. Speeches about service can be a terribly convenient way for politicians to seem to call for sacrifice without demanding much of citizens. At little cost to themselves, advocates of both conservative and liberal individualism can use service to shroud their real intentions behind the decent drapery of community feeling.

William Galston, a scholar who has devoted years of energy to promoting research and action to excite young Americans to public engagement, worries that the failure to link post–September 11 rhetoric about service to actual calls for civic action could well lead to the very sort of cynicism service advocates decry. He is not alone in these pages. "Would Pearl Harbor have been a defining event if it had not been followed by a national mobilization and four years of war that altered the lives of soldiers and civilians alike?" Galston asks. "In the immediate wake of September 11, the administration's failure to call for any real sacrifice from citizens fortified my belief that the terrorist attack would be the functional equivalent of Pearl Harbor without World War II, intensifying insecurity without altering civic behavior."

Theda Skocpol, a wise student of the last century and a half of American civic life, sounds an equally useful warning. "Absent organizational innovations and new public policies," she writes here, "the reinvigorated sense of the American 'we' that was born of the travails of September 11 may well gradually dissipate, leaving only ripples on the managerial routines of contemporary U.S. civic life." In fact, as Galston suggests, mere exhortation to serve will do little to foster public—and especially political—participation if too many citizens see the public realm as broken. As Galston puts it, "If we clean up our politics, rebuild the institutions that ask citizens to participate, multiply opportunities for national and community service, and restore the civic mission of our educational institutions, we have a chance to reverse the cynicism evoked by the politics of the past three decades." A tall order indeed! But the alternative is not pretty: "If we squander this opportunity, the civic impact of the terrorist attacks will continue to fade, leaving young Americans with only a dim memory of what might have been."

The issue of whether Americans have been called to any real sort of sacrifice is, of course, the point of Charles Rangel's essay calling for a renewal of the draft. Rangel, drawing on the finding of columnist Mark Shields, was bothered that of 535 members of the House and Senate voting on the Iraq war, only one had a child—a son, as it happens—in the enlisted ranks of the armed forces. Rangel sees this as a problem for democracy, and he is not alone. Rangel struck a nerve because virtually all Americans know there is a hole in our post–September 11 expressions of patriotism. It is neither race baiting nor class warfare—Rangel was accused of both—to suggest that a democratic society has a problem when members of its most privileged classes are not among the first to rally to the colors at a time of trouble. The sacrifices made in Iraq by the men and women of our nation's military remind us that the subject of this book is not abstract. Service is a serious matter, especially for those of our fellow citizens who render it under fire. Charles Moskos, the nation's premier student of service and the military experience, explores ways of expanding the circle of commitment and promoting the idea of the "citizen-soldier." John Lehman, the navy secretary under Ronald Reagan, offers helpful remedies short of a draft to overcome what he agrees is a fundamental problem: that "the burdens of defense and the perils of combat do not fall even close to fairly across all of our society."

If the problems of inequality are vexing where military service is concerned, they can also be troubling for service at home. Service, badly conceived, can distance citizens from public problems. Those who serve can help people "out there," as if the problems "they" have are disconnected from the society in which the server lives. In a separate essay in these pages, Drogosz extends this argument by insisting that service without politics and democratic engagement will never live up to its promise.

Michael Schudson sees President Bush's ideal citizen as a "Rotarian, moved by a sense of neighborliness, Christian charity, and social responsibility, but untouched by having any sense of a personal stake in public justice." Schudson's point is not to knock Rotarians; it is to argue that self-interest in pursuit of justice is a virtue. As Schudson notes in describing the civil rights movement, the most dramatic expansion of democracy and citizenship in our lifetime was brought about by citizens "driven not by a desire to serve but by an effort to overcome indignities they themselves have suffered." The point is brought home powerfully by Charles Cobb who sees the civil rights movement as being best understood "as a movement of community organizing rather than one of protest." The civil rights movement performed a huge national service—and many specific forms of service, including the registration of thousands of voters. It is worth recalling that this quintessentially civic, "good government" act, the registration of new voters, was also a telling form of rebellion in places that denied African Americans the right to vote.

These are essential points. Yet it is also true that Rotarians are good citizens. Neighborliness, charity, and social responsibility are genuine virtues. It is both good and useful to assert, as Rabbi Chaim of Volozhin did, that "my neighbor's material needs are my spiritual needs." It is just possible that a nation responding to the call to service would, over time, become a nation deeply engaged in questions of public justice.

The debate over national service is a debate over how we Americans think of ourselves. It is a debate over how we will solve public problems and what we owe to our country and to each other. If our nation is to continue to prosper, it is a debate we will have in every generation. For if we decide that there are no public things to which we should be willing to pledge some of our time and some of our effort—not to mention "our lives, our fortunes, and our sacred honor"—we will be breaking faith with our nation's experiment in liberty rooted in mutual assistance and democratic aspiration.

PART ONE
How September 11 Changed Us

2

Bowling Together

ROBERT D. PUTNAM

THE CLOSING DECADES of the twentieth century found Americans growing ever less connected with one another and with collective life. We voted
less, joined less, gave less, trusted less, invested less time in public affairs,
and engaged less with our friends, our neighbors, and even our families.
Our "we" steadily shriveled.

The unspeakable tragedy of September 11 dramatically interrupted
that trend. Almost instantly, we rediscovered our friends, our neighbors,
our public institutions, and our shared fate. Nearly two years ago, I wrote
in my book *Bowling Alone* that restoring civic engagement in America
"would be eased by a palpable national crisis, like war or depression or natural disaster, but for better and for worse, America at the dawn of the new
century faces no such galvanizing crisis."

Now we do.

But is September 11 a period that puts a full stop to one era and opens
a new, more community-minded chapter in our history? Or is it merely a
comma, a brief pause during which we looked up for a moment and then
returned to our solitary pursuits? In short, how thoroughly and how
enduringly have American values and civic habits been transformed by
recent terrorist attacks.

During the summer and fall of 2000, my colleagues and I conducted a
nationwide survey of civic attitudes and behaviors, asking about everything

from voting to choral singing, newspaper readership to interracial marriage. Recently, we returned to many of the same people and posed the same questions. Our survey period extended from mid-October to mid-November 2001, encompassing the anthrax crisis and the start of the Afghan war. Emerging from the immediate trauma of unspeakable death and destruction, these 500 Americans were adjusting to a changed world and a changed nation. The results are shown in table 2-1.

Though the immediate effect of the attacks was clearly devastating, most Americans' personal lives returned to normal relatively quickly. For example, despite anecdotal reports of increased religious observance in the immediate aftermath of the tragedy, we found no evidence of any change in religiosity or in reported church attendance. Our primary concern, however, was not with change in the private lives of Americans but with the implications of the attacks and their aftermath for American civic life. And in those domains, we found unmistakable evidence of change.

The levels of political consciousness and engagement are substantially higher than they were a year ago in the United States. In fact, they are probably higher now than they have been in at least three decades. Trust in government, trust in the police, and interest in politics are all up. Compared with a year ago, Americans are somewhat more likely to have attended a political meeting or to have worked on a community project. Conversely, we are less likely to agree that "the people running my community do not really care what I think." This is no doubt partly the result of a spurt of patriotism and "rally round the flag" sentiment, but it also reflects a sharper appreciation of public institutions' role in addressing not just terrorism but other urgent national issues. The result? A dramatic and probably unprecedented burst of enthusiasm for the federal government.

Using a standard question ("How much can you trust the government in Washington to do what is right—all of the time, most of the time, some of the time, or none of the time?"), we found that 51 percent of our respondents expressed greater confidence in the federal government in 2001 than they had a year earlier. No doubt the identity of the commander in chief has something to do with the somewhat greater increase in confidence among Republicans, southerners, and whites; even

Table 2-1. *Change in Selected Civic Attitudes and Behavior, 2000–01*
Percent

Attitude/behavior	Increased	Decreased	Net change
Trust national government	51	7	44
Trust local government	32	13	19
Watch TV	40	24	16
Express interest in politics	29	15	14
Trust local police	26	12	14
Trust people of other races	31	20	11
Trust shop clerks	28	17	11
Support keeping unpopular books in library	28	18	10
Trust neighbors	23	13	10
Contributed to religious charity	29	20	9
Expect crisis support from friends	22	14	8
Trust "people running my country"	32	24	8
Worked with neighbors	15	8	7
Trust local news media	30	23	7
Gave blood	11	4	7
Volunteered	36	29	7
Expect local cooperation in crisis	23	17	6
Worked on community project	17	11	6
Attended political meeting	11	6	5
Read the newspaper	27	24	3
Visit relatives	43	40	3
Attended club meeting	29	26	3
Attended public meeting	27	26	1
Contributed to secular charity	28	27	1
Attend church	20	19	1
Belong to organizations	39	39	0
Had friends visit your home	39	45	–6

Source: Robert D. Putnam, "Bowling Together," *The American Prospect,* vol. 13, no. 3 (2002).

before September 11, the advent of a Republican administration probably changed the partisan polarity of this question. Nevertheless, the bipartisan, nationwide effect of the terrorist attacks and their aftermath is clear.

Although we found most of the changes in civic attitudes to be relatively uniform across ethnic groups, social classes, and regions, some registered more sharply among younger Americans (those aged thirty-five and under) than among their elders. Interest in public affairs, for example, grew by 27 percent among younger people, as compared with 8 percent among older respondents. Trust in "the people running your community" grew by 19 percent among younger people, as compared with 4 percent among older ones.

Nonetheless, Americans from all walks of life expressed greater interest in public affairs than they had during the national political campaign of 2000. This spike in political awareness has not, however, led most Americans to run out and join community organizations or to show up for club meetings that they used to shun. Generally speaking, attitudes (such as trust and concern) have shifted more than behavior has. Will behavior follow attitudes? It's an important question. And if the answer is no, then the blossom of civic-mindedness after September 11 may be short lived.

Americans don't only trust political institutions more: we also trust one another more, from neighbors and co-workers to shop clerks and perfect strangers. More Americans now express confidence that people in their community would cooperate, for example, with voluntary conservation measures in an energy or water shortage. In fact, in the wake of the terrorist attacks, more Americans reported having cooperated with their neighbors to resolve common problems. Fewer of us feel completely isolated socially, in the sense of having no one to turn to in a personal crisis. At the same time, we are now less likely to have friends over to visit. Television viewing increased from about 2.9 hours to 3.4 hours a day. In that sense, whether because of fear or because of the recession, Americans are cocooning more now than a year ago.

We were especially surprised and pleased to find evidence of enhanced trust across ethnic and other social divisions. Whites trust blacks more, Asians trust Latinos more, and so on, than these very same people did a year ago. An identical pattern appears in response to classic questions measuring social distance: Americans in the fall of 2001 expressed greater open-mindedness toward intermarriage across ethnic and racial lines, even within their own families, than they did a year earlier.

To be sure, trust toward Arab Americans is now about 10 percent below the level expressed toward other ethnic minorities. We had not had the foresight to ask about trust in Arab Americans a year ago, so we cannot be certain that it has declined, but it seems likely that it has. Similarly, we find that Americans are somewhat more hostile to immigrant rights. Other surveys have shown that public skepticism about immigration increased during 2001, but that trend may reflect the recession as much as it does the terrorist attacks. Yet despite signs of public support for antiterrorist law-enforcement techniques that may intrude on civil liberties, our survey found that Americans are in some respects more tolerant of cultural diversity now than they were a year ago. Opposition to the exclusion of "unpopular" books from public libraries actually rose from 64 percent to 71 percent. In short—with the important but partial and delimited exception of attitudes toward immigrants and Arab Americans—our results suggest that Americans feel both more united and more comfortable with the nation's diversity.

We also found that Americans have become somewhat more generous, though the changes in this domain are more limited than anecdotal reports have suggested. More people in 2001 than in 2000 reported working on a community project or donating money or blood. Occasional volunteering is up slightly, but regular volunteering (at least twice a month) remains unchanged at one in every seven Americans. Compared with figures from immediately after the tragedy, our data suggest that much of the measurable increase in generosity spent itself within a few weeks.

As 2001 ended, Americans were more united, readier for collective sacrifice, and more attuned to public purpose than we have been for several decades. Indeed, we have a more capacious sense of "we" than we have had in the adult experience of most Americans now alive. The images of shared suffering that followed the terrorist attacks on New York and Washington suggested a powerful idea of cross-class, cross-ethnic solidarity. Americans also confronted a clear foreign enemy, an experience that both drew us closer to one another and provided an obvious rationale for public action.

In the aftermath of September's tragedy, a window of opportunity has opened for a sort of civic renewal that occurs only once or twice a century.

And yet, though the crisis revealed and replenished the wells of solidarity in American communities, those wells so far remain untapped. At least, this is what that gap between attitudes and behavior suggests. Civic solidarity is what Albert O. Hirschman called a "moral resource"—distinctive in that, unlike a material resource, it increases with use and diminishes with disuse. Changes in attitude alone, no matter how promising, do not constitute civic renewal.

Americans who came of age just before and during World War II were enduringly molded by that crisis. All their lives these Americans have voted more, joined more, given more. But the so-called Greatest Generation forged not merely moods and symbols, as important as those were; it also produced great national policies and institutions (such as the G.I. bill) and community-minded personal practices (such as scrap drives and victory gardens). So far, however, America's new mood has expressed itself largely through images—of the attacks themselves, for instance, or the Ad Council's "I am an American" campaign, which powerfully depicts our multicultural society—and gestures, such as the president's visit to a mosque.

Images *do* matter: what a powerful lesson in inclusive citizenship would have been imparted had FDR visited a Shinto shrine in January 1942! But images alone do not create turning points in a nation's history. That requires institutionalized change. To help foster a new "greatest generation," the Bush administration should endorse the bill offered by Senators John McCain and Evan Bayh to quintuple funds for the AmeriCorps program of national youth service. And given that young Americans are more open to political participation than they have been in many years, educational and political leaders should seize this moment to encourage youths' engagement in political and social movements. The grass-roots movement to restore the Pledge of Allegiance in American classrooms advocates fine symbolism; but the time is right to introduce a new, more activist civics education in our schools as well.

Finally, activists should recognize that wartime mobilization could also spark progress toward social justice and racial integration, much as the experiences of World War II helped to generate the civil rights movement of the 1950s. Americans today, our surveys suggest, are more open than ever to the idea that people of all backgrounds should be full members of our national community. Progressives should work to translate that national mood into concrete policy initiatives that bridge the ethnic and class cleavages in our increasingly multicultural society.

The changes in community-mindedness and civic engagement described in this essay were measured about six weeks after the tragic attacks of September 11. Roughly six months later (in March–April 2002), my colleagues and I posed the same questions to another sample of Americans, some of whom had been interviewed in the initial 2000 survey and some not. What did these subsequent interviews tell us about the durability of the effects of September 11 on community in America?

The immediate surge of social and political trust—trust in government, trust in community leaders, trust in neighbors, trust in other races, and so on—had somewhat declined by the spring of 2002 but remained at levels higher than before September 11. Like researchers at the University of Michigan, the University of Chicago, and the Harris Poll, we find that confidence in political institutions and in other people remained elevated for months after the attacks, although this effect tended to fade over time.

In some respects, the positive effects of September 11 on civic engagement continued unabated and perhaps even strengthened as the months passed. For example, in the spring of 2002, we found evidence of a steady increase in "bridging social capital," that is, social ties that cross social cleavages, such as interracial friendships. Conversely, the spike in anti-immigrant sentiment in the immediate aftermath of the attacks had dissipated by the following spring. (The immediate post–September 11 spike in TV watching had also vanished by the spring.) Some forms of civic participation, such as attendance at political meetings and philanthropic giving, actually rose between November 2001 and the spring of 2002.

In short, the emotional and patriotic effect of September 11—the sense of connectedness with other Americans—seemed to fade with the passage of months but not (or not yet) to have disappeared. On the other hand, civic behavior seemed, if anything, to show some continuing improvement, especially among younger Americans, perhaps as their civic habits adjusted to a new and somewhat higher level of engagement.

3

Will September 11 Revitalize Civic Democracy?

Theda Skocpol

Observers of American life have seen a silver lining in the dark clouds that billowed from the Twin Towers and the Pentagon on September 11, 2001. Along with the horror wrought by the terrorist attacks came an outpouring of solidarity and patriotism—a sudden change of heart for many Americans who, prior to that fateful day, had seemed to be drifting inexorably toward individualism, self-absorption, and cynical disinterest in public affairs. As Stanley Greenberg aptly puts it, suddenly the "we" mattered more than the "me."[1] People reached out to family members, neighbors, and friends while proudly declaring their membership in the American national community.

Seventy percent of Americans reportedly gave time or money to charities attempting to help the victims of September 11.[2] Anonymous commuter suburbs in New Jersey suddenly organized to provide constant care for dozens of families who lost loved ones.[3] In the days and weeks after September 11, more than four-fifths of Americans displayed the U.S. flag on homes, cars and trucks, and clothing.[4] And Americans declared renewed trust in the federal government to "do the right thing." In April 2000, only 29 percent said they felt such trust "always" or "most of the time," but 64 percent expressed such faith in a poll taken shortly after September 11.[5]

Popular reactions to September 11 and the subsequent fight against terrorists in Afghanistan seem to resemble what happened in previous U.S. wars. Despite grievous episodes of repression and exclusion, almost all U.S. wars have promoted civic vitality. In a nation whose citizens are famous for their proclivity to organize and join voluntary endeavors, outbreaks of martial conflict have repeatedly sparked voluntaristic upsurges. In the past, moreover, such upsurges have continued far beyond the immediate crisis, revitalizing American civic life well into postwar eras.

The American Revolution, the Civil War, and World Wars I and II all exemplify the favorable civic impact of U.S. wars. The American revolutionary struggle against Great Britain was waged and won by committees of correspondence and volunteer militias—and the era during and after the revolution brought the first great explosion of voluntary group formation in the new nation.[6] The Civil War of 1861 to 1865 was fought and supported by volunteers (with the military draft responsible for at most 15 percent of the men who fought).[7] In turn, the Union victory unleashed fresh rounds of civic organizing by men and women who modeled peacetime association-building on wartime mobilizations. At national and local levels alike, the foundations of modern American civic life were laid as the Civil War generation matured between the 1860s and the 1910s.[8] Thereafter, U.S. involvements in World Wars I and II brought new partnerships between government agencies and federated voluntary associations. From the Red Cross and the YMCA to trade unions and business and professional groups, from the General Federation of Women's Clubs and the PTA to dozens of fraternal groups, voluntary associations contributed vitally to world war mobilizations—and, in the process, gained new infusions of dues-paying members.[9]

Understandably, the dramatic shifts in attitudes and self-reported individual behaviors registered in post–September 11 surveys encouraged observers to start speculating that America's current wartime crisis may spur another historic round of persistent civic revitalization.[10] But before we accept this happy conclusion, we should consider additional evidence raising questions about how much really has changed since September 11. In a nationally representative panel survey conducted by Robert D. Putnam, the same national sample of men and women answered the same questions in the months before and after September 11 and the commencement of the war against terrorism.[11] The data in figure 3-1 demonstrate net favorable changes in various civic attitudes and behaviors. However, although it quite clearly shows that Americans' feelings toward government and one another became considerably more favorable after September 11, behaviors such as volunteering and joining changed much less. Not surprisingly, given the spectacular nature of the terrorist attacks, the one sort of activity that exhibited a big net upward jump after September 11 was mass TV viewing. But other activities, especially those requiring group involvement, changed very little—and since this panel survey, we have not seen any indications of major changes in shared civic activities. Americans' responses to September 11 and the current war against terrorism may, in other words, fall short of the remarkable upsurges in shared civic activity that this nation has experienced in past war crises. This new war may not fundamentally reshape our capacities to work together toward patriotic and community goals.

Why is a split between attitudinal and behavioral change happening with this conflict? Deeper consideration of the conditions that allowed past wars to contribute to civic engagement suggests why today's response to conflict might turn out differently. In the Civil War and World Wars I and II, new attitudes coincided with government efforts to mobilize the citizenry for war, and preexisting federated membership associations channeled popular participation into local and national activities. But so far in this new crisis, official efforts to mobilize citizens have been sporadic and weak, while existing civic organizations provide few channels for group involvement. Historical comparisons bring into sharper relief the full set of factors that shape the degree and kind of civic upsurge we can expect from a war. Changing attitudes, the role of government, and preexisting civic institutions all contribute to the outcome.

Figure 3-1. *After September 11, 2001, American Civic Attitudes Changed More Than Behavior*

Net respondents who increased attitude or behavior, 2000–fall 2001 (percent)

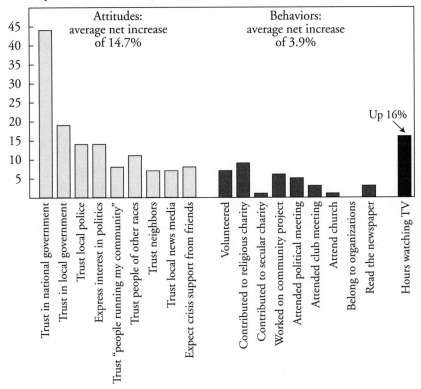

Source: Robert Putnam, "Bowling Together: The United State of America," *The American Prospect*, vol. 13, no. 3 (2002).

Attitudes Shift at the Outbreak of War

For long-past wars, we do not have national surveys comparable to the opinion polls that enable us to track attitudinal changes today. Qualitative evidence nevertheless reveals that outpourings of patriotic and community sentiment accompanied the onset of conflict in April 1861, April 1917, and December 1941. Newspapers, organizational declarations, community demonstrations, and personal memoirs all provide relevant evidence. When wars break out—and especially when the nation is attacked— millions of Americans become aware of their shared national identity and are willing to work together on local and national responses to the crisis. Attitude shifts since September 11 are thus very similar to what happened in the past.

Government Authorities May—or May Not— Call for Mass Mobilization

Although popular attitudes invariably shift with the outbreak of war, the willingness of government authorities to orchestrate voluntary citizen participation varies considerably, depending on the nature of the conflict and the capacities of government. Modern wars require major domestic as well as military commitments, and government bureaucracies only sometimes possess the capacities and resources to act directly.

For example, when the U.S. federal government suddenly found itself challenged by a massive secessionist movement in 1861, President Abraham Lincoln desperately needed organized volunteer contributions. At that point, U.S. standing armies consisted of a mere 16,000 men, mostly deployed in the West and led by a small corps of aging professional officers, many of whom "went South" to fight for the Confederacy. In the North and South alike—but especially in the North—the Civil War was fought by an outpouring of military volunteers assembled by local community leaders, combined into state-level units, and knit together to form the Union Army. To support the troops and organize relief efforts at home, women and older men created similar volunteer federations—the forerunner of what would later become the American Red Cross.

By the outbreak of World War I, federal bureaucracies were more developed than they were in the 1860s. Nevertheless, executive agencies had little capacity to reach directly into local communities and individual homes, so they turned to the national and state leaders of voluntary federations for the organizational networks they needed to run drives to conserve foodstuffs and sell Liberty Bonds and to conduct campaigns for relief, military recruitment, and maximization of economic production. Federal authorities also encouraged professionals and managers to come together in new associations to help manage national projects. Wartime mobilizations spawned many new voluntary associations, and existing groups gained visibility and recruited new members when they cooperated with government.

By the time the United States fought in World War II, government capacities were sufficiently developed that authorities did not need voluntary groups as badly as in 1917. Yet it was clear from the start that this conflict would be massive, lengthy, and costly. Remembering how World War I was fought, U.S. officials saw advantages in getting masses of Americans directly involved. Conservation and fund-raising drives were rerun in much the same way as in 1917–19, with women's groups, fraternal groups, the Red Cross, the Knights of Columbus, the YMCA, and hundreds of professional, business, and ethnic associations called upon to mobilize their members to contribute to the war effort. Again, memberships in voluntary associations surged forward into the postwar era.

In the post–September 11 war against terrorism, U.S. authorities have not been so eager to engage in mass mobilization. Obviously, we are in an era of new kinds of military conflict, waged by highly trained, specialized military personnel backed by a few newly mobilized National Guard units. Military efforts in Afghanistan have not required massive personpower, and war in Iraq is also being waged by relatively small numbers of soldiers. On the home front, moreover, heightened homeland security measures (including early efforts to cope with the anthrax scare) have seemed to call for the expertise of professionals, not citizen volunteers. And as the nation faces a wartime economic slowdown, reigning Republican ideas lead officials to put their faith in tax cuts and consumer spending as remedies. This is the first major war in U.S. history in which the federal government has advocated tax cuts for the rich rather than greater sacrifice across the board.

Given all of this, in the months following September 11, federal officials moved in very different directions than previous U.S. wartime leaders. With limited U.S. military quotas filled, eager volunteers were turned

away after September 11. To be sure, President George W. Bush sporadi-
cally called on civilian Americans to volunteer for service in their communities. But his appeals seemed largely symbolic, not connected to vital
wartime activities. And right after one of President Bush's first speeches
calling for volunteers in the fall of 2001, his homeland security director,
Tom Ridge, publicly wondered what he would do with volunteers should
they materialize, putting a damper on any ideas of large-scale civic mobilization. "Asked about mandatory national service, Mr. Ridge said: 'You
just don't put a volunteer out on the border. There are certain levels of law
enforcement where you really want professionals involved.'"[12]

Commercialism ruled the day along with professional management.
Amidst the efflorescence of patriotism in late 2001 and 2002, President
Bush did not take the opportunity to launch any big new civic effort, such
as mandatory national service for young Americans.[13] Instead, for weeks
after September 11, his most prominent appeals were commercial rather
than civic. The Travel Industry Association of America estimated that two-
thirds of Americans saw the president starring in a television advertise-
ment calling for people to express "courage" by taking more trips. And the
president repeatedly asked people to go shopping to stimulate the economy. If enduring images of World Wars I and II featured posters of Uncle
Sam encouraging citizens to do their duty, perhaps we need a revised version of the poster to capture the main presidential message in 2001.

Civic Organizations Channel Participation

In our past wars, citizens were eager to volunteer and the federal government engaged in mass mobilization and calls for equal sacrifice. Yet the
nature of existing voluntary associations at the time of the Civil War and
the world wars also contributed to wartime mobilizations and helped to
achieve and sustain gains in civic connectedness. The third and final
explanatory factor we must consider, therefore, is the landscape of civic
associations and institutions in place when a war breaks out.

From the early 1800s until the 1960s, American civic democracy was
rooted in membership-based voluntary associations.[14] Leaders in the

United States established civic reputations by helping to organize fellow citizens into major membership associations such as the PTA, the Elks, the American Legion, and dozens, even hundreds, of other groups. In every American community of any size, clubs, lodges, and posts were as ubiquitous as churches and schools, and most local membership groups were linked together into state and national federations—organizations that held regular gatherings at state and national levels so that people from local communities could join forces for broader sets of activities. In fact, voluntary membership associations exactly paralleled the various levels of

U.S. representative government, with local clubs or lodges electing delegates to state and national assemblies. When national crises struck, therefore, U.S. government leaders could readily mobilize fellow citizens for wartime activities by simply asking great voluntary associations to get involved. There were well-worn institutional channels through which Americans from many occupations and walks of life could work together and pool resources.

After the 1960s, however, U.S. civic life was radically reorganized in a much more elitist and managerial direction.[15] In the wake of the civil rights and feminist movements, traditional chapter-based membership federations, most of which had been racially and gender-segregated, understandably failed to attract many younger members. The war in Vietnam, ultimately unpopular and militarily unsuccessful, rendered traditional patriotic voluntary associations less appealing to many Americans.

Challenged by movements and defections from below, traditional voluntary associations were also bypassed in national politics by professionally managed advocacy associations, which proliferated by the thousands in the 1970s and 1980s. In Washington, D.C., and New York City, new "issue-oriented" groups set up offices to lobby government, mount lawsuits, and promote messages in the national media. These new, professionally run citizen-advocacy groups often had no individual members at all, or else recruited monetary contributions through the mail.[16]

At the state and local level, meanwhile, nonprofit social agencies proliferated. Like advocacy groups, these are professionally managed civic organizations that raise money from donors, government agencies, or mailing-list adherents, rather than from members who attend meetings and pay regular dues. Local nonprofit agencies do lots of good things in their communities, but they do not involve most Americans as members in ongoing, shared projects. And they do not elect leaders to coordinate efforts at the state and national level, as traditional voluntary membership associations used to do.

Well before the crisis of September 11, therefore, professionally managed associations and institutions had become central to American civic life—and most membership-based voluntary groups had dwindled into insignificance. To be sure, churches remain vital centers of membership activity in many U.S. communities. But other kinds of membership associations have either disappeared or are carrying on with tiny numbers of older participants. When a national crisis happens nowadays, there are fewer well-established channels through which people can volunteer together—and fewer ways to link face-to-face activities in local communities to state and national projects. Throughout much of American history in war and peace, voluntary membership federations teamed up with local, state, and national public officials to pursue important public projects. But today, partnerships between civic organizations and government are primarily a matter of collaborations among professionals. Managers in government offices either work with their own employees to get things done, or else they try to team up with nonprofit agencies. Ordinary Americans get involved, if at all, only as occasional individual volunteers coordinated by nonprofit professionals. Or they may respond to appeals made by advocacy groups to send checks to fund special projects in response to a national crisis.

Against this background, we can better understand why, following September 11, Americans suddenly displayed new attitudes of social solidarity and trust in government while barely changing their patterns of collective civic participation. Wartime crises may immediately evoke attitudes of civic solidarity, but some combination of government mobilization and available organizational channels is needed to enable people to act together. If this hypothesis is true, we should see less of a gap between attitudinal and behavioral change among Americans already engaged with membership associations prior to September 11, and we also should see positive responses when government offers new opportunities to participate.

There is some evidence that both have happened. According to a report from the Pew Research Center, a large majority of Americans perceived religion to be more important after September 11, yet religious behaviors changed very little, except among people who were already regular churchgoers.[17] Moreover, after President Bush backed modest expansions in national service programs and appealed to Americans to join, applications to AmeriCorps and related programs shot up.

Institutional shifts also help us to understand imbalances in U.S. charity following September 11. Before the 1960s, charitable giving was typically channeled through chapter-based federations, which took advantage of wars (and other major crises) to raise resources both for the immediate crisis and for long-term organizational and community needs. Federations with thousands of local chapters could also move funds around to meet a variety of needs. During World Wars I and II, for example, the American Red Cross built up its chapters, ranks of volunteers, and finances, so that it could deal with all kinds of needs during and after the conflicts.

Yet U.S. charities today are highly professionalized operations, very dependent on media-driven messages to attract money from contributors who expect their money to go exactly where the advertisements promise. After September 11, U.S. charities were inundated with contributions if they advertised plans to help the victims of the terrorist attacks. But if charities tried to bank resources for general needs, they could get into trouble—as did the American Red Cross when a "scandal" broke out over its attempts to devote some post–September 11 donations to other needs.[18] Critics bitterly complained that the Red Cross was banking contributions for needs broader than those connected to September 11 itself, yet this is exactly the sort of thing that federated U.S. charitable associations always did in the past. Furthermore, not only was the Red Cross embarrassed by scandal, but in the months after September 11, charities that routinely help the poor in communities across the United States were starved for necessary resources.[19] Food banks and other local agencies were out of the media limelight as their regular donors gave to September 11 causes.

An Urge to Act—but How?

The American "public feels [an] urge to act—but how?" asked an insightful article appearing in the *Christian Science Monitor* not long after the terrorist attacks of September 11.[20] "What Americans are being called upon to do—live normal lives—hardly seems heroic. Unlike during World War II, citizens aren't needed to roll bandages for GIs or collect scrap metal to make airplanes." My analysis of the roots of war-inspired spurts in civic engagement suggests that, indeed, Americans since September 11 may be

Source: *Boston Globe,* December 27, 2001.

willing to do more than they have been asked to do by government, and more than they may have been allowed to do, given the structure of existing civic organizations.

I do not mean to suggest that September 11 and the war on terrorism will have no enduring impact on American public life. To the degree that they persist, post–September 11 attitude shifts toward patriotism, social trust, and community responsibility may contribute to electoral trends and changes in individual behavior, especially among young people just coming of age. There is, however, little evidence that September 11 and its martial aftermath have led to any immediate upsurge in collective voluntary activities at all comparable to the upsurges associated with historic wars. This twenty-first-century conflict has different requirements, and Americans today live in a very different governmental and civic universe than their forebears—a changed public world in which political authorities and nonprofit organizations rely on professional management and media messages rather than on organized popular participation.

Terrorist attacks and the commitment of U.S. forces to armed combat abroad may have aroused the usual patriotic and communal feelings, but the outbreak of this war could not suddenly remake the institutional face of American civic democracy. Therefore, absent organizational innovations and new public policies, the reinvigorated sense of the American "we" that was born of the travails of September 11 may well gradually dissipate, leaving only ripples on the managerial routines of contemporary U.S. civic life.

4

Patriotism-Lite Meets the Citizen-Soldier

CHARLES MOSKOS

IF THERE WAS any good that came of the terrible events of September 11, 2001, it was the apparent awakening of a long-dormant American patriotism. Everyday observations as well as media coverage recorded abundant signs of national unity. Never in anyone's memory had so many American flags been displayed. Of particular note was the patriotic upsurge among the young. The press reported an increase in the number of people seeking to enter the armed forces, and recruiting offices, it was claimed, were deluged with inquiries.

But truth to tell, there was no increase in recruiting in the days and weeks following the terrorist attacks on the World Trade Center and the Pentagon. And there were also indications that less had changed than met the eye. A poll of Harvard students released a few weeks after the attack revealed that only 32 percent of campus Democrats, 41 percent of independents, and 56 percent of Republicans would be willing to serve in the military if called upon.[1] Despite all the flag waving, it seems likely that recruitment will remain a problem for America's all-volunteer force (AVF) and that privileged young Americans will continue to shun military service.

According to surveys between 1980 and 2000, the number of young Americans saying they definitely would not volunteer for military service increased from 40 to 64 percent.[2] Recruitment problems, however, were alleviated by the lower recruitment objectives resulting from the drawdown in military force levels following the end of the cold war. At the end of this drawdown in the late 1990s, recruitment shortfalls began appearing in all the services (with the exception of the Marine Corps). In fiscal year 2001, recruitment goals were met but with much greater expenditure—about $11,000 per recruit compared with half that figure in the late 1980s.[3] Even with these additional outlays, however, recruiters continue to be hard-pressed to meet goals, especially for reserve components.

How recent innovations in recruitment will fare is yet to be seen. Some appear promising. All the services are moving into online recruitment, complete with "chat rooms," to enlist new troops. In 2000 the army introduced a program offering financial assistance to community-college students in advance of enlistment. But we should not lose sight of one of the verities of recruitment: the best recruiter is a credible veteran with a positive military experience.

Adding to recruitment woes is the surge in attrition since the advent of the AVF. In the peacetime draft era between the Korean and Vietnam Wars, approximately 10 percent of draftees failed to complete their two-year obligation. For enlistees who volunteered for the typical three-year term, the attrition rate was about 20 percent. Since the 1990s, over one-third of enlistees have not finished their first term. Statistical differences in race, gender, and education were significant. White women had an attrition rate of 55 percent, compared with 39 percent for black women. For males the attrition rate was 26 percent for Hispanics, 33 percent for blacks, and 36 percent for whites. Those with a high school diploma had an attrition rate of 35 percent compared to 52 percent for those who entered without a high school diploma.[4] Even though recruitment goals for the active force were met in 2001, there were some disturbing signs of a drop in quality. The number of enlistees scoring in the top half of the Armed Forces Qualification Test has fallen by a third since the mid-1990s. In 2001 the army took in some 380 recruits with felony arrests, a number more than double that of 1998. The number of desertions has also climbed in recent years.[5]

Recreating the Citizen-Soldier

The conventional wisdom within the Department of Defense attributes recruitment and retention fluctuations to the economy. The conventional wisdom is wrong: the real problem is the high rate of college attendance. Today some two-thirds of high school graduates go directly on to higher education. But military recruitment centers on the high school graduate and, recently, on those without diplomas as well. To focus on this population, rather than the expanding pool of college students and graduates, is self-limiting. The military needs to place greater *emphasis* on college recruitment and must recognize that attracting college youth will require changes in the prevailing enlistment philosophy.

The biggest disincentive for college youth is the long enlistment. The armed forces try to get recruits to sign on for three, four, or more years by emphasizing such inducements as high pay and job training. For college youth this is a nonstarter. Rather than stress military career opportunities, recruitment appeals must reinvigorate the ideal of the citizen-soldier. But more than the message must change.

The defense department spent $270,000,000 on recruitment advertising in 2001. To the consternation of many, the army recently adopted a new recruiting slogan: "An Army of One." The hullabaloo over recruitment slogans may be overdone. In a survey of UCLA students I conducted last spring, three quarters said they had not even heard of the slogan![6] Of those who had, over 90 percent said it would not affect their inclinations one way or the other. (Of the small number for whom the slogan had any effect, more said that it would make them less rather than more likely to join.) The extent to which the impact of such advertisements has been exaggerated was vividly brought to my attention when I addressed a large conference of army recruiters in 1996. I asked them if they would prefer to have their advertisement budget tripled or have Chelsea Clinton join the army. They unanimously raised their hands for the Chelsea option.

The most effective way to revive the citizen-soldier ideal would be to introduce a fifteen- or eighteen-month enlistment option. Such a term would involve five or six months of training followed by an overseas assignment. Obvious locales would be Korea, Germany, the Sinai, Bosnia, and Kosovo. Alternatively, the assignment might involve homeland defense. Rather than seeing such duty as onerous, short-termers would see it as a chance to do something entirely different for a year. It would be important to couple such a military enlistment with generous postservice educational benefits linked to a reserve obligation of, say, two years. Dedicated and intelligent reservists will be a vital part of future homeland security missions.

Students who have earned bachelor's degrees often want a break before entering graduate school or the professional world. A short enlistment would also appeal to those who want to take a year off from school at some time during their college career. It could become the military equivalent of the "junior year abroad." A G.I. bill that paid off student loans not just for college but also for graduate school would be especially attractive. The proportion of students with a bachelor's degree who go on to pursue an advanced degree is now higher than the proportion of World War II veterans who used the G.I. bill to attend college.

Indeed, a major obstacle to military recruitment is the substantial amount of federal aid already given to college students. We now spend annually over $20 billion in grants and loan subsidies to college students. We have, in effect, created a G.I. bill without the G.I. If we want to encourage the ideal of service, there must be a push to link federal college aid to enlistment, whether military or civilian. It is noteworthy that a 1995 Gallup poll found that 40 percent of the American public favored this proposition, an amazing level of support for a concept that has not even entered the public debate.[7] A U.S. Army recruiting study showed that linking federal aid to some form of national service would boost military enlistments as well as civilian service.[8]

Short-term enlistments have advantages beyond resolving recruitment woes. Recruits with higher educational levels are less likely to leave service before their enlistment is up. And there is another important factor to consider: the lower enlisted ranks are increasingly populated by married soldiers who bring with them the attendant strains of family life. With more college youth (who tend to marry later in life) entering the military, the proportion of married soldiers and single parents in the junior ranks would drop markedly (and so, too, would the number of service members on food stamps).

Willing to Serve

The above proposal may sound idealistic, but it is supported by empirical data. College graduates are an untapped pool for peacekeeping and humanitarian missions and, surely, for homeland security. Recently I surveyed 430 undergraduates at Northwestern University in my introductory sociology class. The students were asked about various social values as well as military recruitment options. This was the first time such a survey had ever been conducted on a college campus, and the results contain some surprises. But first, some background information.

Northwestern students fall in the 93rd percentile on SAT scores, and 90 percent were in the top 10 percent of their high school graduating class. These students are, in the main, destined for high-paying corporate and professional positions. Slightly over half identified themselves as politically liberal, a third said they were middle-of-the-road, and only 15 percent defined themselves as conservative. These are the kind of young people who are not joining the armed forces. In fact, the military is not even attempting to recruit them.

The survey presented four enlistment options: terms of four, three, or two years, or fifteen months. Each of these options was paired with an educational benefits package of $60,000, $40,000, $25,000, and $15,000, respectively. These benefits could be used to underwrite graduate school or to pay off undergraduate student loans. Those answering "likely" or "possibly" were defined as having some propensity to join the military. The numbers were close to zero for the four- or three-year options, which are the terms of enlistment most favored by recruiters. About one in ten indicated some interest in the two-year or fifteen-month options.

Both women and men generally had similar views. The large majority had negative impressions of military life, with lifestyle, threat of danger, and length of commitment heading the list of their complaints. Such desired goals as travel, personal freedom, and meeting people of different backgrounds were seen as much more attainable in civilian life than in the military.

Toward the end of the survey, the students were asked to pause and await my remarks. I then gave a five-minute talk on my own days as a draftee in Germany during the cold war years of the late 1950s, as well as my research experiences in peacekeeping operations in Somalia, Haiti, Bosnia, and Kosovo. I sought to be as candid as I could by noting the physical demands and regimentation of military service as well as the real danger of combat operations. But I also mentioned the fun and laughter I enjoyed in the company of a cross-section of Americans that I would otherwise never have met. I described peacekeeping as an ennobling experience and as a chance to step into history. I concluded by saying that having such a different experience for a year or two was the best way to refresh oneself before going on to graduate school or a career.

Following these remarks, the students were asked to reconsider the enlistment options given previously. There was no change for the long enlistments, but the propensity to enlist doubled for the two-year option and tripled for the fifteen-month one. Interestingly, enlistment propensity did not correlate with political ideology, the liberals being as willing or unwilling to enlist as the others. The students also did not seem to be attracted by the usual enlistment inducements of pay, skill training, or physical adventure. Rather, the strongest positive correlations were with the probability of serving overseas and with having had a friend or relative with a favorable military experience.

So where does this leave us? If Northwestern students are typical of other college students, it would appear that there is a limited but not insignificant enlistment pool among college graduates. Indeed, if the military could recruit just 5 percent of the 1,200,000 students who graduate from college each year—as opposed to the infinitesimal number who enlist now— our recruitment woes would be over. Equally important, students from elite colleges, who go on to important leadership positions in politics, business, and the academy, would gain some exposure to and knowledge of the armed forces. So what accounts for the defense department's resistance to recruiting college students?

There are three major arguments against short enlistments. First, it is said that the peacekeeping missions for which our military is increasingly deployed require professional soldiers. But let us remember that in World War II, Korea, and Vietnam, most combat soldiers had only six months of training before being sent to war. And the training required to become a military policeman—the role often required for peacekeeping—takes only about six months. Moreover, when we consider that peacekeeping assignments such as those in Bosnia or Kosovo are typically six months long, the logic of a short enlistment seems apparent.

A second, related argument is that today's military requires highly technical skills that cannot be met by short-termers. This overlooks the reality that there are thousands of low-skilled military jobs and that many college students would be coming in with computer skills far exceeding present levels in the armed forces.

The third objection to short enlistments is the fear that they would increase demands on the training base. We have already noted that today more than one-third of our soldiers fail to complete their initial enlistments. High-quality short-termers would reduce attrition dramatically. It is much better to have a soldier serve fifteen months honorably than to be discharged prematurely for cause.

So what are the real obstacles in the way of reviving the citizen-soldier ideal? It is my belief that the senior policymakers in the defense department do not want college graduates because they believe these youth are too good for the military. One such official dismissed my proposal of recruiting college graduates by stating that "they would be pushing brooms." Perhaps so. No one can deny that military service includes drudgery. But if serving one's country were to become more common among privileged youth, more future leaders in civilian society would have had a formative citizenship experience. This can only redound to the advantage of the armed forces and the nation.

A Call to Service

Now is also the time to extend the concept of national youth service to include quasi-military civilian service. The terrorist attacks of September

11 point to an obvious avenue for youth service. The glaring vulnerabilities in our nation's airport security system have come to everyone's immediate attention, and the costs of airport security in the new era will be staggering. But these costs could be contained by some form of national service. Similarly, young people might help guard nuclear plants, patrol the nation's borders, or serve as customs agents.

Recently, President Bush unveiled USA Freedom Corps, a national service initiative with the aim of encouraging American community service and volunteerism. At the forefront of Freedom Corps is Citizen Corps, an agency designed to promote homeland security at the local level and to help prepare communities against the threat of terrorism. The new service program would expand crime-prevention and neighborhood-watch programs, train communities in local disaster and emergency preparedness, and provide volunteer opportunities at local police, fire, and public health agencies. Bush's national service agenda also includes significantly expanding established volunteer programs such as the Peace Corps and AmeriCorps.

Bush has described Freedom Corps as the answer to the post–September 11 question: "What can I do to help?" In this sense, the program echoes the traditional appeal of the armed forces, emphasizing the value of the service performed, not the presumed good for the servers. The benefits of national service for the volunteer can be achieved only when such service is cast in terms of civic duty. After all, our military was not established for the purpose of helping young men and women mature. The military performs this function, to be sure, but its main objectives are not those of a remedial or welfare organization. Thus any new program of national service for homeland security must emphasize the responsibilities of citizenship.

The Price of Citizenship

There is yet another reason why privileged young Americans should serve in the armed forces. Their participation would not only provide a fine example of leadership but might also increase the public's willingness to accept wartime casualties. There has been much discussion about the greater reluctance of Americans to accept casualties than in times past. We need only consider the abrupt American evacuation from Beirut following the 1983 bombing of the Marine barracks, or the turn-around in Somalia following the deaths of eighteen American soldiers, or the unwillingness to use ground troops in the 1999 war against Serbia, to recognize the scope of the problem.

What has changed? Certainly the small number of combat losses in recent military operations contributes to the lower tolerance for casualties. The invasions of Grenada and Panama were over within a matter of days and incurred just eighteen and twenty-three American deaths, respectively. Even with over a half-million troops in place during the Persian Gulf War, we suffered only 183 combat deaths (a quarter of which were incurred by "friendly fire"). In Haiti, only one American soldier was killed by hostile fire. And, remarkably, in the 1999 NATO bombing campaign against Serbia, not a single American was killed in combat. Likewise, the peacekeeping operations in Bosnia and Kosovo have been, at the time of this writing, free of combat deaths.

But the increasing reluctance to accept wartime casualties also suggests a deeper change in society. One school of thought holds that a declining birth rate and smaller families make the loss of children much more traumatic. This explanation has a certain surface plausibility, but what are we to make of the fact that the birth rate in the United States is higher than that of the former Yugoslavia, where willingness to suffer—as well as to inflict—casualties has become legendary?

The most frequently voiced explanation is that the American public will not accept combat deaths unless the national interest—sometimes the adjective "vital" is added—is clearly at stake. On this point analysts are almost unanimous. The civil war in Lebanon and clan warfare in Somalia did not meet the criterion of national interest and hence our quick departure once the going got tough. From economic and political perspectives, the Gulf War more easily fit into the framework of America's vital interests. But the Gulf War was not a true test of American willingness to suffer casualties, for we have little idea of how Americans would have reacted had the combat deaths been in the thousands rather than in the low hundreds.

But all of this is wide of the mark. The answer to the question of what are considered our "national interests" depends not only on the cause itself but also on who is willing to die for that cause. Only when the upper classes perform military service has the public at large defined the cause to be worth young people's lives. Only when privileged youth are on the firing line do war losses become more acceptable. Citizens accept hardships only when their leadership is viewed as self-sacrificing.

Historical experience supports the argument that Americans are more willing to accept casualties when privileged youth serve. In World War II, battle deaths approached 300,000. Yet Americans accepted these casualties because virtually every able-bodied male served in the military. The Korean War—fought mainly by draftees and incurring 33,000 deaths— was never popular but was tolerated for four years. Support for the Vietnam War, where 47,000 Americans died in battle, waned as more and more privileged youth evaded the draft. The army of the Vietnam War had a social base narrower than at any time since before World War II.

The advent of the all-volunteer force in 1973 made it much less likely that privileged children would serve, especially in the enlisted ranks. This social reality, more than any other fact, has lowered our country's willingness to accept wartime casualties, and it explains the apparent paradox of our lower acceptance of combat casualties with a volunteer military than with a draft.

There are only two ways to raise acceptance of combat casualties: bring back a draft that starts conscription at the top of the social ladder, or establish recruitment appeals that will garner some share of privileged youth. Otherwise the all-volunteer force will be an ineffective instrument in any mission unless it is one guaranteed to be almost casualty free. Upon entering what may be a second Thirty Years War, President Bush has candidly stated that there "will be costs." Will we be willing to bear them?

PART TWO
Politics of the Service Debate

5

The Politics of Service

HARRIS WOFFORD

THE CHARGE FROM President Bill Clinton in the summer of 1995 was urgent and strong: find a way to take the new national service program, AmeriCorps, off the partisan political battlefield. Make it, like the Peace Corps, a nonpartisan source of pride for all Americans.

After the 1994 elections, the new AmeriCorps program, enacted by Congress with only a handful of Republican votes, was high on Speaker Newt Gingrich's list for termination. It had been zeroed out in the budget adopted in the House of Representatives. What Clinton called "the transcendent idea" of his administration—and the press called his "pet project"—was imperiled, and the charge to me as the new CEO of the Corporation for National Service was to help save it.

The usually resilient president said we could win—if he stood firm in vetoing any budget that killed AmeriCorps and if our team at the corporation went to work with my former Senate colleagues and with the much more hard-line members of the House Republican majority. My first step was to develop a close collaboration with the Points of Light Foundation established in 1990 by former president George H. W. Bush—and often ridiculed by Democrats. Indeed, on the Senate floor, after the Los Angeles riots of 1992, I had said that the thousand points of light had turned into a thousand fires in Los Angeles. But I had since come to admire the work of the foundation, and an alliance with it offered the most direct way to reach out to Bush.

"Well, I never ridiculed it," Clinton said. "I thought it was the best thing Bush did." The one request Bush had made of him was to take care of his Points of Light. And Clinton had promised to do so.

To assure Congress that AmeriCorps would be entirely nonpartisan, I pledged in the confirmation hearings to stay out of political campaigns altogether and make politics off-limits to national service participants, as in the armed forces. Eli Segal, who had launched AmeriCorps, was an outstanding and creative leader, but he had also been Clinton's campaign chairman. Key Republicans took that as a sign that the new program was an outpost of Democrats. We had to give a different signal.

Patriotism, Not Politics

Why had the idea of national service become such an intensely partisan and controversial issue, and how could we reclaim it as an area of common ground? Several times in the twentieth century the idea had reached high tide and then receded, but beginning with a 1910 essay by William James, "The Moral Equivalent of War," the idea had always had an aura of patriotism, not politics, around it. What was the source of the idea's recurring appeal, and why had it fallen so far out of grace in 1995?

In his first months in office, in response to the emergency of the Great Depression, Franklin Roosevelt persuaded Congress to establish a Civilian Conservation Corps (CCC) to offer 500,000 jobless young men the opportunity to live and serve in the nation's parks and forests. The program soon became overwhelmingly popular, surpassing Roosevelt's goal of a quarter million "boys in the woods" by the end of summer. Before going off to national service of the military kind in World War II, several million young men of the CCC had turned their lives around and made lasting contributions to the environment. The memory of that achievement lingered on through the next decades.

George H. W. Bush, John Kennedy, and many other veterans of World War II shared the idea of large-scale or universal service as a rite of passage for the young and a way of uniting the nation. The call to ask "what you can do for your country" became the most remembered and revered aspect of Kennedy's short-lived presidency. Although small in scale, the Peace Corps, launched by Sargent Shriver, was a symbolic embodiment of that call. In 1961, in sending the Peace Corps volunteers overseas, the president said on the White House lawn, "Someday, we're going to bring this idea home to America."

But the Peace Corps was not born without vehement opposition. In the 1960 campaign, President Eisenhower derided Kennedy's proposal as "a juvenile experiment." Vice President Nixon likened it to "draft evasion," and others called it a "Kiddie Korps." Congress had little interest in the idea.

The surprising enthusiasm of college students, who had been dubbed the silent and apathetic generation, and the good work of the Peace Corps volunteers themselves were the keys to its success. But had Kennedy not been killed, and the Peace Corps enshrined as a central part of his legacy, it might well have become a matter of controversy in the 1964 election.

In the War on Poverty that he later organized for Lyndon Johnson, Shriver started the first domestic Peace Corps, the Volunteers in Service to America (VISTA), and looked forward to hundreds of thousands of VISTA volunteers leading the assault on poverty. He aimed for similar large numbers of Foster Grandparents and participants in the Job Corps and Head Start. On George Washington's birthday in 1965, at the University of Kentucky, President Johnson urged the nation to "search for new ways" through which "every young American will have the opportunity— and feel the obligation—to give at least a few years of his or her life to the service of others in the nation and in the world."

Those Kennedy-Johnson years were the high-water mark, in the twentieth century, of the idea of making citizen service the common expectation of all Americans. Soon the war in Vietnam absorbed the resources needed for an expanding war on poverty. The number of Peace Corps volunteers fell from more than 15,000 to fewer than 5,000. The momentum toward a federally led program of national service faltered. With the assassinations of Robert Kennedy and Martin Luther King Jr., the wind went out of the sails of that or any other such far-reaching idea.

Streams of Service Become a River

During the 1970s, the idea of full-time youth service percolated up from New York City and a scattering of other local communities that formed youth corps. The larger California Conservation Corps, started by Governor Jerry Brown, grew under Republican and Democratic administrations, and similar conservation corps were launched in other states in the image of the old CCC. All were viewed as nonpartisan, but few were microcosms of national service that brought young people of all racial and economic backgrounds together in common work. Most government, foundation, and corporate money targeted "at risk" young people, and the early service corps were composed largely, if not entirely, of poor and minority youth.

The 1980s also saw a considerable increase in volunteer centers that helped place traditional volunteers who wanted to serve a few hours a week. Former Michigan governor George Romney was their greatest champion. Although Ronald Reagan began the decade by invoking the American spirit of service "that flows like a deep and mighty river through the history of our nation," service was not carried much further in his administration. For those of us campaigning for large-scale, full-time national service, the river seemed more like many separate streams: state and local youth service corps programs, volunteer centers, and the civic sector's array of educational, charitable, and faith-based service organizations engaging millions of citizens in traditional voluntary service.

With the 1990s those streams began to come together, and for a few years the river ran high. President Bush appointed the first special assistant to the president for national service, Gregg Petersmeyer. In 1990 Congress enacted the first National Service Act, which authorized funds for the Points of Light Foundation and for a new bipartisan Commission on National and Community Service.

In negotiating a consensus bill, Senate Democrats pressed for a demonstration program of full-time national service. The White House emphasized support for traditional community volunteering. The joint bill embodied both, as well as a noncontroversial program for service learning that reflected a growing movement for student service.

In 1988 Bill Clinton, then governor of Arkansas, endorsed the Democratic Leadership Council's landmark report *Citizenship and National Service*, which called for national service for all who volunteered and proposed that federal college student aid be conditioned on such service.[1] As chair of the National Governors Association, Clinton had formed a working group on national youth service. In the 1992 presidential campaign, the idea clicked: Clinton found that his most popular campaign promise was to create a large-scale service corps, offering college aid as a "carrot" to all who served a year or more in the community.

When the 1993 National and Community Service Act emerged from intense negotiations between the White House and Congress, most of the press treated the authorization of a national service corps of 20,000 members for the first year as an embarrassing falling-off from the campaign promise of a program for all who wanted to serve. Nevertheless, the president launched the new AmeriCorps with fanfare, and almost all governors, most of whom were Republicans, formed the bipartisan state commissions the act required to allocate most of the positions for AmeriCorps members. During the budget crisis and government shutdown of 1995–96, however, the budget of the just-launched AmeriCorps was substantially cut. Thereafter, despite opposition by most House Republicans, the appropriations for the Corporation for National Service increased modestly each year, and the number of AmeriCorps members continued to grow.

Before his death in 1995, George Romney set in motion a plan that led to increasing Republican support. He enlisted the Corporation for National Service and the Points of Light Foundation in realizing a dream he had unsuccessfully tried to sell to three presidential administrations: a summit of all the presidents and leaders from all sectors of society and from hundreds of communities to mobilize civic and government forces to solve some of America's most urgent problems, especially those facing young people heading down the wrong track.

Romney saw the need for a large-scale domestic Peace Corps, such as AmeriCorps, as a cadre of leaders to help the civic sector recruit and organize what he hoped would be an ever-growing army of unpaid volunteers. He saw national service and traditional volunteers as twin engines pulling together to accomplish vitally needed tasks in every community. He argued, "If we were threatened by external forces, our resurgence would be swift and sure, centered around a full-scale mobilization of the entire nation. Our domestic problems demand no less."[2] A summit convened and attended by all the presidents, Republicans and Democrats, would, he believed, take AmeriCorps off the partisan playing field and demonstrate the nonpartisan nature of both national service and community volunteering.

General Colin Powell accepted the chairmanship of the summit and of the ensuing nationwide campaign called "America's Promise—The Alliance for Youth." He became an outspoken champion of AmeriCorps and the other programs of the Corporation for National Service and thus weakened much of the Republican opposition. In the aftermath of the summit, Senator Dan Coates, a conservative who had voted against AmeriCorps, wrote a persuasive article, "Why I Changed My Mind on AmeriCorps."[3]

Republicans Take up the Torch

When Clinton left office, he may not have asked the incoming president to take care of AmeriCorps, but he knew that in Texas, Governor George W. Bush had supported the work of his state's national service commission (though he seldom used the controversial word "AmeriCorps"). Clinton was delighted that forty-nine governors, including those of Texas and Florida, signed a letter circulated by Montana governor Marc Racicot that supported reauthorizing and strengthening AmeriCorps.

Most supporters of national service were nonetheless anxious about the future of AmeriCorps in a Republican administration—until Leslie Lenkowsky was nominated and confirmed as the new CEO of the Corporation for National and Community Service. Lenkowsky had served diligently and constructively on both the board of former president Bush's 1990 commission and the board of the corporation, after Clinton nominated him in 1993.

President George W. Bush also recommended Stephen Goldsmith, the former mayor of Indianapolis and a close campaign associate, as chair of the corporation's board, and he later picked Racicot to be chair of the Republican National Committee. Both shared George Romney's vision of national and community service, and Racicot had taken Powell's place as chairman of America's Promise.

In his campaign for president, John McCain surprised his fellow Republicans by announcing he had been wrong about AmeriCorps—and wrong not to say so sooner. When McCain enlisted Democratic senator Evan Bayh and, later, House Democrat Harold Ford Jr. to call for an increase of AmeriCorps to 250,000 members within five years, no one could foresee that President Bush would join in the bidding. Budgetary limits alone would presumably hold him back.

September 11 changed that. With the assaults on the Twin Towers and the Pentagon, the challenge by outside forces that George Romney had imagined came to pass, and a new reality began. In his 2002 State of the Union address, Bush called for 4,000 hours—or two years—of service by every American and asked for a doubling of the Peace Corps and a 50 percent increase in AmeriCorps in one year, from 50,000 to 75,000 members.

Since then, President Bush has renewed that call in visits and talks around the country and at White House conferences. The Citizen Service Act of 2002 has been approved by the very House committee that had been a bastion of opposition to AmeriCorps and is supported by the leading former opponent, Representative Peter Hoekstra. To drive his call to service, the president created the USA Freedom Corps Council, a cabinet-level council that he chairs, and selected John Bridgeland to direct it. At the council table are AmeriCorps, the Peace Corps, the newly created Citizen Corps for national emergencies—run by the Federal Emergency Management Agency—and the secretaries of the appropriate federal departments.

For some of us who witnessed the origins of the Peace Corps, Bridgeland calls to mind the early Sargent Shriver. And though some of us may disagree with President Bush on tax cuts, environmental decisions, or foreign policy, his determination to build national and community service as a major institution of the civic sector is a common ground on which a large majority of Americans can come together.

For George W. Bush to be the president who presides over the largest quantum leap in national service is not the equivalent of Nixon going to China. But for the president, the secretary of state, and the head of the Republican Party to lead the way in national and community service is to take that party on a new journey.

Quo vadis?

6

Service and the Bush Administration's Civic Agenda

JOHN M. BRIDGELAND,
STEPHEN GOLDSMITH,
AND LESLIE LENKOWSKY

FROM HIS FIRST major speech as a presidential candidate in Indianapolis in July 1999, George W. Bush has made expanding civic engagement and increasing the strength and effectiveness of civic institutions a central aim. He articulated his vision for an active and engaged citizenry in his inaugural address, in which he urged Americans to be "citizens, not spectators; citizens, not subjects; responsible citizens, building communities of service and a nation of character."

The events of September 11 added energy and urgency to this goal, as an active citizenry became an important bulwark against terrorist threats. These policy objectives took their most concrete form in the 2002 State of the Union address, when President Bush called on all Americans to devote at least two years—or 4,000 hours—over their lifetimes in service to their communities, nation, and world. The president announced that he had created the USA Freedom Corps to promote and coordinate government and private sector efforts to give Americans more meaningful service opportunities to answer that call. As part of the USA Freedom Corps, he also formed Citizen Corps to help citizens play appropriate roles in meeting the nation's emerging homeland defense needs, and he called for expanding the Peace Corps, Senior Corps, and AmeriCorps.

The president's embrace of national service programs, while springing directly from his philosophy of compassionate conservatism, no doubt surprised many people who had come to associate such efforts with Democratic presidents. Few people dispute that the voluntary efforts of citizens can make neighborhoods safer, the environment cleaner, children more prepared to face life's challenges, seniors healthier, and communities better able to deal with emergencies. But the challenge for many has been to define the role government ought to play in this arena. Can federally funded service be administered in a way that protects the independence of the civic sector and ensures that citizens, rather than government, take responsibility for the health and safety of their neighborhoods and their nation?

Government and the Voluntary Sector

A long tradition in American politics warns against allowing government to encroach on the private sector. No less a student of American democracy than Alexis de Tocqueville warned that the growth of government could weaken the American tradition of joining civic groups. In the 1950s, sociologist Robert Nisbet, among others, lamented the decline of community, blaming it on the destructive effects of an expanding welfare state. Recently, a host of figures, especially Robert Putnam in his book *Bowling Alone*, have warned that Americans are reaching dangerous levels of civic disengagement, one measure of which is declining interest in volunteering and civic associations.[1]

Not until 1965, however, did many thinkers who were concerned about government encroachment on the voluntary sector begin to develop a positive agenda for the diffuse web of nonprofit groups, associations, schools, and community organizations that came to be known as the "independent sector." Chief among them was Richard Cornuelle, a businessman and political activist, who in his 1965 book, *Reclaiming the American Dream*, championed the right of private, nonprofit organizations to demonstrate that they could successfully tackle tasks such as making college education affordable for the lower and middle classes, reducing poverty and welfare dependency, and improving housing for the needy.[2] Could developing an agenda for the independent sector, he asked, offer a way to address pressing public needs without expanding government?

A decade later, two scholars from the American Enterprise Institute, Peter Berger and Richard John Neuhaus, set out such an agenda. They urged government to make better use of "mediating structures"—neighborhood, family, church, and voluntary associations—to deal with social problems. In their widely discussed *To Empower People,* they set forth two propositions: first, that government policy should stop harming these mediating structures and, second, that it should use them whenever possible to realize social purposes.[3] During Governor George W. Bush's campaign for the presidency, his support for mediating structures and the people they mobilize—now termed "armies of compassion"—figured prominently. He proposed to clear away legal and bureaucratic obstacles, thereby allowing the federal government to provide support to grassroots groups, exactly the kind of mediating institutions that Berger and Neuhaus had in mind.

In Bush's vision, federal service programs fill a special niche—they create more opportunities for people to volunteer. Through AmeriCorps, for example, the intensive commitment members make—up to forty hours a week for one or two years—would be directed to helping organizations locate, train, and mobilize the armies of compassion.

September 11 and Service

In the fall of 2001, the administration was hoping to advance its strategy for citizen engagement through a "Communities of Character" initiative. The president was planning to spotlight places across the nation where people voluntarily came together to solve problems, putting others' interests above their own. The attacks of September 11 made that effort superfluous. Communities across the United States sent medical and relief teams to New York and Washington, while millions of ordinary citizens donated blood and money. "What can I do to help?" became an almost universal refrain, making citizenship and service more important than ever. In response, the president announced plans to increase the role of AmeriCorps members and Senior Corps volunteers in public safety, public health, and disaster relief and to focus their efforts more sharply on homeland security.

In his 2002 State of the Union message, the two halves of the Bush administration's civic agenda came together. Toward the end of an address devoted chiefly to the war against terrorism, homeland security, and the economy, the president called on all Americans to devote at least two years during their lifetimes to serving their neighbors and their nation. Acts of goodness and compassion in one's community, he argued, would be an appropriate way of responding to the "evils" of September 11. And he proposed changes in national service programs to enable more Americans to serve both through these programs and through the grassroots organizations they would support.

These proposals represent a new direction in national and community service. To begin with, they put to rest the idea—which has gained currency in the aftermath of September 11—that national and community service should be made mandatory. Whether in AmeriCorps, the Peace Corps, or in private organizations, service, the president said, was to continue to be a voluntary, individual moral commitment.

The proposed reforms also make clear that service through the federal government is to strengthen, not replace, traditional volunteering. The president anticipated that most Americans would answer his "call to service" by continuing to devote a few hours a week to work with a local church, school, hospital, or nonprofit. But federal programs like AmeriCorps and the Peace Corps would be available for those who wanted an intensive volunteer experience at home or abroad. The president also directed various cabinet departments to explore ways to encourage more Americans to volunteer and to remove any barriers to participation.

A New Role for Federal Service

In the administration's vision of national service, participants take on tasks different from those performed by ordinary volunteers. Volunteerism is not free, in the sense that volunteers must be recruited, organized, and set to work. To make more effective the efforts of millions of individual volunteers, who come to the table with all types of skills, abilities, and experiences, someone has to organize volunteer opportunities so that they meet concrete and clearly defined human needs. The organizations mobilizing the armies of compassion need corporals and sergeants—precisely the role that this administration sees for national service participants. Whether in education, the environment, public health, elder care, or strengthening homeland security, their long-term commitment is of special value to charities and public agencies, which can count on them to show up each day, receive training, and take on long-range tasks and responsibilities that ordinary volunteers cannot—something known in the nonprofit world as capacity building. That difference also justifies paying some of them a small stipend for living expenses, as well as a G.I. bill-type award for education.

Habitat for Humanity already follows this approach. It uses AmeriCorps members and Senior Corps volunteers to recruit, manage, and organize the traditional volunteers on which it relies to build homes for low-income people. Habitat founder Millard Fuller—once skeptical of AmeriCorps but now an enthusiastic supporter—reports that volunteer leveraging by AmeriCorps members serving with Habitat has helped the group build 2,000 extra homes and engage more than 250,000 new volunteers. AmeriCorps members working with Habitat do not replace the volunteers who are building the houses; instead, they help recruit them from college campuses and elsewhere. They also ready the building sites so that when the hammer-swinging volunteers show up, they can get right to work and have a more productive experience. Along with helping Habitat build more houses, AmeriCorps participants thus engage more Americans in civic activities.

Another version of this model is to use AmeriCorps members to build the administrative and technological capacities of grassroots groups. For example, since it was created in 1965, members of Volunteers in Service to America (VISTA), who now make up about 15 percent of AmeriCorps members, have focused their efforts on mobilizing and managing teams of volunteer counselors, developing or expanding programs, and implementing administrative and accounting systems. Those efforts equip nonprofits—or voluntary public health or disaster relief groups—to do more of the work they already do. This fall, for example, VISTA will fund ten members to work with Students in Free Enterprise (SIFE) at strategic points around the country, helping to develop SIFE teams that will teach financial literacy, from balancing checkbooks to investment strategies, to underprivileged populations in inner cities. The VISTA members won't do the actual teaching; rather, they will expand the program by training and developing new teams.

Implementing these strategies requires changing not only how federal service programs have been run but also the laws establishing them. While VISTA members, for example, are allowed to do a wide range of capacity-building activities, other AmeriCorps participants, governed by rules enacted in the 1990s, are now required by law to provide services (such as tutoring or health care) directly to clients. Changes to allow national service participants to perform a wider range of services were incorporated in a set of principles for a Citizen Service Act, which the Bush administration unveiled last spring. The bill includes reforms to mobilize more volunteers who receive nothing from government, make organizations receiving support more effective and accountable, and remove barriers to participation in service programs. It is before the Congress as of this writing.

Finally, the president will use his new White House council, the USA Freedom Corps, to promote the health of the voluntary sector in general. The council will not only coordinate the efforts of all volunteer and service programs in the federal tent, but it will also concern itself with federal policies that affect the well-being of civil society. For example, it can work across federal agencies to improve the effectiveness of school tutoring programs that help students in need. And it can encourage organizations—businesses and nonprofits alike—to respond to the president's call to service by making institutional changes, such as giving employees paid time off for service, enlisting consumers in volunteer service activities, and increasing the capacity of service providers to use volunteers. For the first time, at the highest levels of our government, a presidential council will develop an agenda of citizenship, service, and responsibility. The USA Freedom Corps will link citizens with service opportunities in their communities. In July the president unveiled a redesigned website that features the USA Freedom Corps Volunteer Network, the largest clearinghouse of volunteer opportunities ever created.[4] Thanks to an unprecedented collaboration among many government agencies, for-profit companies, nonprofit organizations, and private foundations, Americans can now find volunteer opportunities anywhere in the country (and even abroad) with just a few clicks of the mouse. The effort represents the power of government to rally diverse (and sometimes competitive) groups to a higher and shared purpose—and offers a glimpse of the public-private partnerships that are possible when government promotes service.

Since the president's call to service, interest in volunteer and national service is up. Key indicators include the increase in the numbers of citizens being matched with local service opportunities, as well as traffic at websites for the USA Freedom Corps and the recruitment websites of Senior Corps and AmeriCorps, where applications have more than doubled. The Peace Corps also reports steady increases in applications. Nonprofit organizations, businesses, schools, faith-based groups, and other institutions are stepping forward to answer the call to service with new commitments and, in many cases, institutional changes that promise to foster a culture of service for years to come.

Service and Cultural Renewal

The Bush administration's civic agenda, together with its reform of national service, represents an unprecedented, cross-sector push to reconnect Americans to their communities and their country—and a new direction in how government views its role in strengthening the voluntary sector. Instead of bemoaning the decline of American mediating institutions, the administration seeks public actions to reinvigorate them. In an era of a high-tech, low-manpower military, it also looks for ways to involve as many Americans as possible in serving their country during a time of war and to encourage institutional changes at every level to ensure that volunteer service remains strong in times of peace. It aims to provide avenues for Americans, especially young adults and senior citizens able to offer sustained volunteer service, to dedicate themselves to reaching out and ministering to the needy and suffering. The president's service agenda clearly reflects the belief that citizens who are closest to the needs of people in local communities are best positioned to bring hope and help to those most needing it and that a renewed effort is needed to mobilize more Americans into volunteer service.

In identifying national and community service as a force for institutional and cultural renewal, the Bush administration has begun to make it an idea that Americans of all political stripes can embrace.

7

Patriotism Means Reaching beyond Our Self-Interest

JOHN McCAIN

AFTER THE EVENTS of September 11, Americans found a new spirit of national unity and purpose. Forty years ago, at the height of the cold war, President John F. Kennedy challenged Americans to enter into public service. Today, confronted with a challenge no less daunting than the cold war, Americans again are eager for ways to serve at home and abroad. Government should make it easier for them to do so.

I strongly believe that it is the obligation of our country's political leadership to provide more opportunities for service to country. During the past presidential campaign, I had the privilege of traveling the country and meeting vast numbers of young people. With energy and passion as contagious as it was inspiring, these young Americans confided their dreams and shared their aspirations, not for themselves alone, but for their country. Their attitude should come as no surprise. Though today's young people, according to polls, have little faith in politics, they are great believers in service. They are doing volunteer work in their communities in record numbers—proof that the urge to serve runs especially deep in them. Indeed, most Americans share this impulse, as witnessed after the September 11 terrorist attacks, when thousands of Americans lined up to give blood and assist in rescue efforts. It is time we tapped that urge for great national ends.

And it is not true, as the cynics suggest, that our era lacks great causes. Such causes are all around us. Thousands of schools in our poorest neighborhoods are failing their students and crying out for talented teachers. Millions of elderly Americans desperately want to stay in their homes and out of nursing facilities but cannot do so without help with the small tasks of daily life. More and more of our communities are being devastated by natural disasters. And our military services face immense challenges, both in fighting the war against terror and fulfilling our other obligations around the world.

Beyond such concrete needs lies a deeper spiritual crisis within our national culture. Since Watergate we have witnessed an increased cynicism about our governmental institutions. We see its impact in declining voter participation and apathy about our public life—symptoms of a system that demands reform. But it's a mistake, I think, to believe that this apathy means Americans do not love their country and aren't motivated to fix what is wrong. The growth of local volunteerism and the outpouring of patriotic sentiment in the aftermath of September 11 suggest a different explanation: that Americans hunger for service to the nation but do not see ways to personally make a difference.

What is lacking today is not a need for patriotic service or a willingness to serve, but the opportunity to do so. Indeed, one of the curious truths of our era is that while opportunities to serve ourselves have exploded—with ever-expanding choices of what to buy, where to eat, what to read, watch, or listen to—opportunities to spend some time serving our country have dwindled. The high cost of campaigning keeps many idealistic people from running for public office; teacher certification requirements keep talented people out of the classroom; and the all-volunteer military is looking for lifers, not those who might want to serve for shorter tours of duty.

The one big exception to this trend is AmeriCorps, the program of national service begun by former president Bill Clinton. Since 1994 more than 200,000 Americans have served one- to two-year stints in Ameri-Corps, tutoring school children, building low-income housing, or helping flood-ravaged communities. AmeriCorps members receive a small stipend and $4,725 in college aid for their service. But the real draw is the chance to have an adventure and accomplish something important. And AmeriCorps' achievements are indeed impressive: thousands of homes constructed, hundreds of thousands of senior citizens assisted to live independently in their own homes, and millions of children taught, tutored, or mentored.

Beyond the good deeds accomplished, AmeriCorps has transformed the lives of young people who have belonged to its ranks. They have begun to glimpse the glory of serving the cause of freedom. They have come to know the obligations and rewards of active citizenship.

But for all its concrete achievements, AmeriCorps has a fundamental flaw: in its seven years of existence, it has barely stirred the nation's imagination. In 1961, President John F. Kennedy launched the Peace Corps to make good on his famous challenge to "ask not what your country can do for you, but rather what you can do for your country." Since then, more than 162,000 Americans have served in the Peace Corps, and the vast majority of Americans today have heard of the organization. By contrast, more than 200,000 Americans have served in AmeriCorps, yet two out of three Americans say they have never heard of the program.

If we are to have a resurgence of patriotic service in this country, then programs like AmeriCorps must be expanded and changed in ways that inspire the nation. There should be more focus on meeting national goals and on making short-term service, both civilian and military, a rite of passage for young Americans.

National service is an issue that has been largely identified with the Democratic Party and the left of the political spectrum. That is unfortunate because duty, honor, and country are values that transcend ideology, and thus national service, both civilian and military, can embody the virtues of patriotism that conservatives cherish.

More than a decade ago, the patron saint of modern conservatism, William F. Buckley Jr., offered an eloquent and persuasive conservative case for national service. In the book *Gratitude*, Buckley wrote, "Materialistic democracy beckons every man to make himself a king; republican citizenship incites every man to be a knight. National service, like gravity, is something we could accustom ourselves to, and grow to love."[1]

Buckley was right, but it's fair to say that it took a while before we conservatives accustomed ourselves to the idea. Indeed, when Clinton initiated AmeriCorps in 1994, most Republicans in Congress, myself included, opposed it. We feared it would be another "big government program" that would undermine true volunteerism, waste money in "make-work" projects, or be diverted into political activism.

We were wrong. Though AmeriCorps' record is not untarnished, the overall evidence for its effectiveness is hard to deny. For instance, Ameri-Corps members tutored over 100,000 first-through-third graders during the 1999–2000 school year. On average, those children scored significantly higher on reading performance tests than would otherwise have been expected, according to Abt Associates, an independent evaluation firm.[2] Having seen results like these—and having often seen AmeriCorps members at work on the ground—more and more of my GOP colleagues have changed their minds about the program. Forty-nine of fifty governors, twenty-nine of them Republicans, signed a letter last year urging Congress to support AmeriCorps. One of the signers was then-governor of Texas George W. Bush.

Part of what conservatives admire about AmeriCorps is that it strengthens "civil society"—the rich web of neighborhood, nonprofit, and faith-based groups outside of government that provide services to those in need. This is built into the decentralized design of the program. Most AmeriCorps funding is in the hands of state governors, who give it to their national and community service commissions; these, in turn, make grants to local nonprofits, who then recruit and hire AmeriCorps members. The vast majority of AmeriCorps members are thus "detailed" to work for organizations like Habitat for Humanity, the Red Cross, or Big Brothers/Big Sisters. They become, in effect, full-time, paid staff members of these often understaffed organizations.

Rather than elbowing out other volunteers, as many of us feared, AmeriCorps members typically are put to work recruiting, training, and supervising other volunteers. For instance, most of the more than 500 AmeriCorps members who work for Habitat for Humanity spend less time swinging hammers themselves than making sure that hammers, nails, and drywall are at the worksite when the volunteers arrive. They then teach the volunteers the basic skills of how to hang drywall. As a result, studies show that each AmeriCorps member generates, on average, nine additional volunteers.[3]

The ability to provide skilled and motivated manpower to other organizations is what makes AmeriCorps so effective. But it also creates a problem. AmeriCorps members often take on the identity of the organizations they're assigned to. In the process, they often lose any sense of being part of a larger national service enterprise, if they ever had it at all. Indeed, staffers at nonprofit groups sometimes call AmeriCorps headquarters looking for support for their organizations, only to find out that their own salaries are being paid by AmeriCorps. It's no wonder most Americans say they have never heard of the program. And a program few have heard of will obviously not be able to inspire a new ethic of national service.

I believe AmeriCorps needs to be expanded and changed in ways that do not alter those aspects of the program that make it effective but rather build greater esprit de corps among members and encourage a sense of national unity and mission. There is no doubt that this can be done because some smaller programs within AmeriCorps are already doing it. One example is City Year, an AmeriCorps effort that began in Boston and is now operating in thirteen American cities. City Year members wear uniforms, work in teams, learn public speaking skills, and gather together for daily calisthenics, often in highly public places such as in front of city hall. They also provide vital services, such as organizing after-school activities and helping the elderly in assisted-living facilities.

Another example is AmeriCorps' National Civilian Community Corps (NCCC), a service program consciously structured along military lines. NCCC members not only wear uniforms and work in teams, as City Year members do, but actually live together in barracks on former military bases and are deployed to service projects far from their home base. This "24-by-7" experience fosters group cohesion and a sense of mission. AmeriCorps' NCCC members know they are a part of a national effort to serve their country. The communities they serve know that, too.

Only about 1,000 of AmeriCorps' 50,000 members are a part of NCCC. City Year accounts for another 1,200. Congress should expand these two programs dramatically and spread their group-cohesion techniques to other AmeriCorps programs. Indeed, the whole national service enterprise should be expanded, with the ultimate goal of ensuring that every young person who wants to serve can serve. Though this will require significantly more funding, the benefits to our nation will be well worth the investment. At the same time, we must encourage the corporate sector and the philanthropic community to provide funding for national service, with federal challenge grants and other incentives.

We should also be concerned by the growing gap between our nation's military and civilian cultures. While the volunteer military has been successful, fewer Americans know and appreciate the sacrifices and contributions of their fellow citizens who serve in uniform. The military is suffering severe recruitment problems.

In the past, it has been a rite of passage for our nation's leaders to serve in the armed forces. Today, fewer and fewer of my congressional colleagues know from experience the realities of military life. The decline of the citizen-soldier is not healthy for a democracy. Although it is not currently politically practical to revive the draft, it is important to find better incentives and opportunities for more young Americans to choose service in the military, if not for a career, then at least for a limited period of time.

If we are to have a resurgence of patriotic service in this country, then programs like AmeriCorps must be expanded and changed in ways that inspire the nation. There should be more focus on meeting national goals and on making short-term service, both civilian and military, a rite of passage for young Americans.

That is why Senator Evan Bayh and I have introduced legislation to revamp national service programs and dramatically expand opportunities for public service. Many tasks lie ahead, both new and old. On the home front, there are new security and civil defense requirements, such as increased police and border patrol needs. We will charge the Corporation for National Service, the federal office that oversees national volunteer programs, with the task of assembling a plan that would put civilians to work assisting the Office of Homeland Security. And because the military will need new recruits to confront the challenges abroad, our bill will also improve benefits for members of our armed services.

At the same time, because the society we defend needs increased services, from promoting literacy to caring for the elderly, we will expand AmeriCorps and senior service programs to enlarge our national army of volunteers. Currently, more than 50,000 volunteers serve in AmeriCorps. Under our bill, 250,000 volunteers each year would be able to answer the call—with half of them assisting in civil defense needs and half continuing the good work of AmeriCorps.

We must also ask our nation's colleges to promote service more aggressively. Currently, many colleges devote only a small fraction of federal work-study funds to community service, while the majority of federal resources are used to fill low-skill positions. This was not Congress's vision when it passed the Higher Education Act of 1965. Under our bill, universities will be required to promote student involvement in community activities more vigorously.

We also seek to better enable seniors age fifty-five and older to serve their communities in a variety of capacities, including education, long-term care, and acting as foster grandparents. Our legislation removes the low-income requirement for participation in all three Senior Service programs, provides low-income seniors with a stipend for service, and creates a competitive grant program to provide seniors with training both to prepare and encourage them to serve.

And for those who might consider serving their country in the armed forces, the benefits must keep pace with the times. Although the volunteer military has been successful, our armed forces continue to suffer from significant recruitment challenges. On May 10, 2002, the Senate Armed Services Committee passed the military service program that was part of the original McCain-Bayh national service legislation.[4] This program would offer a new short-term enlistment option for the armed services. Individuals who volunteer under the new program would be required to serve on active duty for fifteen months after completion of initial entry training. They then complete the remainder of their military service obligation by participating in the Selected Reserve and subsequently in the Individual Ready Reserve or in a civilian national service program such as the Peace Corps or AmeriCorps.

I strongly believe that public service is a virtue. This is the right moment to issue a new call to service and give a new generation a way to claim the rewards and responsibilities of active citizenship.

In America our rights come before our duties, as well they should. We are a free people, and among our freedoms is the liberty to care or not care for our birthright. However, those who claim their liberty but not their duty to the civilization that ensures it live a half-life, indulging their self-interest at the cost of their self-respect. The richest men and women possess nothing of real value if their lives have no greater object than themselves.

Success, wealth, celebrity gained and kept for private interest—these are small things. They make us comfortable, ease the way for our children, and purchase a fleeting regard for our lives but not the self-respect that, in the end, matters most. Make a sacrifice for a cause greater than self-interest, however, and you invest your life with the eminence of that cause.

National service is a crucial means of making our patriotism real, to the benefit of both our country and ourselves.

8

The Duties of Democracy

WILLIAM J. CLINTON

ONE OF THE MOST gratifying responses to the tragedies of September 11 was the sudden desire of millions of Americans to give something back to their country for the blessings of democracy and freedom. Many citizens, especially young ones, would do much more if given the opportunity to serve. A system of voluntary national service would harvest this new growth in our civic capital by mobilizing Americans to meet the big challenges facing our country, including the urgent new one of homeland security.

Citizen service is as old as our republic. Observers of America as early as Alexis de Tocqueville recognized that the young country's defining characteristic was voluntary citizen participation in associations and community life. But the idea of citizen service is also as new as the astonishing spread of democracy and the institutions of civil society around the world during the past decade. Citizen service—as important a part of a healthy democracy as voting participation or a stable political system—bridges isolated individuals, local communities, the national community, and, ultimately, the community of all people.

One of my proudest accomplishments as president was to help revive our tradition of citizen service through the AmeriCorps national service initiative. AmeriCorps was modeled after the citizen service program, City Year, and is based on the simple idea that we should offer young people a chance to serve their community and country for a year or two and then receive help paying for a college education or paying off college loans. The initiative started small and unfortunately got caught in the fierce political crossfire of the 1990s.

Republican opposition to AmeriCorps turned first into grudging acceptance, then into enthusiastic support. In 1997 Colin Powell—now secretary of state—organized a summit for service that called for an expansion of national service opportunities. Governors lauded the work of AmeriCorps: forty-nine of them asked Congress to continue to support it. Sen. John McCain (R-Ariz.), once an AmeriCorps opponent, had a change of mind and heart and made expansion of national service a central theme in his 2000 presidential campaign. By the time I left office, over 200,000 young people had served in AmeriCorps, more than in the entire forty-year history of the Peace Corps.

AmeriCorps continues to thrive, and I am proud of everything that has been accomplished through the program and continue to enjoy working with young people from across the country as they fulfill their voluntary national service commitments. We are expanding the program in America and internationally, particularly in South Africa, where there are currently eleven City Year fellows working to develop pathways for engaging others in service and strengthening democracy in their home country through advocacy, dialogue, and workshop training.

A New Rite of Passage

Participation in AmeriCorps is a badge of honor for some of our brightest, most promising young people. The value of AmeriCorps to the people and the communities that benefited from its work was enormous: houses were rehabilitated, poor children learned to read, neighborhood-watch networks were established, hundreds of thousands of new trees were planted, and hundreds of thousands of new volunteers were organized and trained, all due to the efforts of AmeriCorps members.

But I also think we should do more to instill a desire to participate in service programs when people are younger. Maryland is the only state in the country that requires school students to engage in community service to earn a high school diploma. Students can begin to fulfill this requirement when they are in middle school, and through service-learning they are able to contribute to pressing community needs while improving their academic knowledge by applying what they have learned in class to real-life situations. This is a good thing to do, and I wish every state did it.

Voting

In addition to national service, one of the most critical components of a healthy democracy is an active voting body. Ideas of citizenship and service are not complete without encouraging the young people of this country to participate and be heard through the ballot box. It was Lyndon Johnson who once told us: "Voting is the first duty of democracy." We must never forget this responsibility nor can we forget the people who, for generations, fought to give us that right.

Yet I can understand how even smart, engaged, and self-confident young people can become discouraged by the feeling that so many of the problems they see in the world seem beyond the reach of ordinary citizens. Even if 100 percent of the people who participate in some kind of national service program actually vote, that still leaves a lot of people who feel left out, left behind, and unengaged. So the trick is to get more people into service and more people voting. How can we do this?

If every student voted in every election from the time they start the first grade until they get out of high school, it would dramatically increase the number of people who would keep voting as adults. I think schools should hold mock elections every two years when states have their elections, and every school child should vote after learning in class about each candidate and some of the issues. Then the votes would be tallied and reported.

It is important that young people get into the habit of participation through voting and citizen service. We cannot afford to continue this trend of ever decreasing participation among young adults. America will be a better country if our young people both serve and vote.

Heeding the Nation's Call

In 2002 Senators McCain and Evan Bayh (D-Ind.) offered the best, most ambitious legislative proposal for taking national service to a national scale. President Bush, in his January 2002 State of the Union address, joined the national service movement by calling on Americans to give something back through service and by asking Congress to expand Ameri-Corps and other service opportunities.

We must take full advantage of the current convergence of political support for national service and the deep desire of so many Americans to serve. While every new ounce of civic capital is important, we should not be satisfied with incremental expansions of service opportunities; it is time for a quantum leap. And while all Americans should be asked to set aside such time as they have for service, it is also time to ensure that those willing to serve full time have the opportunity to do so.

Now is the right time to make national service an integral part of our society and a regular rite of passage for our citizens. It is also the time to address our pressing need to increase the number of Americans voting. Terrorism is not simply a security threat; it is also a challenge to our faith in democracy and to our willingness to work for and live by the values the world understands as "American." Voting will transform our voices into action. Citizen service will help us manifest our faith and secure our future.

9

Thinking Bigger
about Citizenship

WILL MARSHALL AND MARC MAGEE

OVER THE LAST decade, voluntary national service has secured a small but vital beachhead in national policy. Now a powerful confluence of factors suggests the possibility of a breakout that could take national service to a truly national scale. Most important, of course, was the September 11 attack on America, which sparked an intensely patriotic response that has manifested itself in a yearning for national unity and a surge in applications to programs such as AmeriCorps and the Peace Corps. As Americans ask what they can do to protect their country against a terrifying new barbarism, national service offers a potential vehicle for mobilizing citizens to contribute to the common defense at home and abroad.

Another key factor has been the sterling performance of AmeriCorps, the nation's main national service initiative. Now at 50,000 strong, AmeriCorps has proven its ability to match young volunteers to work that is highly valued by the communities they serve. At the same time, AmeriCorps has become a training ground for multiethnic democracy, one of the few public venues in which youths from different ethnic and class backgrounds routinely interact. All this has spawned growing public and political support for national service around the country. State and local elected leaders as well as local nonprofit groups have welcomed the help of the highly motivated and disciplined service members organized by such groups as City Year, Public Allies, and Teach for America with financial support from AmeriCorps. Faith-based organizations like Habitat for Humanity have shown how AmeriCorps members can help them recruit and oversee a growing force of volunteer homebuilders without violating constitutional safeguards against public support for religion. Businesses also are chipping in hundreds of millions to support national service projects in their communities.

The gathering momentum of national service, however, could be checked without enlightened national leadership. What is needed now is a new push from the top to enlarge national service so that more citizens can serve. Our ultimate goal should be to make national service a common expectation—a civic rite of passage for young Americans and an opportunity for older Americans to pass something on to their children and grandchildren. Despite great strides, national service remains a small demonstration project on the margins of big government. It should become a truly national enterprise that helps usher in an era of big citizenship where Americans from all backgrounds are brought together in common efforts to tackle the great challenges of our time, such as

—tutoring and mentoring disadvantaged children, including those from broken families and those with a parent in prison;

—providing long-term care and other assistance for the elderly, to help America age successfully as the baby boomers retire;

—securing our homeland against terrorist attacks; and

—sharing the burden of fighting in America's defense.

This new experiment with national service has reached the point where it must take a great leap forward or risk going the way of the Peace Corps and Volunteers in Service to America (VISTA), noble endeavors that languished after an initial burst of inspiration and failed to reach critical mass. While the era of big government is over, big challenges still remain. Scaling up America's national service programs will make it possible for us as a nation to tackle these big challenges with big citizenship.

In this chapter, we examine the evolution of the national service experiment from conception to its current state, explore tensions and competing interpretations of service, and propose a set of benchmarks for realizing what we see as the transformative promise of national service.

A Brief History of National Service

The concept of national service has intrigued Americans since William James first proposed it in his famous 1910 essay, "The Moral Equivalent of War."[1] Like his Gilded Age contemporary, Teddy Roosevelt, James worried that America's newfound wealth would make its young soft and selfish, sapping the hardy pioneer spirit that had built the nation. He envisioned service as a way to "inflame the civic temper" and foster the sentiments of solidarity and common endeavor that characterize societies at war but often dissipate in peacetime.

As U.S. leaders have learned in trying to rally the nation to confront ills ranging from poverty to oil dependence to drugs, there probably is no moral equivalent of war. Nonetheless, the idea of enlisting the nation's youth to serve their country has proved remarkably durable, resurfacing in one form or another for decades. It was not until the late 1980s, however, that a serious attempt was made to give it concrete expression in national policy. The catalyst was the founding of the Democratic Leadership Council (DLC), whose leaders made national service the centerpiece of their campaign to revive a politics of civic reciprocity and mutual responsibility.

New Democrats challenged the impoverished conception of citizenship that prevailed on both ends of the left-right spectrum. The left's demand for expanding rights and entitlements, they said, eroded civic responsibility by promising "something for nothing." The right's social Darwinism, with its remorseless, "every-man-for-himself" ethos, saw Americans as unencumbered by obligations to each other or to the larger community. By proposing a large-scale national service plan that linked public benefits (chiefly college aid) to public service, New Democrats sought to strike a new balance of citizen rights and responsibilities. The DLC, then chaired by Senator Sam Nunn, described its 1988 proposal as a new "G.I. bill" expanded to include civilian as well as military service to the nation. Its blueprint synthesized elements of earlier research on national service, especially the work of Northwestern University sociologist Charles Moskos, into a proposal of unprecedented scope and scale.[2]

In January of 1989, Senators Nunn, Charles Robb, and Barbara Mikulski and Representative David McCurdy introduced the Citizenship and National Service Act, based on the DLC proposal. The bill proposed a large-scale (800,000-member) Citizen Corps that would offer young Americans an opportunity to earn federal tuition vouchers by serving in their communities or as short-term "citizen-soldiers" in the armed forces. While in the end Nunn and his allies were forced to settle for a small demonstration project in 1990, his successor as DLC chairman, Arkansas governor Bill Clinton, kept the national service flame alive. In 1992 Clinton made national service a touchstone of his New Democrat campaign, and in 1993 President Clinton steered through Congress the National and Community Service Trust Act, which created AmeriCorps.

After taking control of Congress in the 1994 midterm election, however, the new Republican majority tried repeatedly to smother the fledgling AmeriCorps in its crib. The newly elected Speaker of the House, Newt Gingrich, led the attack against AmeriCorps, labeling it "coerced volunteerism" and arguing that its participants were "not only useless but dangerous." Gingrich was joined in his attacks in the House by Representative Dick Armey, who dubbed AmeriCorps "a welfare program for aspiring yuppies." In the Senate, Rick Santorum derided AmeriCorps as a program "for hippie kids to stand around a campfire singing 'Kumbaya' at taxpayers' expense."[3] Year after year, House GOP leaders "zeroed out" funding for AmeriCorps, only to see it restored in the end-of-the-year scramble to pass appropriations bills.

After the 2000 election and Clinton's departure, New Democrats saw an opportunity to move beyond the rancid partisanship of the 1990s and forge bipartisan support for national service. As AmeriCorps grew and worked out some early kinks, it won over many of its erstwhile detractors. By 2000 forty-nine governors (including George W. Bush of Texas) had signed a letter urging Congress to restore full funding to AmeriCorps.[4] In the Senate, thanks to the missionary efforts of former Democratic senator Harris Wofford, head of the Corporation for National Service, such outspoken GOP critics as Charles Grassley and Santorum had changed their tune.

In November 2001, amid the aftershocks of the September 11 attacks, Sen. Evan Bayh (D-Ind.) teamed up with Sen. John McCain (R-Ariz.) to propose a dramatic expansion of national service. Their Call to Service Act marked a milestone in the evolution of national service in four crucial respects. First, it called for scaling up civilian national service by expanding the Senior Corps in preparation for the coming wave of baby boomer retirees and for quintupling AmeriCorps' annual enrollment to 250,000. Second, the Bayh-McCain plan yoked national service to homeland defense, requiring that half the new funding for AmeriCorps be dedicated to work on domestic security or public safety. Third, the bill weaved military and civilian service into a seamless fabric by creating a new "citizen-soldier" option for young Americans who want to serve their country in uniform without choosing a military career. Fourth, the Bayh-McCain bill marked a new, bipartisan stage in the politics of national service. And as prominent conservatives like McCain embraced national service, they also brought new ideas and emphases to this evolving civic experiment.

The September 11 attacks seemed to have altered President Bush's outlook on national service. Before the attacks, the White House had been planning to unveil a "Communities of Character" initiative that would "spotlight places across the nation where people voluntarily came together to solve problems, putting others' interests above their own."[5] This approach was consistent with the first president Bush's approach to service, which extolled private volunteerism and derided national service as "paid volunteerism."

After the attacks, however, the president ditched those plans and instead unveiled, in his January 2002 address to Congress, his USA Freedom Corps initiative. As described by the president, the USA Freedom Corps is designed to increase opportunities for Americans to fulfill his call "for every American to commit at least two years—4,000 hours over the rest of your lifetime—to the service of your neighbors and your nation." The initiative would provide new funding for existing part-time volunteer programs, such as Neighborhood Watch and Volunteers in Police Service, that encourage Americans to volunteer a few hours a week in their communities, and new funding for part-time Senior Corps programs. Crucially, however, the initiative also called for a 25,000-member expansion of AmeriCorps—a move that infuriated adamantly anti-Clinton Republicans such as former majority leader Dick Armey, who groused, "I do not understand why anyone would embrace AmeriCorps. I think the conceptual framework of AmeriCorps is obnoxious."[6] The Bush plan is thus an amalgam of GOP conservatives' preference for "Points of Light" volunteerism and New Democrats' conception of national service as full-time, year-round public work.

Unfortunately, the White House failed to push the plan vigorously in 2002, as the president spent his political capital on the midterm election rather than securing bipartisan legislative accomplishments. National service advocates nonetheless scored a major victory in 2002: on December 2 the president signed into law a modified version of the Bayh-McCain citizen-soldier enlistment option, potentially the most important change in military recruitment policy since the end of the draft. It enables volunteers to sign up for fifteen months of service on active duty (the average enlistment now is four years) followed by service in the reserves and then either a period of availability in the nondrilling Individual Ready Reserves or civilian service in AmeriCorps or the Peace Corps. A big push to recruit more enlistees through this short-term citizen-soldier program, together with a national call to service, would not only help spread the risks of defending America more widely and equitably, but would also help ease the strains on the reserves created by the war on terrorism and contain the military's growing manpower costs.[7]

Having made unexpected progress in the creation of this citizen-soldier enlistment track, national service proponents should press for a robust expansion of this innovative program while also redoubling their efforts to secure a major expansion of civilian service, especially AmeriCorps. Now that Republicans control both houses of Congress, the ball is squarely in the president's court, and it remains to be seen whether he will give his Freedom Corps proposal the high priority he attached to it when unveiling it last year.

Volunteerism versus National Service

If conservatives' opposition to national service is waning, it may be because their attempt to cast AmeriCorps as big government in a new guise was not very credible to begin with. As conceived by progressive centrists, national service is more than a government program; it is a new form of civic activism that relies on private citizens rather than public employees to tackle urgent national problems. Senator Barbara Mikulski memorably described national service as the latest example of a venerable American tradition of "social inventions" intended to promote mutual aid and self-help.[8] Like settlement houses and night school, which helped America absorb waves of immigrants, national service opens new paths of opportunity and upward mobility for young Americans and for the people they serve. And, like the G.I. bill, national service should be seen as a long-term investment in the education, skills, and ingenuity of our people.

Although President Bush's Freedom Corps proposal tends to conflate volunteerism and national service, it is clear from this definition that they are very different things. National service supporters, of course, have no beef with private volunteerism, which is one of the glories of a free, self-governing democracy. We believe, rather, that occasional and diffuse acts of volunteerism aren't sufficient to help us grapple with an array of national problems that require a more focused and systematic response. Because the president's proposal blurs the lines between national service and volunteerism, it is worth discussing those differences in greater detail.

Tackling National Needs

Volunteerism creates no systematic way to address America's most pressing needs. By definition, it sets no national priorities; instead, it enjoins Americans to engage in any kind of volunteer activity they choose. That could mean anything from contributing a few hours of service each week to the local garden club or little league to helping the homeless.

National service, in contrast, aims at mobilizing citizens in focused, disciplined, and results-oriented efforts to solve our biggest problems: offering hope and opportunity to the millions of American children trapped in a cycle of poverty, meeting the challenges of long-term aging in the face of the coming wave of baby boomer retirees, and securing the homeland from the new threats from abroad.

Uniting Military and Civilian Service

National service encompasses both military and civilian service to our country. By creating a citizen-soldier option for youths who want to serve in uniform without choosing military careers, national service strengthens the all-volunteer force by spreading the risks of defending America more widely and equitably, easing the strains created by long-lasting conflicts and helping contain rising manpower costs.

Volunteerism is geared to civilian service and doesn't address the nation's military needs. It is curious that although America is engaged in a far-reaching war on terrorism to defend our freedom, President Bush's Freedom Corps plan makes no mention of military service to the nation.

Rewarding Those Who Serve

Volunteerism offers no tangible incentives for service. The first president Bush best summed up this philosophy: "You don't need to be bribed with incentives and threatened with penalties to get engaged in community service. Service is its own reward, satisfaction guaranteed."[9]

National service, in contrast, is charged not with satisfying volunteers or making them "feel good about themselves" but instead with enlarging our civic capacity to solve our common problems. It is not simply or even primarily an exercise in altruism. Instead, its purpose is to create new opportunities for citizens to help themselves by helping others. It is a civic compact that says: public benefits should be linked to public services. In the best, Madisonian tradition, it fuses self-interest and civic responsibility rather than cultivating a patronizing spirit of noblesse oblige.

Investing in Human Capital

Whereas volunteerism is an investment of private time and energy, national service provides a dual investment in both the service members and those who are served. By linking full-time service with education scholarships, national service invests in America's human capital—the skills and brainpower of our people. Like the G.I. bill—which for each dollar spent generated three dollars in taxes from the better educated, higher earning veterans it produced—large-scale, voluntary national service will create a more resourceful and productive work force and stimulate broad prosperity by expanding federal support to higher education.[10]

Four Ways to Scale Up National Service

It is important to bear these distinctions in mind as the national service debate unfolds in the next Congress and possibly in the 2004 presidential campaign. We believe national service advocates should insist on the following steps.

Recruit More Citizen-Soldiers

The inclusion of the short-term citizen-soldier option in last year's defense authorization bill represents a historic leap forward for advocates of national service. By shortening the length of enlistment and basing recruitment on a call to service rather than the current focus on cash incentives, this citizen-soldier option offers the nation's most fortunate sons and daughters a voluntary equivalent of the old draft—a way to contribute to America's defense without choosing a military career.

However, the ultimate success of this effort to reconnect national service and national defense will be determined by how this citizen-soldier option is implemented beginning in October of this year. Although the president signed last year's defense authorization bill, he never endorsed the citizen-soldier option and did nothing during the course of the last year to advance its prospects. For this initiative to fulfill its promise of sharing the burden of fighting in America's defense more widely and equitably, it must be scaled up over the next several years until it is a central component of America's military recruitment efforts.

There are three steps that can be taken this year to ensure the creation of a robust citizen-soldier program. First, recruitment efforts in this citizen-soldier initiative should focus on college students, which the data show are both the most underrepresented group in today's armed forces and the group most receptive to short-term enlistments. Second, recruits brought into the armed forces through this citizen-soldier program should be given the opportunity to serve in important occupations with short training programs, such as military police, infantryman, and military intelligence. Third, national service advocates should insist on an ambitious set of recruitment targets beginning with the goal of recruiting 25,000 citizen-soldiers in the program's first year.

Expand AmeriCorps and Senior Corps

The Bayh-McCain bill offered the most ambitious proposal for scaling up AmeriCorps. It earmarked $15.5 billion over eight years to increase AmeriCorps from 50,000 to 250,000 members a year by 2010. Half of the new spending was for expanding the work AmeriCorps is already doing, while the other half was dedicated to homeland security. President Bush's Freedom Corps plan called for increasing AmeriCorps by 50 percent to 75,000 members. In order to expand opportunities for senior service in preparation for the coming wave of baby boomer retirees, the Bayh-McCain bill also provided an additional $50 million a year for Senior Corps and created a new "Silver Scholarship"—a $1,000 education award for 500 hours of tutoring or mentoring that a senior volunteer can designate for a grandchild. Bush's Freedom Corps plan mirrored these proposals.

However, the White House stood by last year as the House GOP leadership stripped the 2003 Corporation for National Service reauthorization bill of the president's proposed increase in AmeriCorps, blocked even this watered-down bill from coming up for a floor vote, and slashed the funding for AmeriCorps grants by one-third in the 2003 appropriations bill. As a result, the number of Americans serving in AmeriCorps is set to decline dramatically in the coming year. Prospects for getting the expansion of AmeriCorps back on track depend on the president's willingness to face down ideologues in his own party and keep his promise to expand AmeriCorps by 25,000 members. New Democrats should support the president's proposed expansion but also continue the push for the larger goal of a 250,000-member AmeriCorps program by 2010.

Link National Service and Homeland Security

The Bayh-McCain and White House proposals offered two distinct models for meeting the challenge of homeland security through an expansion of civilian service. Building on the existing AmeriCorps disaster preparedness, crime prevention, and crisis response programs, Bayh-McCain sought to scale up this service infrastructure to match the new challenges America faces in homeland security. By contrast, the White House plan relied on an as-yet-to-be-created network of Citizens Corps Councils to recruit part-time volunteers for homeland security tasks and put the Federal Emergency Management Agency (FEMA) in charge of organizing and providing support for these projects.

We believe the Bayh-McCain approach to homeland security is superior for three reasons. First, FEMA has no experience managing national service projects, whereas the Corporation for National and Community Service has built up considerable experience managing national service projects over the last eight years. Second, a proven model for integrating national service and disaster response activities already exists in AmeriCorps*National Civilian Community Corps programs, where the Corporation manages the projects and organizations such as FEMA and the Red Cross assist in the training of service members. Third, building an alternative system of service from scratch would take considerable time and result in a costly duplication of the existing national service infrastructure.[11] Given the pressing needs of homeland security and the proven ability of the Corporation for National Service to manage effective service projects, national service advocates should insist that the majority of funds for civilian homeland security efforts go to projects within the existing service infrastructure as advocated under Bayh-McCain.

Replace Work-Study with Serve-Study

The Federal Work-Study Program underwrites the cost of college for nearly one million students at a cost of $1 billion a year. According to Harris Wofford, now chairman of America's Promise, the program was originally designed to serve two purposes: providing low- to middle-income students with additional money to pay for college and increasing the number of students participating in community service activities. Yet the overwhelming majority of work-study students today do their service on campus, not in the community. In effect, they constitute an enormous pool of cheap labor for college administrators.

Both the Bayh-McCain and White House proposals sought to restore the program to its original purpose. The former sought to increase work-study funds specifically targeted for work in community service organizations from the 7 percent currently required in the Higher Education Act to 25 percent by 2010. This change would result in an additional 125,000 students serving in community service organizations per year, at virtually no cost to taxpayers. The White House proposal went even further, boosting the percentage to 50 percent by 2010.

Yet both met scorched earth resistance from college administrators and the powerful higher education lobby, who claimed a shift from campus-based to community service would force them to jack up tuition fees and interfere with students' education. But a UCLA study conducted in 2000 suggests that community service activities, far from being a burden on college students, are connected with a number of positive outcomes, including better performance in the classroom.[12] National service advocates and the White House should join forces to insist that Congress not wait another year to begin the process of replacing on-campus jobs with real community service.

Conclusion

These four ways to scale up national service all point toward the same end: replacing big government with big citizenship by helping voluntary national service achieve critical mass. By bringing tens and eventually hundreds of thousands of citizens together to meet the great challenges of our time, we will hasten the day when it will become routine for Americans to ask each other, what did you do for your national service? We are confident that Americans are ready to serve; all they need is for the nation's leaders to afford them the opportunity.

10

Solving Problems through Service
Labor and National Service

ANDREW L. STERN

To MAKE A REAL difference, initiatives for national service and civic participation must not be limited to recent college graduates or retirees who are able to volunteer their time or work for subsistence wages. Working together, unions, employers, and government can increase opportunities for participation by low-income workers who would add diversity to the ranks of national service and benefit from the learning experience that civic participation provides.

The 1.5 million members of the Service Employees International Union serve our nation every day. They care for the sick as nurses and doctors, nursing assistants and medical technicians, home care and nursing home workers. They protect workplace health and safety as security officers and janitors. They work in children's services, law enforcement, and environmental protection. A true national service initiative could unleash their talent and energy.

One way to expand civic participation would be to designate election day as "National Citizenship Day" and require employers to provide a paid holiday to encourage working people to vote and perform community service as local election board poll workers or on behalf of nonpartisan election day activities. Unions already help workers register and vote, without regard for political affiliation. But many workers cannot find time to vote, let alone participate in other aspects civic life and community service. Many are holding down two or three jobs to make ends meet. In nearly two-thirds of married-couple households with children, both parents are working. Mandatory overtime keeps many on the job well beyond the eight-hour day. Meanwhile, most working families are scrambling to piece together childcare and elder care and to secure health care. If the United States is to be a nation "of the people" and "by the people," working families need time set aside when they can choose elected leaders and the policies they will be pledged to carry out.

Millions of the hardest-working people in America today are recent immigrants. They harvest and serve our food, care for our children and our sick, and build and clean our homes and offices—yet their legal status keeps them on the fringe of our communities. Unions are often immigrants' entry point into civic life. We help them achieve living wages, affordable health care, and career ladders. We provide English classes so that workers can improve their job status and better understand their adopted country. But hard-working, taxpaying immigrant workers cannot become full participants in this country without a national commitment to legalization.

Not so long ago, President Bush was an outspoken advocate for providing a clear and achievable pathway to citizenship. After September 11, he and others backed off that conversation with the American people, but it is now time to resume it. National service by itself is not an answer to legalization, but it could be part of a renewed discussion about the need to acknowledge the contributions immigrants make to American society. Why not make a two-year commitment to national service one pathway to legalization? Union leaders and employers together could identify eligible current and future workers for screening by appropriate authorities. After legal checks, undocumented workers (and legal immigrants who are more than two years away from citizenship) could participate in national service jobs and gain credit toward legal status and, ultimately, citizenship. During their service, workers could attend English and citizenship classes.

The nation could also benefit from a concerted program to give workers who have been convicted of a felony an opportunity to reenter society. More than 3.8 million people who have been convicted of a felony are denied voting rights and full participation in our communities. Some states have passed laws that allow reinstatement of full citizenship after release, parole, and probation periods. Why not find appropriate national service opportunities to enable these men and women to earn credits toward restoration of full citizenship at the same time that they gain work experience and new skills?

Establishing a National Citizenship Day on election day, rewarding hard-working immigrants, and reintegrating those who have served time for past crimes are just three ways to expand national service and civic participation programs to include working people. If we are going to achieve the mission of the Corporation for National and Community Service to "foster civic responsibility, strengthen the ties that bind us together as a people, and provide educational opportunity for those who make a substantial commitment to service," working people must be part of the process.

11

Doing Well and Doing Good
The Business Community and National Service

JEFF SWARTZ

I AM THE THIRD generation of my family to run the Timberland Company. My grandfather was an immigrant to this country. A man of few words, big dreams, and real values, he built boots, the same ones we market today all over the world. And he taught his sons, and they taught me, what it takes to run a business or to live a purposeful life: a commitment to humility, humanity, integrity, and excellence—values that are the cornerstone of our company today in the global economy.

For the business community, doing well and doing good should not be separate or separable efforts. Every day, everywhere, we compete in the global economy, but at the center of our efforts should be the premise of service, service to something larger than self-interest, a demand more pressing even than this quarter's earnings. While we are absolutely accountable to our shareholders, we must also recognize and accept our responsibility to share our strength—to work, in the context of for-profit business, for the common good.

For me, service is about "the Work"—doing the Work and working to perfect the universe. That such an aspiration, normally housed in a faith construct, can be applied in a day-to-day business is the beauty of service at Timberland. I can benefit the shareholder and the customer and fulfill a larger mission at the same time.

Understanding the role of service in perfecting the universe was not an intellectual experience for me. It was visceral. I received a letter one day, the standard, well-intended plea for charity from yet another worthy nonprofit. This one, City Year, was an urban peace corps of sorts starting up in Boston, near where I live. The letter described fifty young people, out to save the world, lacking only boots for their feet. Would I send along the boots?

Who knows why I did or why the cofounder of City Year decided to come to my office and challenge me to spend four hours doing community service with him and a small group of young leaders near our headquarters in New Hampshire. But I sent the boots, Alan Khazei paid the visit, and I accepted the challenge to serve. Thus I found myself, not a mile from our headquarters, face-to-face with the stories you read in the newspaper, face-to-face with a vision for America not unlike the one that drew my grandfather to leave Russia in steerage so many years ago. I spent four hours with the corps members from City Year and some young recovering drug addicts in a group home. As I painted some walls, I also felt the world shaking under my feet. In America? At this time of plenty?

Behind my desk again, deeply unsettled but also moved by my own sense of having served, albeit briefly, a larger purpose, I felt that all that mattered was figuring out how service could become part of daily life at Timberland. In fact, each of the ten of us who served that day experienced a personal transformation, and as a result, we worked together to create the Path of Service.

Formally launched in 1992, the Path of Service galvanized the spirit of volunteerism and citizenship that permeates our company. It engages the skills and talents of employees to create long-term solutions for critical community needs. In addition, the lessons learned from such service then shape our actions each day with and for shareholders, customers, employees, and communities. The Path of Service is the canvas on which our ideals and beliefs are expressed. As Marian Wright Edelman wrote, "Service is the rent we pay for being. It is the very purpose of life, and not something you do in your spare time."[1]

In 1997 we expanded the Path of Service and founded Serv-a-Palooza, an annual celebration of community and service that unites employees, vendors, community partners, and youth from our home community and twenty nations worldwide in a day of transformational service. For one full day each May, the sun never sets on Timberland employees' service. How is that for an alternative definition of globalization? With passion, innovation, and a singular sense of purpose, we have sought to improve our communities and the condition of those beside whom we live and work. And we have benefited: we have been given wisdom, humility, and a stronger sense of justice.

If the United States is to establish a national service agenda, corporate America as a whole must take action. Thus I recently joined a group of seventeen other corporate leaders, representing a variety of industries, to create Businesses Strengthening America, a long-term effort to engage hundreds of America's business leaders in helping corporations, employees, and consumers answer President Bush's State of the Union call to service. Its premise is that a strong commitment to volunteering and civic responsibility serves corporate interests, as well as community, national, and global needs, by increasing employee productivity and employee, consumer, and shareholder loyalty. With this in mind, organizing a company around the value of service is more than beneficial: it is a necessity.

12

Flying Colors
Americans after September 11

DAVID WINSTON

EXACTLY WHAT HAPPENED to America in fall 2001? In focus groups I have conducted since September 11, I have been constantly amazed at the number of people who watched live on television as the second plane crashed into the World Trade Center. All were deeply shaken by the sight of hundreds of innocent men and women dying in an instant. When the two towers collapsed, the horror was magnified and forever etched in people's minds.

In the hours and days after the attack, however, Americans saw something else—something surprising that would give them strength, make them proud, and show the world what this country is made of. Average Americans, suddenly forced into horrific situations, simply did their jobs and, in doing so, became true heroes. They were there when the country needed them.

Comments from focus groups conducted for the Ripon Society capture this changed attitude toward America: "I think everybody banded together. Everybody was an American and we all just worked together."[1] This revelation appears to have been startling. In the back of many people's minds, doubt had lingered as to whether this generation of Americans had what it takes to stand up to a tough challenge, the way the

"Greatest Generation" did in World War II. One focus group participant put it this way: "I think it's made me more grateful to be an American. I have never been patriotic, but I felt it for the first time really. My father was a Holocaust survivor who lived through hard times. My grandfather was a World War II veteran. And I think this is really our first test, although we haven't really had to do anything personally. This is really the first thing that has happened to my generation, the first terrible thing that we've really had to confront."

Before September 11, Americans harbored many doubts about themselves. Television, newspapers, radios, and magazines depicted a vain and self-centered society where average Americans made little or no individual contribution, the exchange of ideas had been reduced to television screaming matches, and politics had become ideological food fights intended to score partisan points rather than solve people's problems.

September 11 radically changed the political environment, at least for average Americans. Many surveys just before September 11 found Americans growing less certain about the direction of the country as the recession began to take its toll on the public's optimism. According to the August 29–30, 2001, New Models survey, 40 percent of the country thought we were headed in the right direction, while 44 percent thought we were headed off on the wrong track.[2] So logic dictated that after the attack in September, people's attitudes toward the direction of the country would likely become worse. Reporters, politicians, and pundits all predicted a terrible economic shock, and when the stock market reopened a week after the attacks, their forecast seemed on the money as stock values plunged. But the "direction of the country" numbers didn't follow Wall Street's negative path. Instead, optimism surged. An October 25–28, 2001, CBS–*New York Times* survey showed that people felt the country was headed in the right direction by a two-to-one margin.[3] A sense of pride in who we are as a country and as individuals overcame negative economic news in an unprecedented way. People saw that the heroism of New York's firefighters, police, and emergency personnel was more important than stock prices. The freedom that for many had been an abstract lesson in a civics class suddenly took on real meaning. Americans found themselves measuring their lives and their country not in economic terms but in values like family, friends, and community, with a newfound respect for each other. This new sense of community and bonding together as a people has created a unique opportunity for increased civic activity and involvement.

Following the horrific scenes of terror, people began talking with each other, asking questions most had rarely, if ever, asked themselves. Who are we as a country? Do we have good values? What does it mean to be an American? What does freedom mean? What is our responsibility as a nation and as individuals? What is really important to me personally? Are there good and evil in this world? That conversation resulted in four significant shifts in public opinion.

First and foremost, as people found a renewed faith and pride in their fellow Americans, patriotism surged. The spirit that swept America was not just a typical "rally round the flag" reaction to threats against the nation and its people. It sprang, in large part, from the country's sudden realization that we liked who we were as a people—a feeling that has generated a new sense of community.

Second, people turned away from cynicism and moral relativism. They began to believe once again in the concepts of right and wrong, of good and evil. For decades, the media, politicians, academicians, and other leaders shied away from moral judgments. Actions, good or bad, were often presented in ambiguous terms, rarely in black or white but in shades of more "comfortable" gray. September 11 changed that. Moral clarity replaced moral relativism for millions of Americans.

The third major shift was a new focus on key values. Before September 11, most Americans' political attitudes were usually determined by their views on specific issues, whether prescription drugs or education or foreign affairs. After September 11, issues were seen through a new, value-oriented perspective as Americans reassessed their principles and priorities. As a Ripon post–September 11 study found, the American public underwent a fundamental change. It no longer judged the state of the union solely in economic terms, as it had for decades, but instead moved to a more value-based estimation that, in turn, also shifted the traditional right track–wrong track evaluation from one based on issues to one based on values.[4]

Finally, the American public rejected partisanship. This trend away from ideological or partisan problem solving was under way before September 11. After September 11, however, the country saw the two parties and the two ideologies come together and get things done. Now Americans know the two parties can work together, and they expect it.

Most Americans understand that the nation faces "a clear and present danger" here at home and overseas. Yet, as the right track–wrong track data showed shortly after the terrorist attack, the challenges of September 11 reinvigorated the optimistic spirit of America in a way we hadn't seen in more than half a century.

As of this writing, after weeks of corporate scandals and a battering in the stock market that has devoured the retirement and college savings of millions of Americans, the right track–wrong track results have finally moved into the negative column. But it took a near-historic downturn and an assault on two major areas of concern—retirement security and the ability to fund their children's college education—to do it. And unlike negative right track–wrong track assessments in the past, recent Winston Group surveys indicate that people aren't blaming either party for the market's economic woes, and a majority is generally optimistic about the long-term future of America.[5]

This newfound resiliency, even in the face of serious economic troubles and continued terror threats, confirms that Americans' reassessment of values and their newfound sense of community since September 11 are neither shallow nor temporary.

In spring 2003, as the military stages of Operation Iraqi Freedom wound down, we saw Americans again expressing very positive attitudes. In one survey, roughly 60 percent saw the country headed in the right direction, despite continuing reservations about the economy. The reason was familiar: a close-up view of ordinary men and women "just doing their job" with bravery and dedication inspired national confidence. Through the embedded news reporters, soldiers became national figures and local heroes much as the police and fire fighters did on and after September 11.

13

A New Greatest Generation?

PETER D. HART AND MARIO A. BROSSARD

YOUNG PEOPLE TODAY are getting a bad rap. If you ask the typical forty-
or fifty-year-old what he or she thinks of today's young Americans, you'll
hear descriptions ranging from amoral and cynical to self-indulgent and
money-grubbing. But several surveys focusing exclusively on young people have been released this year, and all paint a portrait of a generation that
is both striking and encouraging. The surveys find that young Americans
are, in fact, among the most optimistic, least cynical adults; they are
actively engaged in helping to make their communities better places; and
they are tolerant and civically engaged.

In April 2002, Peter D. Hart Research Associates conducted a major
survey among 814 Americans aged eighteen to thirty for Public Allies, a
national service organization based in Milwaukee, to commemorate its
tenth anniversary.[1] The organization, an AmeriCorps program, identifies
talented young adults from diverse backgrounds and advances their leadership through full-time paid apprenticeships in nonprofit organizations,
weekly leadership training sessions, and team service projects. Another
poll on this topic, released in March 2002, was conducted the preceding
January for the Center for Information and Research in Civic Learning
and Engagement (CIRCLE) among 1,500 young people aged fifteen to
twenty-five.[2]

Instead of finding young Americans downcast about the implications
of the nation's recently declared war on terrorism and their seemingly

diminished employment prospects in the poorly performing economy, these surveys suggest that young Americans remain positive and quite optimistic about the future. By a two-to-one margin, youth aged eighteen to thirty say they think this is a good time in America's history for people their age, with lots of opportunities to get ahead and achieve their goals.[3]

This may come as a surprise because over the past couple of generations, American pollsters have recorded diminished levels of optimism and found that the trust many Americans place in their most important institutions has waned. Looking closely at results from recent NBC News–*Wall Street Journal* national surveys, however, we see that young people generally display more trust in certain American institutions— Congress, the FBI, the CIA, and the national news media—than do other adults. (See table 13-1.)

More important than how they look at institutions is how invested they are in making a difference. While their parents were activists in social protest and worked to make society more open and accepting, this generation's call to action is social issues and human rights. They are especially impressive because, unlike their parents, they are not protesters and marchers but participators and doers. They want to be involved one-to-one, and they want to make a difference. Their volunteerism is up close and personal.

Just as important, this generation displays a strong sense of self-confidence, believing they personally can make a difference. Almost half of young Americans aged fifteen to twenty-five say they believe they personally have the power to make at least "some" difference in solving the problems they see in their communities.[4] And the problems they are most interested in fixing tend to be those that allow them to have a direct impact on improving the everyday lives of the less fortunate in their local communities. Across the nation, 85 percent of those aged eighteen to thirty say that volunteering to help individuals in a direct way is a "very"(58 percent) or "fairly"(27 percent) effective way for them personally to bring about needed changes in our country.[5] Half (49 percent) of respondents in the CIRCLE survey say volunteering in local community activities to address local problems is the most important kind of activity in which a citizen can engage, and 23 percent say the same about participating in national organizations trying to change our society.[6]

Table 13-1. *Trust in American Institutions: A Generation Gap*
Percent

Questions and responses	Under age 30	Aged 30 and over
Confidence in Congress		
A great deal/quite a bit	47	35
Very little/none at all	7	19
Confidence in the national news media		
A great deal/quite a bit	38	28
Very little/none at all	25	0
Feelings toward the Federal Bureau of Investigation		
Very/somewhat positive	49	38
Very/somewhat negative	25	35
Feelings toward the Central Intelligence Agency		
Very/somewhat positive	37	30
Very/somewhat negative	27	8

Source: NBC News–*Wall Street Journal* polls. Questions about Congress and the news media are from a January 2002 poll; those about the FBI and CIA, from a June 2002 poll.

More important, they translate their words into deeds. The Public Allies survey finds two-thirds saying they have helped their communities within the past three years through activities such as volunteering their time, belonging to an organization, or advocating on a public issue.[7]

This generation is not volunteering as a way to pad resumes or look good on college applications. Almost half of those aged fifteen to twenty-five say they volunteer because it makes a difference (21 percent) or makes them feel good (24 percent)[8], while more than a third of those aged eighteen to thirty indicate that their impetus is a personal experience or issue they care about (22 percent) or that their spiritual or religious faith is the single greatest influence on their desire to improve their communities (14 percent).[9]

Although their preferred mode of service is one-to-one, their service has broad residual effects. Almost three quarters (74 percent) of Public Allies respondents say their service increased their interest in following news about a public issue or area of the community in which they had not previously been interested. Just as large a share of young adults—72 percent—say their service has enhanced their understanding of public issues, politics, government, or civics.

Significantly, a majority (55 percent) of all young adults surveyed say their activities have increased their tolerance or changed their views on people of different racial, ethnic, or religious backgrounds. A majority also indicate that their volunteering has changed their view on a public issue. Service, these results suggest, not only helps transform those being served but also helps convert those doing the serving into engaged, enlightened, and tolerant members of our civic society.

The types of service opportunities and organizations in which young adults express most interest explain some of these personal changes. Beyond tutoring and mentoring youth (75 percent), Public Allies finds that young adults display a "great deal" or "fair amount" of interest in volunteering to help build affordable housing for low-income families (65 percent), help community residents gain access to health care and other social services (60 percent), educate people about environmental conservation (53 percent), and assist with homeland security by helping communities prepare for threats of terrorism (53 percent). These independent surveys show that young people are not simply paying lip service to civic engagement—they take their role in our larger national community quite seriously.

The cry of the 1960s youth was "Never trust anyone over thirty." Ironically, the challenge to that now-aging generation is to begin to trust and believe in this new under-thirty generation. Although less than 10 percent of under-thirty Americans now know even a "fair amount" about the Bush administration's Freedom Corps, they are eager to participate in their communities on the most important issues of the day. It is time to salute them and provide them more avenues for participation.

PART THREE
Universal Service?

14

The Obligations of September 11, 2001
The Case for Universal Service

ROBERT E. LITAN

AMERICANS ARE A generous people. The attacks of September 11 produced an outpouring of donations to help families of the victims. Americans took pride in the heroism of public servants—firefighters, the police, FBI agents, and men and women in the military—who responded to the call of duty. It was also widely felt that September 11 would change the lives of many young Americans, who not only would have the images of the attacks seared into their memories but also would pursue careers in public service or the "helping" professions.

Time will tell whether those initial impulses toward helping others will last. But time alone won't determine the outcome. Public policy can and will have an impact. If Americans want more of their children to pursue service careers or at least devote time to activities that help and support others, whether in the public or private sector, it will certainly help if government encourages or provides opportunities for such service. The same is true for adults wishing to serve in some capacity, as many apparently were willing to do in the weeks following September 11.

President Bush, for one, has recognized the role of public policy by supporting a much-expanded voluntary national service program. In his fiscal year 2003 budget, he called for the creation of the USA Freedom Corps, which would combine and expand the Peace Corps and Ameri-Corps programs and add a new Senior Corps as well as a volunteer program for college students. Bush proposed increasing the funding of all national service programs by nearly $300 million and eventually placing more than 2 million Americans a year in some kind of formal national service (75,000 in full-time AmeriCorps programs). He also called on Americans to give two years over the course of their lives to service.

The Bush proposals tap into two strong American traditions—a commitment to volunteerism and a resistance to compulsory service except in wars requiring a massive call-up. With the exception of some community service programs in some high schools in certain states, this nation has never required its young citizens to perform civilian service.

The president's call to service may be working. Applications by college graduates to AmeriCorps are up 75 percent and applications to the Peace Corps are up 18 percent, according to a June 2002 survey in *Time*.[1] But the surge in interest may also be linked to the poor job market this past year for college graduates.

In short, there are limits to volunteerism. Can we do more? Here I lay out the case for moving beyond even the president's new initiative toward some kind of universal service requirement, one that would offer all young Americans a choice, preferably after finishing high school, to enter military or civilian service for at least a year. Those opting and qualifying for the military would be given additional monetary incentives to do so.

Having a reasoned debate about universal service before September 11 would have been unthinkable. It isn't (or at least shouldn't be) anymore.

The Case for Universal Service Now

As the Bush administration has reminded us, we are at war—this time, against an enemy whose main targets of attack are American civilians. Unlike past wars, this new war on terrorism, we are told, could last a generation or more. In addition, in March 2003 the United States led a coalition of nations in a war with Iraq aimed at dismantling that country's weapons of mass destruction. The question thus arises: why should the burden of these wars—and the risks of getting injured or killed—rest only on the shoulders of those who volunteer to fight them?

There are answers to this question, of course. One is that the armed services look fully able to handle both military campaigns. They fought Iraq in 1991 with roughly 500,000 troops; this time around, the highest projections seem to fall in the 350,000 range (the drop in numbers being more than compensated by improved war-fighting technology). A second answer is that the men and women in uniform are paid to put themselves in harm's way, and they volunteered to assume any risk of war that may come about.

But unlike America's past foreign wars, the war on terrorism requires a vigilant homeland security effort in addition to an offensive military (and intelligence) campaign abroad. This time around, it is not just those in the military who are in harm's way. We are all potential targets or victims—and thus all of us have some obligation to help secure America. As a practical matter, neither the economy nor society could function if everyone stood guard duty or devoted their time to protecting the homeland. Paid professionals have and will continue to carry out these duties. But if this new war is, as it is said to be, a generational event, then why not also ask the next generation—all of whom may be at risk—to help shoulder the security burden?

The need is there. Young people in service, provided they were properly trained, could substantially augment the guards now in place at a wide range of public and private facilities. The nation could also use many more inspectors at its ports—perhaps our greatest vulnerability today—where only a tiny fraction of incoming containers is examined. Some highly motivated young people may even decide to train for security-related careers—as police officers, customs or immigration officials, or FBI agents—and serving in all of these jobs should qualify for universal service.

Though one good reason for adopting universal service now is to respond to the military and homeland threat, universal service makes sense in other ways in this time of national peril.

First, universal service could provide some much-needed "social glue" in an embattled American society that is growing increasingly diverse—by race, national origin, and religious preference—and where many young

Americans from well-to-do families grow up and go to school in hermetically sealed social environments. Twenty years ago, when America was much less diverse than it is now and is going to be, the editorial page of the *Wall Street Journal* (of all places) opined that mandatory service would constitute a "means for acculturation, acquainting young people with their fellow Americans of all different races, creeds, and economic backgrounds."[2]

Those words are as compelling today as when they were written. A service program in which young people from different backgrounds work and live together would do far more than college ever could to immerse young Americans in the diversity of our country. It would also help sensitize more fortunate young men and women, at an impressionable point in their lives, to the concerns and experiences of others from different backgrounds and give them an enduring appreciation of what life is like "on the other side of the tracks."

Second, universal service could promote civic engagement, which, as Harvard social scientist Robert Putnam has persuasively argued in *Bowling Alone*, has been declining—or at least was before September 11.[3] Some who perform service for the required period may believe their civic responsibilities will thereby be discharged, but many others are likely to develop an appreciation for helping others that could change the way they lead the rest of their lives.

Third, young people serving in a civilian capacity in particular would help satisfy unmet social needs beyond those associated with homeland security: improving the reading skills of tens of millions of Americans who cannot now read English at a high school level, cleaning up blighted neighborhoods, and helping provide social, medical, and other services to the elderly and to low-income individuals and families. Allowing individuals to delay their service until after college would enable them to bring skills to their service that could prove even more useful to society and thus may be a desirable option. But doing so would also reduce the benefits of added social cohesion from universal service because it would tend to create two tiers of service, one for those who don't go to college and another for those who do.

Finally, universal service would establish firmly the notion that rights for ourselves come with responsibilities to others. Of course, the Constitution

guarantees all citizens certain rights—free speech, due process of law, freedom from discrimination, voting—without asking anything of them in
return. But why shouldn't citizens be required to give something to their
country in exchange for the full range of rights to which citizenship entitles them?

Countering the Objections

As Bruce Chapman makes clear in the chapter that follows, imposing a
universal service requirement would raise serious objections aside from the
philosophical one—opposition to any form of government compulsion
and the temporary loss of liberty it entails. Probably the most serious argument against universal service is its cost. Roughly 4 million students graduate from high school each year. A good benchmark for costs is the Ameri-
Corps program. According to official figures, the federal government
spent roughly $10,000 for each AmeriCorps volunteer in fiscal year 2001.
A plausible assumption is that the states and the private sector added perhaps another $7,000. (A 1995 study by the General Accounting Office
suggested that these costs amounted then to about $5,500 per person, so
they might be close to $7,000 now.)[4] Given the relatively small numbers
enrolled in AmeriCorps—about 50,000 annually—its per person costs
may be higher than those for a much larger universal program, which
would be able to amortize overhead costs over a much larger population.
On the other hand, not all AmeriCorps volunteers live in a dormitory setting. Providing dormitories for all participants in a universal civilian program would raise the cost relative to AmeriCorps.

Balancing these factors, I assume here for illustrative purposes a per
person cost of $20,000, which, if funded entirely by the federal govern-
ment, would bring the total annual gross cost of the entire program to
about $80 billion. From this figure, it would be necessary to subtract the
costs of those who already serve in AmeriCorps and the Peace Corps, as
well as high school students who now volunteer for the military. In addition, some participants in a universal service program might be performing functions now carried out by paid workers. Taking all these offsets into

account could bring the annual net incremental cost of the program down to, say, the $70 billion range—still a very large number.

Given the recent dramatic deterioration of the federal budget, a program of that magnitude would seem now to be a political nonstarter, and it may well be. Nonetheless, one potentially fair way to reduce costs and thereby make the idea of universal service more palatable from a budgetary perspective would be to implement the requirement initially as a lottery, much like the system that existed toward the end of the Vietnam War. Depending on the cutoff point, the program could be sized at any level that the political traffic could bear.

However large the program could become, those who may be tempted to dismiss as too costly a universal service requirement of any size must consider its benefits. A 1995 GAO cost-benefit analysis, for example, positively evaluated the findings of a 1995 study by George R. Neumann, Roger C. Kormendi, Robert F. Tamura, and Cyrus J. Gardner that had cited quantifiable monetary benefits of $1.68 to $2.58 for every dollar invested in three AmeriCorps programs.[5] These estimates did not count the nonquantifiable, but very real, benefits of strengthening local communities and fostering civic responsibility. Nor did they include the broader benefits of added social cohesion that a universal program would entail. On the other side of the ledger, it is quite possible that there would be diminishing returns from a program much broader than AmeriCorps, and thus at some enrollment level, the costs of a universal requirement could exceed the benefits. But even this result—which is hardly ensured— would not credit the nonquantifiable social benefits of a broader program.

The bottom line: even a universal service program as large as $70 billion a year could well produce social benefits in excess of that figure and thus represent a very real net economic and social gain for American society as a whole.

Of course, the gains from universal service would be realized only if the participants were doing valuable work. And some fear that under a universal requirement, many participants—in the civilian program, in particular—could be doing make-work (raking leaves is the image) without contributing much in the way of social value. Indeed, to the extent this happened—and some assert that it happens in the AmeriCorps program—the affected participants would come away from their service with a negative view of government and civic responsibility.

The concern is real. AmeriCorps tries to address it by decentralizing its activities, relying on both state governments and the private sector to develop programs that are essentially certified at the federal level. A civilian universal service program could work largely the same way, but on a much-expanded scale. At the same time, certain programs, especially those associated with homeland security, would have to be run out of Washington.

Still, it would be a challenge to develop meaningful work for all of the high school graduates who would enter the civilian program each year. Meeting this challenge provides another reason, besides cost, to begin the program on a less than universal scale, run it first as a lottery, and eventually expand it into a true universal system.

An Idea Whose Time Is Coming

Universal service is an idea whose time may not be quite here, but it is coming. For reasons of need, social cohesion, and social responsibility, universal service is a compelling idea. If adopted, it could be one of the truly transformative federal initiatives of recent times, perhaps having an even greater impact on American society than the G.I. bill, which helped educate much of the post–World War II generation. At the very least, universal service should be on the public agenda and actively debated. The discussion alone would be a fitting postscript to the horrible events of September 11 and the continuing search for ways to engage all Americans in serving their country.

15

A Bad Idea
Whose Time Has Passed
The Case against Universal Service

BRUCE CHAPMAN

IF EACH WOMAN in China could only be persuaded to lower the hem of her skirt one inch, some nineteenth-century English merchants reasoned, the looms of Manchester could spin forever. Like that romantic calculation, the idea of universal service assumes a mythical economic and cultural system where people behave as you would like them to, with motivations of which you approve. Unlike it, universal service adds coercion to ensure compliance.

Universal service never was a good idea, and it grows worse with time. It fails militarily, morally, financially, and politically.

For almost a century, universal service has brought forth new advocates, each desiring to enlist all youth in something. Only the justifications keep changing. Today's justification is "homeland security." But is it realistic to suggest that youth who help guard a "public or private facility" (let alone those who stuff envelopes at some charity's office) are "shouldering the burden of war" in the same way as a soldier in Afghanistan?

I don't want to attach to Robert Litan all the customary arguments that universal service advocates have been promoting for years, especially because he states that a "reasoned debate about universal service before September 11 would have been unthinkable" (at least to him). Except in times of mass conflict, such as the Civil War and the two world wars, there has never been much of a reason for universal service. Still, the varied arguments for it need to be addressed.

No Military Case

Universal service is not needed on military grounds. We eliminated the draft three decades ago in part because the armed services found that they needed relatively fewer recruits to serve longer than conscription provided. As the numbers that were needed shrank, the unfairness of the draft became ever more apparent—and offensive. Youth, ever ingenious, found ways to get deferments, decamp to Canada, make themselves a nuisance to everyone in authority—and make those who did serve feel like chumps. Many of the young people who objected to military service availed themselves of alternative service, but no one seriously believed that most conscientious objectors were shouldering the burden of war in a way comparable to those fighting in the field.

The government took advantage of its free supply of almost unlimited manpower by underpaying its servicemen, thereby losing many recruits who might have chosen a military career. Raising the pay when the volunteer force was introduced changed the incentives and—surprise— eliminated the need for the draft. The all-volunteer force has been a big success.

Leaders in today's increasingly sophisticated, highly trained military are now talking of further manpower cuts. They have no interest in short-term soldiers of any kind and give no support to a return to conscription. The idea of using universal service to round up young men and women who, instead of direct military service, could be counted on to guard "public and private facilities," as Litan proposes, is naive. In Litan's plan, youth would be obligated for only a year—slightly less if AmeriCorps were the model. Philip Gold, a colleague at Discovery Institute and author of the post–September 11 book *Against All Terrors: This Nation's Next Defense*, points out that "if the object is fighting, a person trained only for a few months is useless. In a noncombat defense position, he would be worse than useless. He would be dangerous."[1]

Litan's interest in compulsory service grew partly out of recent work on Israel. According to Gold, armed guards in Israel do protect day care centers, for example. But all have had serious military training and two to three years of active duty, followed by service in the active reserves. A population with widespread military training and service can accomplish things that a civilian volunteer program cannot.

Litan anticipates nothing comparable from short-term universal servicemen and -women. A one-year obligation, under the AmeriCorps example, works out to only 1,700 hours—roughly ten months of forty-hour weeks. By the time the compulsory volunteers were trained, it would be time for them to muster out. The system would be roiled by constant turnover. It is surely unrealistic to expect to fill security jobs with youths who will be around for only a few months. Ask yourself, would you rather have a paid and trained person or a conscripted teenager inspecting the seaport for possible terrorists?

No Moral Justification

Trying to justify universal service on moral grounds is also a mistake, and a serious one. Morally, service isn't service to the extent it is compelled. Involuntary voluntarism is like hot snow. And allowing the pay to approach (let alone surpass) that available to ordinary workers of the same age performing the same tasks as the stipended and officially applauded "volunteers" stigmatizes the private sector. (The military recruit of today is sometimes called a volunteer only because he is not conscripted. His service is more commendable morally than that of some other paid employee because he is prepared to risk his life.)

Universal service advocates such as Litan are on especially shaky ground when charging that citizens should be "required to give something to their country in exchange for the full range of rights to which citizenship entitles them." This cuts against the grain of U.S. history and traditions.

Citizens here are expected to be law-abiding, and they are called to jury duty—and to the military if absolutely necessary. They are encouraged (not forced) to vote and to render voluntary service—which Americans famously do. But to require such service before the rights of citizenship are extended is simply contrary to the purposes for which the country was founded and has endured. The Founders had a keen awareness of the ways that the state could tyrannize the people, and taking the people's liberty away to serve some specious government purpose unattached to national survival is a project that would horrify them.

I also raise this practical question: exactly which citizenship rights will Litan deny those people who decline to perform government-approved national service? What will be done to punish the activist who thinks he can do more to serve humanity through a political party than through pre-scribed government service? Or the young religious missionary who would rather save souls than guard a pier for a few months? How about—at the other end of the virtue spectrum—the young drug dealer who is only too happy to help guard the pier? Will he be kept out of the service of his choice and compelled to do rehab as his form of "service"?

Outside of mass mobilization for war—or in the special case of Israel, a small nation effectively on constant alert—the only modern nations that have conscripted labor to meet assorted, centrally decreed social purposes have been totalitarian regimes. In those lands, the object, as much as any-thing, has been to indoctrinate youth in the morality of the state. Litan may not have such goals in mind, but many universal service advocates want to use conscription to straighten out the next generation—to their approved standards. No doubt many—perhaps most—think they can inculcate a sense of voluntary service through compulsory service.

In reality, however, no previous generation of youth has been so encouraged to volunteer for various approved, state-sponsored social causes. In many high schools in the United States, students cannot get a diploma without performing a certain number of hours of approved "community service." Does a child who must perform service to graduate from high school develop a high sense of what it means to help others? Does a student who learns that almost anything counts toward the service requirement—as long as he doesn't get paid—develop a keen sense of civil calling? Or does he hone his skill at gaming the system? And why, if we have this service requirement in high school—and in some colleges—do we need yet another one for the year after high school?

Unintended Consequences

Universal service (indeed any national service scheme that achieves demographic heft) is a case study in unintended consequences. One surprise for liberals might be a growing disillusionment with the government and the way it wastes money. Today's youth trust the government and are immensely patriotic, but bureaucratized service requirements could cure that. Another unintended consequence might be instruction in how government make-work is a tax on one's freedom and an irritating distraction from educational goals and serious career development. Conservatives of a sardonic nature might come to appreciate the prospect of generations growing to adulthood with firsthand experience of government's impertinence. It would not be necessary thereafter to exhort the veterans of such unnecessary compulsion to resist the claims of government over the rest of their lives.

Universal service likewise would be an invitation to scandal. The military draft was bad enough, dispatching the budding scientist to pick up paper on a base's roadsides and sending the sickly malcontent to deliver meal trays to patients in base hospitals. People with powerful parents got cushy positions, while the poor got the onerous tasks. When labor is both free and abundant, it will be squandered and abused. If that was true in eras when mass armies were raised, what can one expect in a time when only a small fraction of the population is needed to operate our high-tech military?

No Financial Justification

The cost of universal service would be prohibitive. Direct costs would include those for assembling, sorting (and sorting out), allocating, and training several million youth in an unending manpower convoy. Indirect costs include clothing and providing initial medical attention, insurance, law enforcement associated with such large numbers (no small expense in the army, even with presumably higher discipline), housing, and the periodic "leave" arrangements.

The $20,000 per involuntary volunteer estimated by Litan is too low. The more realistic total figure would be more like $27,000 to $30,000. First, the federal cost for a full-time AmeriCorps member is about $16,000, according to AmeriCorps officials.[2] (The $10,000 figure cited by Litan appears to average the cost of part-time volunteers with that of full-time volunteers.) And that, recall, is for an average ten-month stint; so add another $3,000 or so for a twelve-month term of service. Giving the involuntary volunteers the AmeriCorps education benefit of some $4,000 brings the total to about $23,000 of federal contribution for the full-time, one-year participant. When local or private matching funds are added, the total cost will easily approach $30,000 per person. Few unskilled young people just out of school make that in private employment!

Because organized compulsion costs more than real volunteering, however, the indirect expenses for governments would be still greater. Chief among these are the hidden financial costs of universal national service to the economy in the form of forgone labor. That problem plagued the old draft and would be more acute now. The United States has suffered a labor shortage for most of the past two decades, with the dearth of educated and trained labor especially serious. Yet universal service advocates want to pluck out of the employment ranks some 4 million people a year and apply a command-and-control approach to their optimal use. How can we even calculate the waste?

Litan says that in 1995 the GAO "positively evaluated" a cost-benefit study of three AmeriCorps programs that found them to produce quantifiable monetary benefits of $1.68 to $2.58 for every dollar invested. But he overstates the GAO's positive evaluation of the private study's findings.[3] These assumptions (of future benefits and their dollar values) are inherently problematic, based as they are on projected data. And neither the GAO nor the private study whose methodology it checked says anything about the applicability of the study's results to some universal service

program. Inferring GAO endorsement for some putative financial benefits from a national service scheme—let alone a program of compulsory
national service—is not good economics.

By contrast, a recent review of the literature and evidence of government spending by William Niskanen, former chairman of the President's
Council of Economic Advisors (under Ronald Reagan), concluded that
"the marginal cost of government spending and taxes in the United States
may be about $2.75 per additional dollar of tax revenue." As the late
Nobel economist Frederick Hayek said, "There is only one problem with
socialism. It does not work."

The cost of universal service for one year would not be $80 billion,
with certain additional economic benefits, as Litan would have it, but
roughly $120 billion, with considerable additional losses to the economy
as a whole.

No Practical or Political Worth

There is no demand for all these volunteers, as charities themselves have
pointed out. Nonprofits can absorb only so many unseasoned, unskilled,
short-term "volunteers," particularly when some of the volunteers are
reluctant, to say the least. So what is the point? Is it political?

Some universal service advocates (not Litan) have cited a January
2002 survey by Lake Snell Perry and Associates and the Tarrance Group
that shows strong support among youth for universal service.[4] But these
advocates usually neglect to mention that this support is based on a stated
assumption in the survey question that such service would be "an alternative to (compulsory) military service should one be instituted." A truer
reflection of youthful opinion is found in the survey's largely unreported
question on community service as a requirement for high school graduation. That program is overwhelmingly opposed—by a 35 percent margin
among current high school students. Interestingly, the same survey shows
that "instituting civics and government course requirements in schools is
favored by a 15-point margin by current high school students."[5]

This should tell us something: putting $120 billion, or even $80 billion, into a universal national service scheme would be a waste. But how

about spending some tiny corner of that money on teaching kids about real—that is, voluntary—service? How about paying to teach students about representative democracy and their part in it as voters and volunteers or about the way our economy works and how to prepare for successful participation in it? Or to teach them American history (for many, it would be a new course) in a way that inspired them with the stories of men and women, great and humble, who have rendered notable service in their communities, nation, and world.

The way to get a nation of volunteers is to showcase voluntary service, praise it, reward it, and revere it. The way to sabotage voluntary service is to coerce it, bureaucratize it, nationalize it, cloak it in political correctness, and pay for it to the point where the "volunteer" makes out better than the poor soul of the same age who works for a living. Voluntary service blesses the one who serves as well as those to whom he renders service. Universal service would be civic virtue perverted into a civic vice.

COMMENT

The Case for
Universal Service—Again
A Reply to Bruce Chapman

ROBERT E. LITAN

BRUCE CHAPMAN MAKES a powerful case against universal service. Indeed, he may be right about every one of the practical downsides of the idea. It may be more expensive than the $80 billion back-of-the-envelope estimate I advanced in my initial chapter. It may well be true that only one year of service would result in an excessive degree of turnover and thus training costs. And it may be the case that the government is unable to find suitable things to do for all 4 million high school graduates who would enter the program each year.

In my original piece, I acknowledged each of these problems with universal service and concluded, therefore, that a truly universal service requirement—one that offered all those eligible a choice between military and various kinds of civilian service (including actual jobs in certain "helping professions")—was not ready for immediate implementation. Instead, I suggested that the only practical way to begin would be with a lottery and then eventually to ramp it up to a broader program.

But why even maintain the idea of a broader, universal program as a goal—perhaps much like the "man on the moon" objective announced by

President Kennedy for the end of the 1960s? Because there are significant benefits from or reasons for the idea, which Chapman really never directly addresses in his critique.

First, the post–September 11 world in which we and our children live is a different world from the one we inhabited less than two years ago, and correspondingly, there is a greater *need* for citizens to pitch in for homeland defense. Of course, Chapman is right that not everyone, or even a majority of those eligible for universal service, is equipped by age and experience to perform guard duty or other functions useful to the homeland security effort. But surely some of the recruits would be able to help out where needed and if they were trained. More to the point, I suggested that the year of universal service could be fulfilled by actually taking, or training for, positions in fields directly related to the homeland security effort: as police officers, customs or immigration officials, FBI agents, or medical workers. To this extent, the universal service requirement could induce more young Americans to go into the helping professions permanently, which could be a powerful side-benefit of the program, even if the total numbers of such individuals employed in these fields did not increase. At the very least, the talent pool for these jobs would be significantly enlarged, leading to more qualified individuals serving in them in the future.

But even if September 11 had never occurred, there were and remain ample opportunities for young people to make important contributions in civilian jobs that address a wide variety of unmet social needs. Without repeating the list of possibilities provided in my initial piece, consider this one additional idea: allowing many of those serving to be teachers' aides or tutors in inner city schools, where class sizes already are too large and poorly performing children do not receive sufficient personalized attention. With roughly one-third of American children living in poverty and lacking the opportunities for advancement open to those in middle- and upper-class households, who can say straight-faced that there aren't unmet needs that could be filled, at least partially, if the people were available to provide the assistance—even if they were equipped with only a high school education?

And then there are the needs of the military. My case for universal service does not rest on the moral argument that in times of war it is only fair that the risks be shared broadly, nor on the argument that because the United States has deliberately chosen to be policeman for the world, its need for more men and women in uniform has expanded. Both arguments are compelling, but they do not require that all 4 million of those annually eligible for universal service go into the military. Nonetheless, there may be a case for adding some modest fraction of those eligible to those serving in the armed forces. But as I suggested in my initial piece, individuals with a service obligation still would *choose* whether to sign up for military service, although they would be encouraged to do so by additional monetary incentives above those paid to those serving in civilian capacities. Moreover, service in the armed forces would extend beyond the one-year minimum set for all others.

Indeed, Chapman's most compelling argument against the plan I offered is that one year of service may be too short. If he is right, however, that does not defeat the idea of service but only changes its nature. I proposed one year initially out of an effort to balance the personal costs of serving against the social obligation of service. I readily admit I may have struck this balance in the wrong place. (But this should be open for debate.)

What about the other arguments for universal service—that it could help enhance social cohesion in an increasingly diverse society and that it meets a legitimate objective of asking what every young person can do for his or her country as a condition of citizenship? Chapman never really grapples with the first of these arguments, except to suggest that the government would so botch things up that individuals would find new reasons to be antigovernment as they enter adulthood. Of course, government will not be perfectly efficient in finding everyone the right kind of job that provides true meaning to those in service. But this danger at least can be minimized (with respect to the civilian service) by decentralizing the operation of the program to the state and local levels where the needs are best identified. Indeed, this aspect of any universal service program ought to be appealing to conservatives, who tend to put more faith in state and local governments rather than the federal government (to the extent they trust *any* level of government).

The same ought to be true with the notion that individuals should have some responsibility to serve their nation in some capacity as a condition for enjoying the rights of citizenship. Chapman essentially asserts that this claim is "un-American" and asks what rights I (or other advocates of universal service) would take away for those who do not serve? I am not proposing to take away any rights, only to build upon the fundamental idea that the rights we all enjoy are not free, in the sense that we can do anything we want and still enjoy the freedoms that our constitution protects. We take away the freedom of those who break *the law*, whether it be the injunction against murder or theft, the obligation to pay taxes, and yes, the obligation to serve in the military if Congress should require it (allowing exceptions for those who conscientiously object to such service). A universal service requirement would be one additional law to obey, but one that at least allows individuals to choose their form of service. In this sense, the "requirement" is truly conservative in nature by allowing choice. And one would think that conservatives would also support the notion that rights come with responsibilities.

Chapman also agues that a universal service requirement would invite all kinds of evasion or maneuvering by those seeking to avoid service or to find "cushy" jobs that might fulfill the service obligation. Evasion would be virtually impossible, since even those with physical limitations could be placed in appropriate civilian jobs. I admit, however, that there would be some jockeying for "good jobs." All I can say is that this has always been true of military service, and it would likely continue to be true to some degree if a civilian choice were offered. But to a significant degree, those filling the "good jobs"—or those demanding the highest skills—would in fact be those with greater work force skills. This tendency would reduce some of the inefficiency Chapman believes to be inherent in any universal service program.

There is one aspect of the transition toward a universal service program—the need for a lottery to randomly fill the limited number of places that could be initially afforded—with which I am somewhat uncomfortable. It will strike those who are picked as unfair for them to serve while their peers with "high numbers" get off scot-free. Many certainly felt this way about the draft during the Vietnam War, and it no doubt would be the same if a new "somewhat" universal service program—with a lottery—were implemented now. I know of no way to avoid this problem, since a lottery is a concession to current economic and political reality. If Chapman had chosen to attack this part of the proposal, I would have felt more vulnerable. But his wider attacks on the very concept of universal service strike me as a bit strident and give insufficient due to the personal and social benefits of the idea.

16

A Solution in Search of a Problem

MICHAEL LIND

NATIONAL SERVICE IS a solution in search of a problem. Most public policy proposals are supported by constituencies who seek to achieve a particular result. National service is an unusual exception. Within the small but vocal community of national service enthusiasts, there is far more agreement on the policy of national service than on its purpose.

Most proponents of national service agree that it would be a good thing if all Americans, on their own initiative or under compulsion, spent a year or two engaged in service of some kind to the public. Few, however, can agree on the rationale. Is it to build the character of the participants? To meet "unmet needs" of society? To increase national integration among different classes, races, and religious and regional subcultures? All too often national service enthusiasts allege that all of these diverse goals—and perhaps others—will be promoted by the same policy.

To date, the American public and its political representatives have not been persuaded. Every few years there is a flurry of interest in the idea of mandatory national service. The flurry quickly subsides, however. I have followed the national service debate since the 1980s, when I helped to research William F. Buckley Jr.'s thoughtful book on the subject, *Gratitude*, and when Sam Nunn and other centrist Democrats were enthusiastic about the idea.[1] My support for national service was always qualified, and over the years my skepticism has grown. I now believe that national service, in its familiar form, is a bad idea, in the United States and in comparable countries. In this essay, I will explain why I think that national service is not only misguided but also illiberal and even un-American. There is only one approach to national service that is not vulnerable to the convincing objections against national service in its familiar form. But this "republican" version of national service, as I will call it, has little to do with the versions being peddled today, and it is far from clear that most proponents of national service would approve of it.

It is necessary to limit the conversation at the outset to compulsory, universal service. All too often enthusiasts for national service confuse the issue by labeling voluntary programs, like AmeriCorps, as examples of "national service." But the rather marginal AmeriCorps program, in which few Americans participate, should not be confused with genuine national service, conceived of as a universal or nearly universal program. By the same token, the Job Corps, the Peace Corps, and VISTA are not national service programs. Only a tiny minority of Americans of any generation take part. Despite the hopes of the national service lobby, it is unlikely that such small, voluntary programs will ever prove to be the seeds of universal programs, which would necessarily be compulsory. On the contrary, AmeriCorps and similar programs may well prove to be substitutes for genuine national service, not pilot projects for it.

If national service is to be meaningful, then it has to be universal; and if it is to be universal, it must be mandatory. It must be based, in other words, on universal conscription—a draft or a comparable mandatory requirement, like jury attendance. National service must impose a duty on citizens, the evasion of which is punishable by fines, imprisonment, or both.

An alleged duty to serve the country that is optional and fulfilled on a voluntary basis by a minority of citizens is not a genuine duty at all. As John Stuart Mill observed in *Utilitarianism* (1863): "It is a part of the notion of duty in every one of its forms that a person may rightfully be compelled to fulfill it. Duty is a thing which may be exacted from a person, as one exacts a debt. Unless we think that it may be exacted from him, we do not call it his duty."[2]

The idea of national service as a universal, mandatory program was part of the original definition in the late nineteenth and early twentieth centuries. William James, who defined national service as "the moral equivalent of war," conceived of a national service program as a civilian equivalent to a mass army.[3] Most national service theorists have envisioned a period of prolonged compulsory service during which young Americans would live and work together like soldiers in the military. In some schemes, military and civilian service would be alternatives, as is the case in some European countries where compulsory civilian service (*Zivildienst*) is offered as an alternative to military conscription.

If you are going to draft all or most eighteen-year-olds in the country; take them away from their families, friends, and neighborhoods; and impose tasks on them for a period of months or years, then you had better have a good reason. The two reasons usually offered by proponents of national service—character formation and meeting "unmet needs"—are not good enough to justify a draft.

Character formation was the purpose of national service in the mind of William James, who is widely recognized as one of the patron saints of this public policy tradition in the United States. In 1910 he wrote: "To coal and iron mines, to freight trains, to fishing fleets in December, to dish-washing, clothes-washing, and window-washing, to road-building and tunnel-making, to foundries and stoke-holes, and to frames of skyscrapers, would our gilded youths be drafted off, according to their choice, to get the childishness knocked out of them, and to come back into society with healthier sympathies and soberer ideas."[4] Proponents of national service often quote this line with approval. Less often quoted is another phrase from the same essay: "the martial virtues, although originally gained by the race through war, are absolute and permanent human goods."

James's famous essay must be read in the context of the time-bound obsessions of his class and generation. Many members of the Northeastern elite in the United States in the late nineteenth and early twentieth centuries were deeply ashamed because they, or their fathers, had avoided service in the federal armies during the Civil War, when it was legal for the rich to buy their way out of the draft through working-class or poor "substitutes." In addition to this local American factor, there was a trans-Atlantic fad of concern about "degeneration" and "decadence." Note James's reference to the need for "gilded youth"—like those of his own class and his Harvard students—to "get the childishness knocked out of them." Getting the childishness knocked out of them was not necessary for most of James's fellow Americans at a time when child labor was widespread and graduation from high school had not yet become routine.

To accept the relevance of James's rationale for national civilian service as "the moral equivalent of war," one must agree with him that "the martial virtues . . . are absolute and permanent human goods" that must be maintained by artificial, civilian methods during times of peace and prosperity, in order to prevent social and moral decadence. Between James and us is the twentieth century, in which at least a hundred million people died unnaturally as a result of world wars, genocide, and communist famines, and in which whole societies, like those of the communist and fascist nations, were organized as giant armies. The conception of war as a kind of character-building sport, like high school football or junior high soccer, shared by James and jingoistic contemporaries like Theodore Roosevelt, did not survive the trenches and machine guns of World War I. This is a problem for proponents of national service today: if you do not think that galloping on a horse waving a saber builds character, then neither will you believe in James's "martial" argument that fishing the seas in December will do so.

To be fair, most contemporary proponents of national service do not share the romantic belief of James that war or compulsory state service creates better people than peacetime, private pursuits. Some proponents of national service today would like the military draft to be restored, but most are concerned chiefly or exclusively with civilian national service. The virtues that they want to promote among young people are not toughness and valor but rather sensitivity and compassion and a sense of being part of a larger community. Helping the sick and the elderly often tops the list of their examples of national service.

But this contemporary version of the character-formation argument, like the original rationale, suffers from a fatal flaw. The kinds of character-forming activities favored by national service proponents are already undertaken by the institutions of "civil society"—churches, secular charities, philanthropic foundations, and so on. In recent years, scholars have debated the health of American civil society. But there is little doubt that civil society is far more dynamic and creative and active in the United States than it is in other industrial democracies, particularly in continental European and East Asian countries where a relatively passive citizenry is accustomed to waiting for the state to do things that are undertaken by voluntary groups in the United States. One need not agree with conservative proposals to unload functions that are properly performed by the state, even in the United States, onto the institutions of civil society—such as the proposal to replace government welfare programs with "faith-based" church charity—in order to agree with libertarian critics of the character-formation theory of national service. What is wrong with the Boy Scouts and Girl Scouts; the churches, synagogues, and mosques; secular charities and ethnic community groups; sports teams and hobby associations? Have they, in addition to parents and schools, failed so miserably at their task of turning out young people of good character that the federal government needs to take the drastic step of drafting young Americans and regimenting them for a year or two to turn them into moral and civic-minded adults?

Even if American civil society had failed in its function of acculturation and moral indoctrination, it is hard to believe that a compulsory civilian service program administered by the federal government would do a better job. The secret of moral education is intimacy and authority. Parents, along with religious leaders and perhaps scoutmasters and coaches, possess these advantages; federal civil servants, even the best of them, do not.

What is more, moral acculturation takes place best in "thick" communities like families and subcultures, in which customary standards can be enforced, if necessary, by shame and exclusion. A civilian-service barracks full of drafted adolescents from radically different backgrounds, in which federal camp counselors are narrowly restricted in what they can say or do by laws governing civil rights, sexual harassment, offensive speech, and so on, is a "thin" community at best. Here the military model for civilian national service is completely irrelevant, because the kind of emotional brutalization that is sometimes required in stripping identities away from conscripts or recruits, in order to assimilate them into a homogeneous military subculture, would not be tolerated by today's Americans in the case of a civilian national service program. And that kind of total-immersion socialization would be pointless, too, if the program only lasted a few months or a couple of years.

The character-formation argument for national service is invalid, then, not because character-formation is not a social goal—there are few social goals more important—but because it is best undertaken by the nuanced and delicate methods of civil society rather than by the necessarily abstract and hence crude methods of the national government.

The other common rationale for national service—meeting "unmet needs" of society—is based on the same kind of error. In both cases, the goal is legitimate, but just about the least effective way imaginable to achieve it would be to draft eighteen- and nineteen-year-olds in a civilian army.

If William James is the patron saint of the character-formation school of national service, then Edward Bellamy is the patron saint of the unmet-needs wing of the movement. In his novel *Looking Backward*, Bellamy envisioned an "industrial army" of conscripted young people.[5] Bellamy was a socialist—a non-Marxist, nontotalitarian socialist, but a socialist nonetheless. Those who make the unmet-needs argument for national service may not be conscious of the fact, but they are socialists, too.

Here is the reason why. In a capitalist economy, in theory, there should be no "unmet needs." Genuine needs should be met by entrepreneurs in the marketplace. Even conservatives and libertarians admit, of course, that there are market failures and public goods that justify government provision of some services, based on taxation or user fees. But even when this is conceded, the fact remains that, as far as the economy is concerned, the market and the government should meet all legitimate material needs between them.

Even if unmet needs can be identified, it does not follow that they should be provided by a Bellamy-style industrial army. On the contrary, if the American public decides that a particular economic need is not being adequately met by either the market or the government, then the rational response is to reform one of the two. The rules of the market might be reformed, to provide incentives to entrepreneurs to meet the unmet need, or perhaps to give resources to disadvantaged groups. Alternatively, the unmet need can be added to those routinely provided by the government. In neither case is there any economic rationale for national service.

Consider eldercare, which national service enthusiasts often point out as an example of an unmet need that could be met by national service conscripts. If there is a shortage of eldercare, it is necessary to examine the reason. If the problem is a lack of qualified nurses and attendants because of low wages, then wages should be raised, to encourage the diversion of American workers from other fields into eldercare. (The other alternative, flooding the low-wage labor market with unskilled immigrants who can care for the elderly, imposes far greater costs on society as a whole.) If the problem is inequality in access to eldercare, then the government should subsidize its private provision or provide it directly. Whether eldercare is provided by the free market, a government-subsidized market, or the government, the eldercare providers ought to be well-paid, skilled professionals remunerated with good wages and good benefits—not incompetent teenage draftees who may do their mandatory work grudgingly. When I am old and sick and hospitalized or institutionalized, I want to be helped by contented, well-paid career nurses, not by resentful nineteen-year-old conscripts forced by the government to empty my bedpan.

Labor unions have usually opposed national service proposals, with good reason. They fear that the industrial army of Bellamy and other left-of-center national service enthusiasts will be used as an industrialist's army of "scabs." Organized labor has always argued that any tasks that fit the definition of unmet needs should be performed by well-paid adult—preferably unionized—workers. I agree.

Neither the character-formation theory nor the unmet-needs theory, then, is plausible as a rationale for universal, compulsory national service (the only significant kind, given the marginality of all noncompulsory, nonuniversal service programs). If a society, such as the United States, can be viewed as having three spheres or sectors—government, civil society, and the market—then the error of both national service rationales has been to assign to government a task best undertaken by one of the other two sectors of society. Character formation should be the responsibility of the institutions of civil society along with the family, while meeting unmet needs is the task of the market, perhaps with the help of the government in its limited role as a provider of utilities and a few other economic public goods.

The failure of national service proponents to realize their vision, then, has been a benefit, not a loss, to American society. It is always better *not* to do something misguided, and the idea of drafting eighteen-year-olds to make them better people or to have them serve as an industrial army is misguided.

Although the conventional rationales for national service are unconvincing, there is one that might justify the infringement on personal liberty entailed by a draft. This is what I will call the "republican rationale" for national service. The greatest influences on the national service tradition come from the socialist and progressive traditions of the late nineteenth and early twentieth centuries. But now and then one encounters a few relics of an older, smaller republican ideology—particularly in discussions of the duty to serve in the military. It is that older republican tradition that I propose to excavate, and renovate, in the remainder of this essay.

The American republican tradition is little understood, even by most American historians and scholars. In the nineteenth and twentieth centuries, Greek "democracy" has been more influential than Roman "republicanism." But the American Founders drew on a tradition of neo-Roman republicanism, which they derived from their own interpretation of Cicero, Polybius, Livy, and other Roman authors, along with early modern philosophers such as Machiavelli and Harrington in continental Europe and Britain.[6]

The neo-Roman republican ideology is pessimistic about individuals and optimistic about institutions. The state is always in danger of tyranny (lawless power) or faction (laws passed to promote special interests at the expense of the whole). The constitution of a republic, like Rome's aristocratic republic or America's democratic republic, is a complicated machine designed to limit the effects of both tyranny and faction. Democratic election and rotation in office are only two of the deterrents to abuses of power. The separation of powers and checks and balances form additional precautions against both tyranny and faction.

Yet another category of precautions in a republican constitution includes institutions that permit the governed to take part in governance itself. Juries permit the citizenry to participate in the administration of justice; initiatives and referenda permit the citizens to take part in legislation;

and a militia permits citizens to take part in national defense and policing (functions that only in recent generations have been strictly separated). Participation by the populace in the passage of laws and their
enforcement by courts and coercive agencies is justified not by the superior wisdom of ordinary citizens but rather by the imposition of practical
impediments to the corruption and cooptation of so many people by a
tyrant or a faction. (As I said, the neo-Roman republican view of politics
is a pessimistic one.)

In the early American republic, neo-Roman republicanism (which
also influenced France) inspired political practice to a degree greater than
in any other society of modern times. Particularly in rural frontier communities, as a result of necessity, citizens—at least white male citizens—
often took part in juries, militias, and referenda (in states and other
government units where those were allowed). Urbanization and industri-
alization, however, eroded the republican institutions of American society.
Initiatives and referenda remain important in some states (the institution
does not exist at the national level), but voter turnout has declined for various reasons. Few Americans serve on juries today. The militia gave way,
first to professional police forces, fire departments, and paramedic services, and then to a professional, highly specialized military.

In my view, republican political philosophy is as valid in the twenty-
first century as it was in the eighteenth and nineteenth (and not only in
the United States). Unfortunately, leaders and thinkers in the United
States and other nations have failed to devise creative ways to update
republican institutions. Consequently, in the twentieth century, the
republican philosophy of the American Founders became displaced by
two traditions, both of European derivation: a left-of-center statism influenced by German, British, and Scandinavian models, and a hard-line libertarianism with its roots in European classical liberalism—like that of the
"Austrian school" of economics—rather than in America's own Lockean
liberal republican heritage. (For obvious reasons, contemporary liberals
and contemporary libertarian conservatives try to pin the paternity of
their public philosophies on the American Founders rather than on various nineteenth- and twentieth-century European sects such as Swedish
social democracy and Austrian libertarianism).

To speculate on what new institutions, in the spirit of old American republican ideals, would look like in general would take me too far beyond the scope of this essay. I will limit myself to discussing the relevance of neorepublicanism for national service.

The idea of the citizen militia provides a rationale for a kind of national service distinct in both purpose and form from the national service traditions identified with William James and Edward Bellamy. Like the militia, and unlike the national service programs of the followers of James and Bellamy, civic service would be local, not national (indeed, "national service" is something of a misnomer, although I will use the term). The purpose of this third kind of national service would be to establish a twenty-first-century version of the militia, open to membership by citizens of both genders and all racial and ethnic groups, unlike most of the American militias of the past.

The purpose of the new militias would be the same as that of the old ones—to ensure, by mandating the participation of citizens in both military and police work, that a separate caste of soldiers or police officers, with interests and an identity distinct from that of the American majority, does not form. The governed can restrain the governors by taking part in government alongside them. Whether this improves the moral character of citizens or not is irrelevant. The point is to prevent individuals or groups from abusing public power for their own benefit, just as citizen participation in the judicial process by sitting on juries acts as a check on the power of judges.

The National Guard cannot fulfill this function because in the course of the twentieth century it became an integral part of a permanent U.S. military. Most soldiers and police officers are, and should remain, specialized professionals. As both military and police technology develop, to say nothing of fire-fighting and paramedic technology, the role of amateurs or short-term conscripts will continue to diminish. However, citizens can be required to fulfill functions in noncombat roles, behind the front lines of military and police work, by driving trucks or ambulances, operating phone banks, monitoring computers, or delivering supplies. In new militias, unlike in the older versions, there would be a division of labor between civilians and professionals. Civilians would, of course, have an opportunity to undergo training in order to join the professional military, police, and paramedic forces.

Conscription for such noncombat purposes would render conscientious objector status irrelevant. Everyone would be required to serve, but no one would be required to do so as a soldier or police officer. Some pacifists, of course, might object to serving in logistical functions that support state-sponsored violence against foreign enemies or domestic criminals, but the same logic would enable them to withhold taxes that go to the military. An argument that is not convincing in the case of taxes on income, property, or wealth is no more convincing in the case of the draft, which could be considered a tax on labor. And there can be no conscientious objection to compulsory participation in units that provide backup to firefighters and other emergency and disaster relief workers.

A new militia program of this kind would differ from conventional national service programs in three respects. First, no long period of collective communal residence would be necessary. Citizens of all ages—not just young people—might receive their training in their neighborhoods, on nights and on weekends, and would be expected to devote a certain amount of time each year to militia service, as well as being subject to call-ups in emergencies.

Second, the program would be administered chiefly at the state and local level, even if service were mandated by a federal draft. In this respect, too, it would differ from those proposed national service programs that seek to promote a sense of national unity by bringing people together from across the country. A new militia program might break down social barriers within a city or county, but that would be incidental to its practical purpose.

Finally, and most important, a new militia program would be limited to civilian participation in the military, police, and emergency services. The point of creating a modern militia would be lost if the program were given responsibility for other tasks, most of them better performed by civil society, the market, or specialized government agencies. Picking up litter alongside highways and attending to old people in nursing homes would not be legitimate activities. Helping police, military, or emergency personnel identify and pursue criminal fugitives, mobilizing supplies for war, and aiding victims of hurricanes, floods, and fires would be legitimate functions of a neorepublican militia.

It is not clear that a neorepublican militia, of the kind I have outlined, would appeal to the minority of Americans who support national service. And it is far from clear that a majority of Americans would support making such a program mandatory. According to a fall 2002 survey by Harvard University's Institute of Politics, 67 percent of U.S. college students opposed a military draft. Only 24 percent said that if they were drafted, they would "eagerly serve," while 28 percent said they would "serve with reservation," and 44 percent said they would "seek an alternative" to service if drafted.[7]

One thing seems clear, however: a narrowly defined, local militia program of this sort might appeal to many of the Americans who continue to be unpersuaded by the character-formation and unmet-needs arguments for national service. Conventional national service programs are unlikely to be enacted. It is worth changing the debate, therefore, to new programs, in an American republican tradition far older than the national service traditions of William James and Edward Bellamy.

17

In Power, but Not in Peril

MARK SHIELDS

LET US PAUSE on the eve of war to reflect on the Americans who will die. In any war, nearly all of the fighting and dying are done by the youngest soldiers who hold the lowest rank. Of the 58,152 Americans killed in the Vietnam War, three out of four were between the ages of seventeen and twenty-two, and three out of four were under the rank of staff sergeant.

Today there are 1,182,412 enlisted men and women on active duty in the United States military. It is from their ranks that most of all American combat casualties in the next war will come. If you need further proof of the complete separation of the people in power in Washington from the people in the Persian Gulf, just consider this: not one of the 435 members of the U.S. House of Representatives, which gave the president authority to go to war has a son or a daughter on active duty in the enlisted ranks of this nation's military. Sergeant Brooks Johnson of the army's 101st Airborne Division, who has already served in Afghanistan and before that in Kosovo, Bosnia, Korea, and Germany, is the only American enlisted man now on active duty who is the son of a member of Congress: his father is Senator Tim Johnson (D-S.D.).

A wise and just manpower policy is the foundation of our national defense. The all-volunteer army, it was agreed by its supporters, was to be

Adapted from "In Power, but Not in Peril," *Washington Post*, October 15, 2002, and "Rumsfeld's Draft Dodge," *Washington Post*, January 18, 2003. Reprinted with permission of Creators Syndicate.

a peacetime service. Any major military engagement was to be the signal for the resumption of the military draft. The argument was straightforward: if the stated goals of the nation were worth fighting for, then we must not hesitate to ask all Americans to shoulder the duty and the risk of that fighting. In the words of the conservative scholar Michael Barone, "War demands equality of sacrifice."

That is certainly not the case today in proudly "classless" America. The American Establishment—political, economic and journalistic—has no personal stake in the men and women who defend the United States. The American military defending our nation today is increasingly integrated by race and increasingly segregated by class.

To be fair, Air Force Major Bill Bunning, an officer, is the son of the Kentucky Republican senator, and Representative Duncan Hunter (R-Calif.) has a son and namesake who joined the marines after September 11, 2001, and is now a second lieutenant. One House member, Ike Skelton (D-Mo.), has two career-officer sons (whose names Skelton will not provide to the press) on active duty—one is an army major who won the Bronze Star in the first war against Iraq, and the other is a navy commander.

Back when the nation had a draft, fully three out of four high school graduates and three out of four college graduates served in the military. At that time, a full third of college graduates were found in the enlisted (nonofficer) ranks. And then, too, in World War II and Korea, the nation accepted combat casualties and deaths for causes judged to be in the vital national interest.

But Defense Secretary Donald Rumsfeld disparaged draftees for having "added no value, no advantage really to the United States armed services" and emphasized, "We're not going to re-implement the draft. There is no need for it at all. . . . We have people serving today—God bless 'em—because they volunteered. They want to do what it is they're doing." This sounds good, except that it is not true. Two days after the secretary's unequivocal words, the U.S. Marine Corps—which reports to the secretary of defense—froze for the next twelve months every one of its 174,312 members currently in active duty. Marines who have completed their voluntary enlistments or their twenty years and had chosen to return to civilian life or retirement will instead remain involuntarily in the service.

Marines being marines, they will answer their country's call. But let us be clear: this action, along with other more limited freezes imposed by other services and affecting thousands in uniform, means the U.S. military is no longer all volunteer. The question that now must be answered by Rumsfeld and the president is not whether Americans should be "drafted" to defend the country, because we are already doing that, but exactly which Americans should be drafted. Why is it more just to retain on active duty involuntarily an American who has fulfilled his or her voluntary obligation to the country than it would be to bring to active duty involuntarily those Americans who have yet to serve?

The country's preeminent military sociologist, Northwestern University's Charles Moskos (himself a former army draftee), offers a more interesting explanation. "The answer to the question of what are vital national interests is found not so much in the cause itself," he says, "but in who is willing to die for that cause." Moskos adds, "Only when the privileged classes perform military service, only when elite youth are on the firing line, does the country define the cause as worth young people's blood and do war losses become acceptable."[1]

The all-volunteer force all but ensured that the children of the elites would not be found in the military and would be almost missing from the enlisted ranks. Moskos concludes that "citizens accept hardships only when their leadership is viewed as self-sacrificing."

If one listens to our confident leaders, the war against Iraq entails no home-front shortages and no rationing and would impose no civilian sacrifice. The tragedy is that probably nobody at any Washington dinner party tonight—liberal or conservative, Bush appointee or Democratic holdover—personally knows any enlisted man or woman now defending the nation. Absent the resumption of draft without deferments, what we have is a guaranteed formula for both indefensibly unjust military manpower policy and a national unwillingness to accept any war unless it is virtually casualty free.

18

Bring Back the Draft

CHARLES B. RANGEL

PRESIDENT BUSH AND his administration have declared a war against terrorism that may soon involve sending thousands of American troops into combat in Iraq. I voted against the congressional resolution giving the president authority to carry out this war—an engagement that would dwarf our military efforts to find Osama bin Laden and bring him to justice.

But as a combat veteran of the Korean conflict, I believe that if we are going to send our children to war, the governing principle must be that of shared sacrifice. Throughout much of our history, Americans have been asked to shoulder the burden of war equally. That's why I will ask Congress next week to consider and support legislation I will introduce to resume the military draft.

Carrying out the administration's policy toward Iraq will require long-term sacrifices by the American people, particularly those who have sons and daughters in the military. Yet the Congress that voted overwhelmingly to allow the use of force in Iraq includes only one member who has a child in the enlisted ranks of the military. Just a few more have children who are officers.

I believe that if those calling for war knew that their children were likely to be required to serve—and to be placed in harm's way—there

Reprinted from the *New York Times*, December 31, 2002.

would be more caution and a greater willingness to work with the international community in dealing with Iraq. A renewed draft will help bring a greater appreciation of the consequences of decisions to go to war.

Service in our nation's armed forces is no longer a common experience. A disproportionate number of the poor and members of minority groups make up the enlisted ranks of the military, while the most privileged Americans are underrepresented or absent. We need to return to the tradition of the citizen-soldier, with alternative national service required for those who cannot serve because of physical limitations or reasons of conscience.

There is no doubt that going to war against Iraq will severely strain military resources already burdened by a growing number of obligations. There are daunting challenges facing the 1.4 million men and women in active military service and those in our National Guard and Reserve. The Pentagon has said that up to 250,000 troops may be mobilized for the invasion of Iraq. An additional 265,000 members of the National Guard and Reserve, roughly as many as were called up during the Persian Gulf War in 1991, may also be activated.

Already, we have long-term troop commitments in Europe and the Pacific, with an estimated 116,000 troops in Europe, 90,000 in the Pacific (nearly 40,000 in Japan and 38,000 in Korea), and additional troop commitments to operations in Afghanistan, Bosnia, Kosovo, and elsewhere. There are also military trainers in countries across the world, including the Philippines, Colombia, and Yemen. We can expect the evolving global war on terrorism to drain our military resources even more, stretching them to the limit.

The administration has yet to address the question of whether our military is of sufficient strength and size to meet present and future commitments. Those who would lead us into war have the obligation to support an all-out mobilization of Americans for the war effort, including mandatory national service that asks something of us all.

19

Dodgy Drafters

CASPAR W. WEINBERGER

CONGRESSMEN CHARLES RANGEL (D-N.Y.) and John Conyers (D-Mich.) have pushed some bad ideas before, but their proposal—to bring back the Vietnam era in the form of a military draft—is far and away the worst. Attempting to play both the race and class warfare cards, the congressmen said the U.S. "must debate whether it should continue with a fighting force comprised disproportionately of people from low-income families and minorities." In another burst of unconscionable demagoguery, they also say that the burden of defending the country is resting too heavily on the shoulders of the blacks and minorities.

This is all utter and pernicious nonsense. The congressmen never mentioned that the burden of defending the country is resting on the shoulders—white, black, brown—of those who want that "burden," and whose volunteering gives it to them.

If some statistical genius has computed that our all-volunteer force may have slightly more black and Hispanic volunteers than is "proportionate"(to what?), I would reply that that simply demonstrates that there is a higher degree of patriotism among black and Hispanic youths of draft age than among whites of draft age. That should be a matter of praise and gratification. But no! The congressmen simply ignore the fact that however

Reprinted from the *Wall Street Journal*, January 10, 2003.

"proportional," our military is what it is because it is made up of people who want to be there.

Messrs. Rangel and Conyers want to scrap all that, roughly like the people who wanted to break up the New York Yankees because they were too good. The congressmen talk as if there is some racist administration forcing young blacks and Hispanics into the danger of war while leaving the children of the white and the rich free to evade military service and practice greed or whatever.

That is the picture they would like to paint. But that simply does not exist. The true picture is that if there are "disproportionately" too many black and Hispanic volunteers, that is because "too many" of them are volunteering to defend us all. Mr. Rangel and others like him prefer force and compulsion, not reason, on behalf of their causes, and so their solution to the "dilemma" of too many patriotic blacks and so forth seems to be twofold. One, refuse them admission to the military until the "numbers are corrected," or two, draft everyone aged eighteen to twenty-six into a vast unneeded pool of people, all of whom, no matter how unsuitable, would have to be given military training or forced into some unspecified national service.

This would cost enormous sums—far higher than Messrs. Rangel and Conyers would vote to authorize—all to give the country many million more unneeded government employees. But neither a draft nor a refusal to allow patriotic young blacks and Hispanics to volunteer are needed or favored by the military or the majority of citizens. Instead, the stage would be set for the fierce opposition to a draft that marked the Vietnam years, when the nation was polarized.

Would any of this improve the military? Hardly. The purpose of the Rangel-Conyers draft is not to improve the military but to build public opposition to war with Iraq. A collateral result would be to fill the military with people who do not want to be there.

An editorial that appeared January 6, 2003, in the *Wall Street Journal* exploded the idea that the children of low-income or minority parents are at greater risk in war.[1] Those who insist that blacks will become the brunt of combat casualties "have it exactly backwards," as the *Journal* correctly pointed out. The Rangel-Conyers problem is that none of the standard demagogic appeals to racism or class warfare apply to a military comprised exclusively of volunteers. So the congressmen have to invent a scenario in which to invoke their mumbo-jumbo.

Here is the bottom line, to which every American concerned about national security should pay heed: trained and eager volunteers are far more effective soldiers than conscripts. I volunteered for the army and the infantry as a private after graduating from law school in 1941 and trained and served with both drafted soldiers and volunteers. There was no doubt in anyone's mind that volunteers were far more effective than draftees and eager to train and to fight.

Once, early in 1982, President Reagan and I reviewed a force of young American soldiers newly enrolled. Afterwards he said to me, "You know, Cap, I would infinitely rather look each of these young people in the eye and know that each wants to be here."

Let's keep it that way.

20

Degraded into a Trade

JOHN LEHMAN

IN CALLING FOR a new look at resurrecting the draft, Representative Charles Rangel raises a very good point. Our all-volunteer force, for all its many virtues, is not representative of American society. The privileged are largely absent from it. Thus the burdens of defense and the perils of combat do not fall even close to fairly across all of our society.

But the disparity is not one of race. The representation of minorities differs only slightly from that in the population at large. A black Ivy League graduate is as unlikely to serve as a white graduate. Nor is the problem today one of elitist disdain for the uniform. The cause of this very serious problem is instead found in the bureaucracies that encrust our fighting forces.

In the three decades since the draft was abolished, the characteristics of our forces have changed enormously under the hand of the recruiting bureaucracies. Using tools of the behavioral scientists, they have given top priority to finding candidates who above all will stay for a full career. This screening is producing a force of broad racial and gender diversity but of a boring sameness in other respects.

There is, for instance, surprisingly little social, economic, or political diversity. Eighty percent identify themselves as Republicans. Nearly a

Reprinted from the *Washington Post*, January 26, 2003.

third of the cadets and midshipmen at the service academies come from career military families. A force made up overwhelmingly of career professionals has become more and more separate from civilian culture, with housing, schooling, worship, shopping, recreation, and health care all provided within securely guarded bases.

This is a fine culture built on service and patriotism, but it is also a culture of orthodoxy, resistant to and isolated from change. More important, as Rangel has said, it does not represent a cross section of the United States.

This is not a new phenomenon. It has been a characteristic of service life between all our major wars. In each period the onset of war brought in a tide of citizen-soldiers and sailors from every social stratum—disruptive, irreverent, unorthodox, and renewing. In every era they brought new ideas and attitudes and were a catalyst for innovation and transformation. It is the need for this creative leavening of large numbers of noncareer enlisted personnel and officers drawn from every neighborhood that attracts people to the idea of resuming the draft.

An important source of this leavening should be our top universities, where admission is based not on money but on merit. Edward Gibbon wrote in *The Decline and Fall of the Roman Empire* that Rome fell when the most talented and well-educated young Romans no longer served their time in the Roman cavalry.

A similar trend has emerged in the United States these past decades, and nowhere more than in the navy. In the World War II navy, 95 percent of the officers were reservists from civilian universities, with the Ivy Leagues prominent. Six of the last nine presidents were among them. Such people are now very scarce in the service.

Recruiters have long blamed the elite campuses for harboring an antimilitary bias, but that is no longer a valid excuse. Students from the best campuses all over the country are applying to the services in large numbers, but except for the now very rare ROTC units, they are finding that they are not particularly welcome. As an associate fellow at Yale and an overseer at the University of Pennsylvania, I am frequently asked for help by outstanding students who have gotten a cold shoulder from recruiters. If they are given any encouragement at all, they are offered officer candidate school class dates a year or more off.

Rich and poor, these are kids who are genuinely motivated by a sense of duty and love of country, though they would never put it quite that way. Yet they find they get a very cool reception from navy recruiters. Priority is now reserved for career enlisted candidates whom the navy pays to put through college. A fine program in itself, it has been greatly expanded because the recruiting bureaucrats believe commissioned former enlisted sailors are certain to stay for at least twenty years, whereas Joe College is more likely to serve the minimum obligated service and then defect to the reserves. (In fact, OCS graduates from civilian universities have the same retention rates as Annapolis graduates.)

To further deter such candidates, the minimum active-duty requirement has been considerably lengthened. A candidate who wants to fly, for example, must agree to a minimum of ten years on active duty. Thus the lively ready-room mix of academy graduates, Ivy Leaguers, and small-college and ex-enlisted graduates is gone. Today's mix is very different and the culture more conservative, career conscious, and orthodox.

Another important source of diversity used to be the "six by six" program, still used sparingly by the National Guard. Such programs attracted college-bound kids to take a gap year by enlisting for six months of active duty and then six years in the drilling reserves.

Rangel is right. We have a real problem, and the draft in concept is an appealing answer. But it is not a practical answer in the United States, where the services could take only one out of thirty eligible eighteen-year-olds, thus replacing one kind of unfairness with another.

The real answer is to take recruiting policy away from the green-eyeshade bureaucrats who want only "lifers" and restore common sense. We should actively seek to attract the most talented from all backgrounds with service options that allow them to serve their country and experience the character-building unique to military service without having to commit to six to ten years' active duty. Under present policies, naval and military service is being, in Gibbon's words, "degraded into a trade."

21

Military Service and the Middle Class

A Letter to My Sons

STEPHEN HESS

This brief essay was written in November 1981 and appeared in a number of newspapers around the United States. Addressed to my two sons, who were then seventeen and twenty years old, it was a reflection on the lessons I had learned as a draftee in the army from 1957 through 1958, during which time I served in the Third Armored Division and rose to the rank of private first class. This kind of experience my sons and their friends were not to have with the advent of the all-volunteer army.

My sons turned out to be pretty useful citizens. I cannot say how different they might have been if they had had to serve in the army. I can only say that after rereading my words more than two decades later, I have not changed my mind about how worthwhile my two years in the army proved to be for me.

DEAR SONS:

I've just read a disturbing report, *Military Service in the United States*, which, as your teachers say, should be "recommended reading" since you're both at the age that produces a nation's soldiers.[1] The thirty-four experts who were gathered together by the prestigious American Assembly, an arm of Columbia University, state, "Current manning of the military forces in the United States is inadequate to our national needs."

The report does not believe, as some contend, that the all-volunteer force has been a disaster. Indeed, it is called a "quantitative success" in that it has generally met the manpower goals that were set for it. (The experts think, however, that the goals are low.) The report claims the problem is qualitative, "a shortage of recruits from the higher mental categories, particularly the Army."

The experts, instead of advocating a return to compulsory military service, argue that more bright young people can be lured into the military by increased economic incentives. I think they are wrong—at least judging from conversations with you and your friends. But I'm certainly willing to spend the additional dollars to test the proposition.

Still, my hunch is that before long, we will again have to think the unthinkable: a return to the draft.

I pray that you will never have to fight in a war, as I never had to. (I do suspect that domestic politics makes it harder for our leaders to declare war if there is a largely nonvoluntary army.) But I'm not writing you about war. I've no doubt that you would want to defend your country.

Rather, I'd like you to know from my experience what you might someday conclude about being drafted. I say "someday" because I'm not about to tell you I loved my two years as an army private, or that what I did was other than boring or seemed to be other than wasted time at the time.

There is a good deal of learned writing about the army as a "socializing agent." Those who do this writing are in the middle class, usually professors and journalists. They mean that army service can be a good for the lower class. It can teach skills that inattentive students don't get in school, instill discipline, take up the slack in the job market, and so forth.

What I can't recall reading about is the army as a socializing agent for those of us who are privileged, who have the opportunity to go to college, and who rarely will be without a good job if we seek one.

Being forced to be the lowest rank in a peacetime army, serving for long enough that you can't clearly see "the light at the end of the tunnel," is as close as you will ever come to being a member of society's underclass.

To put it bluntly, you will feel in your gut what it is like to be at the bottom of the heap.

The army, by definition, is a gross institution. By that I mean that its primary concern is not with the individual. Why should you want to be deprived of your individuality? You shouldn't, of course. But many people are, and you should want to know how this feels, especially if you someday have some responsibility over the lives of other people.

You can acquire knowledge of being at the bottom in many ways—by reading, observing, serving in a poverty program—but I doubt you will ever truly feel what it is like unless you have been there, even for a short time.

At the same time, the middle class draftee learns to appreciate a lot of talents (and the people who have them) that are not part of the lives you have known, and, after military duty, will know again for the rest of your lives. This will come from being thrown together with—and having to depend on—people who are very different from you and your friends. Moreover, if you can't fix a jeep or dig a hole in the frozen ground, these other people are a lot more valuable than you are. It is no small lesson to recognize their worth. And it is equally useful to learn how to fit together with them in a community. For you, too, will have skills that are valuable to them.

So my two years were not wasted. In fact, I now think they were more useful to my education than anything else I might have been doing for two years at that time. If you should be required to have this experience, perhaps you will find that the old man is right.

Your loving dad.

PART FOUR
Experiences of Service

22

The American Military and the Idea of Service

LOUIS CALDERA

MILITARY SERVICE CAN be a transformative life experience. It was for me, and it continues to be so for today's young servicemen and -women. As young Americans consider their options for national and community service today, however, military service is rarely even on the agenda. What must we do to increase the interest of our young people in serving their country in uniform?

Recent proposals to bring back the draft are certainly not the right way to challenge every young American to ask, "Whose responsibility is it to serve in uniform if not mine?" The draft is a discredited and obsolete tool for manning today's more professional and highly skilled, all-volunteer force. However, a system of universal national service in which military service is but one option among many would increase the opportunities for all young people to have the experience of giving something back to their country, including in uniform.

I volunteered to serve, driven by the immigrant spirit to give something back to the country that had given so much to my family and to me. Bookish, shy, a sheltered son of struggling, Spanish-speaking parents, I knew little of the world outside my own cloistered neighborhood. The military, with its emphasis on leadership development, moral and physical courage, and command presence and voice, opened my eyes to the vast possibilities of life. I learned that the world had much more to offer me than I had ever imagined and that no doors were closed to me except the ones I chose not to open. Our mission in the army—to be prepared to defend the nation and to serve wherever called in support of our nation's interests in the world—gave me a deeper appreciation for the forces, events, and people that shape the world we live in. Inchoate notions of duty, service, and citizenship began to become tangible and permanent.

Throughout my recent tenure as secretary of the army, I heard young men and women express what service means to them. Often deployed far from home, they would say there was no place they would rather be because they knew they were making a difference. Whether helping to save lives and leading recovery efforts in Central America after Hurricane Mitch or preventing genocide in Bosnia-Herzegovina, they could palpably feel the gratitude of those for whom their presence and aid meant hope for a better life for themselves and for their children. Standing watch on the world's hot spots or training to deploy there if necessary, they knew that what they were prepared to do was essential to protecting our nation. These young people did not come, by and large, from America's most privileged families. Yet they were the ones who had internalized the sense that we are abundantly blessed as Americans and called, out of our own principles and enlightened self-interest, to lead and to help others in places driven by hatred and calamity.

Why does military service not figure more prominently in calls for a renewed commitment to service? In part, it is the benign result of the structure of such service initiatives as AmeriCorps and America's Promise, which address urgent domestic needs. In part, it results from the end of the mass-mobilization periods in American history: relatively few parents, teachers, and other role models of today have ever worn the uniform of our country. It may also come from misconceptions about the nature of modern military service, discomfort with the fundamental role of the military, lingering suspicion and hostility arising from an antiwar movement that spanned three decades, and unhappiness with current policies toward openly gay service members. Whatever the reasons, few adults challenge today's young people to consider serving their country in uniform.

Some would say that nothing short of a return to the draft will bring more young people—especially the most socially and economically privileged—into the military ranks. This argument is heard with increasing frequency at times when military confrontation is on the horizon. It is being pressed by Rep. Charles Rangel (D-N.Y.), who has introduced legislation that would require universal service of citizens and permanent residents aged eighteen to twenty-six. First call on those inducted would go to fill the needs of the armed forces, but all would be required to give two years of service in some capacity.

Rangel, a decorated veteran who opposed war with Iraq, wanted to bring the notion of shared responsibility closer to home for all Americans. Noting that few members of Congress have children in the military, he wrote in a *New York Times* op-ed piece (reprinted in this book) that "if we are going to send our children to war, the governing principle must be that of shared sacrifice. . . . A disproportionate number of the poor and members of minority groups make up the enlisted ranks of the military, while the most privileged Americans are underrepresented or absent."[1]

While it is worth debating whether there is something wrong about how the burdens and benefits (yes, benefits) of military service are being allocated within our society, it is not useful to frame this debate in the context of a return to the draft. First, the Vietnam-era draft that most people recall was hardly a model of fairness. It was riddled with loopholes and was susceptible to being gamed. Its biggest failing was that, unlike earlier drafts, the burden it allocated was far less than universal: fewer than 10 percent of eligible-age men served during that period. Today, a lottery-style draft would be even more unfair as well as unnecessary—unfair because far fewer members of a much larger population are needed to fill today's much smaller force, and unnecessary because the armed forces currently get all the volunteers they need to fill the ranks. Second, the draft is not a good path to military quality. Today, the professional military of the United States is undeniably the world's greatest because sufficient numbers of highly qualified men and women volunteer or reenlist every year.

Moreover, these highly motivated volunteers are willing to sign up for the longer enlistment tours necessary for the military to train them to become proficient users of the high-tech weaponry, communications, and information systems now deployed. That valuable training, as well as a strong sense of purpose and commitment among those who serve, is the reason that recruitment and retention rates remain high in a force that is both diverse and cohesive. That diversity is one of the military's strengths. There is nothing pernicious about the fact that many minorities seek to serve—and not just in the enlisted ranks. Indeed, some minorities are underrepresented in the enlisted ranks, and all are underrepresented in the senior officer ranks, though diversity is on the rise there also.

Although the draft is no longer a useful or viable way to fill the ranks of our nation's military, we should do more to teach all of America's young people that the benefits of military service far outweigh its burdens. Although there are unique risks and hardships that come with military service, the courageous and patriotic men and women who serve today take these on willingly out of a sense of duty and love of country. By serving they are learning invaluable lessons about themselves, about others, and about our country and all it stands for. Those are lessons that even America's most privileged youth would do well to learn. We should inspire them to want to serve, not coerce their service through conscription.

President Bush has included the military in his recent national service proposals, but creating new opportunities for military service that parallel those for civilian service will not be easy. The military itself has struggled to find ways to embrace the concept of more young people serving shorter tours of duty without compromising the requirements of military cohesiveness and readiness, particularly in the era of the high-tech battlefield. Today's recruitment and training costs are high. Because service members often train for a year or more before arriving at their first unit, the military services prefer four- to six-year enlistment contracts and put a premium on retaining skilled careerists. Moreover, high personnel turnover at the unit level degrades unit cohesiveness. Teams never quite gel as new recruits keep moving in and out of the ranks. Trainers and leaders rarely get to hone higher-order team competencies as they constantly work to rebuild basic ones. So it will not be as simple as mandating shorter tour options—a proposal that many in the military suspect will bring into the ranks soldiers who are not really committed to the proposition that they must train as if war is imminent and that they will be the ones to fight it.

Despite these difficulties, we should try to create some workable opportunities for shorter-term military service, and we should work with employers, educators, and government leaders to create an enhanced framework of realistic enlistment and reenlistment incentives. Above all, we should make military service an important part of the national conversation about the obligations and benefits of service. Young Americans deserve to know about this opportunity to see firsthand our country's principles put into action, to work with people of all backgrounds and walks of life, and to challenge themselves to live by the high standards the military demands of those who respond to the call of duty. For them, as for me and for so many others, military service can be the foundation for a lifelong commitment to public service and the source of a deep appreciation for the importance of civic engagement in a democracy.

23

Empowering Communities
The Gift of the Civil Rights Movement

CHARLES COBB JR.

HAS THERE EVER been a time when community service was not valued or, indeed, held high as a standard of citizenship in this country? Roosevelt's "New Deal" still stands as a model of government linking to community service. The power of John F. Kennedy's 1961 inaugural call—"Ask not what your country can do for you"—rested on a consensus of obligation to community service.

But whose community? What do we mean by "community" anyway? Although the 1960s opened with Kennedy's almost romantic call to service, those who responded within the framework of the civil rights struggle were often resisted—and not just by redneck racists but at the highest levels of government.

In the early 1960s, government—and I would argue the nation in general—was uncertain whether African Americans were part of the "community," except as recipients of charity. The kind of blatant racial discrimination found in the South embarrassed and offended, yes. But the denial of citizenship to blacks was not really on the national radar screen. It affected nothing that those in power recognized as important.

Embedded in civil rights, and in the easier-to-digest "community service," is the idea of empowerment—an idea that is not readily embraced if it means empowering those perceived as being outside of our own "community." The southern civil rights movement, of which I was a part, got the nation's attention and affirmed black citizenship. The way the movement accomplished that end offers valuable lessons for anyone considering ideas of community service today.

First, the southern civil rights movement is best understood as a movement of community organizing rather than one of protest. Movement organizers committed to a specific idea of service—the "redemption and vindication of the race," to use an old phrase—sought ways to encourage the black community to find its own voice. And though prominent advocates had long spoken up for civil rights, what finally effected change was *ordinary* people—sharecroppers, day workers, maids, cooks, and nursemaids—finding their own voices. Across the long-silent black belt, people who were usually spoken for began speaking for themselves in tones loud enough to be heard. They said—meeting much resistance, some of it violent—"This is what we want!"

The movement is a powerful illustration of how much commitment can compensate for a lack of material resources. Typically, an organizer entered a town or county and, working with a handful of local people, built local organizations—freedom schools, political groups like the Lowndes County Freedom Organization in Alabama, rural labor unions, or small enterprises like Mississippi's Poor People's Corporation. The point to understand is that community organizers do not lead. Instead, they cultivate leadership—grassroots leadership.

One tool that turned out to be critical was the meeting, which shifted, as the movement unfolded, from being a gathering where a person or panel of people presided, delivering information and strategy to others who listened and accepted, to a gathering where people actively engaged problems in various arenas ranging from local violence and denial of civil rights all the way up to politics and law at the national level.

Such grassroots empowerment was a radical idea. Even long-established civil rights figures and their long-time liberal allies were uncomfortable with the Fannie Lou Hamers speaking with their plantation voices. At one point during the challenge by the Mississippi Freedom Democratic party at the Democratic party's national convention in 1964,

Senator Hubert Humphrey bluntly rejected a core idea of the civil rights movement—meaningful participation in the decisionmaking affecting their lives—and said of Mrs. Hamer: "The president will not allow that illiterate woman to speak from the floor of the convention."

Nonetheless, civil rights organizing produced a politically literate network of people who challenged and changed the status quo. They were not formally credentialed people. For the most part, they, like Mrs. Hamer, did not even have high school diplomas. They were not members of labor unions or national church associations. They were not big shots in civil rights organizations. When I think of these ordinary people and the extraordinary struggle they waged, I think of Ella Baker, whose hands shaped a half-century of civil rights organizing. To effect change, Ms. Baker once told us, you have to face a system "that does not lend itself to your needs and devise the means by which you begin to change that system."

Does the Bush administration have this in mind when it posits the value of a new initiative for community service? Do the powerful of America?

24

Is the Era of Recreational Government Bashing Over?

ALICE M. RIVLIN

ONE OF AMERICA'S great national pastimes is baseball. Another is government bashing. It is such fun to encounter a troublesome government regulation or a public official who does not see things your way. You can roll your eyes and say, "Isn't that just like the government?"—and then tell your story at the office or the next dinner party to appreciative audiences guaranteed to nod and smile.

If you have a similar experience, and we all do, with a private company—its product does not work or the bill is wrong—it is no fun at all. You cannot say, "Isn't that just like the private sector?" and get any nods or smiles. You just have to solve the problem.

Of course, government bashing is mostly recreational. In 1995 when I was director of the Office of Management and Budget, Congress voted to close the federal government rather than compromise with President Clinton over budget priorities. The congressional leadership, coming off an unusually strident government-bashing campaign, expected its decision to be wildly popular. But citizens were outraged that they could not picnic at their national park, get their passport renewed, have their FHA housing loan approved, or get their student loan application processed.

Congress was reminded then that government did useful things that citizens need and take for granted. We were all reminded of that again on September 11, when police officers and firefighters and soldiers and airmen that we take for granted most of the time suddenly became the people we were all depending on to save our lives and our way of life.

One recreational benefit of government bashing is that it saves us from facing up to how hard it is to make public policy in a free market economy. Over the past half-century, it has become apparent to the whole world that market economies work much better and produce a far higher standard of living for everyone than centrally planned ones. What is not recognized is that the easy part of a free market economy is the market part. The hard part is making the public policy within which the market can operate effectively.

We rarely think about how demanding a task we have given our policymakers. Indeed, Americans are in almost continuous high dudgeon over the failure of policymakers and politicians. We shake our heads and mutter that if only we had better people or stronger political leadership, everything would be okay. Or we blame democracy, at best a messy way to make decisions, without realizing that most of the problem is not the democratic process. Instead, it is that making public policy for a market economy is genuinely and continuously hard.

What is so hard? Well, first, if markets are to work, there have to be rules about property, bankruptcy, contracts, accounting standards, and not injuring others in specified ways, and the rules have to be enforced. Second, there have to be social, environmental, and other public policies to handle the fact that people and companies operating in their own interest tend to load costs onto others when they can and leave behind those unable to fend for themselves. And, third, there are genuine public goods—armies and navies, police, roads, parks, public health services—that will not be provided by private investors on their own.

Dealing with these questions is the intellectually and morally challenging aspect of a free market system. In centrally planned economies, authorities make policy by fiat, telling somebody to do or not to do something. But in free market systems, making most kinds of public policy requires adjusting incentives and regulations just enough to accomplish a public purpose and to move activities in one direction or another without impeding the main action of the private-sector players and the productivity of their operations. The process is complex and contentious, and the participants can never get it right; they have to keep tinkering as conditions change.

Interestingly, although Americans fail to recognize how challenging public service jobs can be, they firmly believe that these jobs are onerous and unappreciated. They are sure that we who do them would much rather be doing something else.

Not on your life. Most people I know who have had careers in public service have loved their work. It used talents and ingenuity we did not know we had and we did not get to use elsewhere. It gave us the satisfaction of making the world—or some little piece of it—a little better.

In truth, we love our work the way baseball players love playing baseball. Baseball players do not want that known, for if people knew they played for fun, they would not get all that money. And we in public service do not want it known either, or we would not get awards.

25

Service in the Pursuit
of Social Justice

DANIEL BLUMENTHAL

In 1969–70, as the only physician in VISTA, I was assigned to Lee County, Arkansas, a county of 16,000 people in the Mississippi River delta. Said to be the seventh poorest county in the nation, Lee was 60 percent black, 70 percent poor, and virtually untouched by the civil rights movement. It was an unreconstructed, segregated piece of the "Old South."

About thirty VISTA volunteer "health advocates" were assigned to five counties of eastern Arkansas that year, with seven dispatched to Lee. Those seven included my wife (a child psychologist), a nurse, and four recent college graduates trained briefly in health-related areas such as nutrition as well as in community organizing. Together we set up four grassroots "community action councils" and, with the help of a small federal grant, a community-controlled health center, the Lee County Cooperative Clinic. Our goal was to provide health care to the poor (who desperately needed it), but, even more important, to offer them some sense of empowerment—that is, the ability to control resources such as health care rather than having to rely on charity. The clinic was run by a board of directors elected by the patients, who were considered members of the clinic cooperative.

White resistance to the clinic and to VISTA's organizing efforts was formidable. The four-member medical staff of the county's twenty-bed hospital denied me admitting privileges. We were unable to house the clinic at any white-owned property. When the black funeral parlor director finally rented us a five-room house, the county's government tried to block our federal grant. The struggle gained media attention, with front page stories in major newspapers and features on national television.

The conflict mobilized Lee's poor and African American population and transformed the county. A black political organization spun off from the action councils and offered the first black candidates for local public office since Reconstruction. Blacks demanding economic justice boycotted white-owned businesses; students demanding educational justice boycotted the public schools. Buildings were burned and shots fired. Miraculously, no one was killed or injured.

Today, all that is history. Lee County government is integrated. The clinic put up its own building in 1972 and has been a member of the county Chamber of Commerce for many years. The hospital has long since closed, as have most rural hospitals of its size. Marianna, the county seat, now has a biracial work force but could hardly be called prosperous. The county's poverty rate has dropped to a "mere" 38 percent.

And I have been gone from eastern Arkansas for more than thirty years. For the past twenty-one, I have taught public health and supervised the public health faculty at the Morehouse School of Medicine. Public health is that branch of the health profession that tries to ensure that all kids are immunized, everybody has access to safe water and food, everybody gets screened for cancer and high blood pressure, and ultimately, somehow, that everybody has access to health care. The key word is "everybody." We like to say that "public health is social justice."

Striving for social justice comes naturally to Morehouse, a predominantly African American medical school. Blacks still have the poorest health indices in the United States, and few blacks have been trained as public health professionals.

As a volunteer in Lee County, I had the privilege of working for a more just society, of helping to change the conditions that kept people in poverty and denied them their basic rights. In another way, I have the same privilege now. Many of my fellow VISTA volunteers were not so fortunate; their duties were to drive people to the welfare office or distribute used clothing or the like. Those jobs constitute service, to be sure, and they need to be done, but in the long run, they don't change anything. Many volunteers who were doing that sort of work in 1970 felt a sense of frustration and often failed to complete their year in VISTA.

Sometimes today I am asked to address groups of VISTA volunteers, now known as AmeriCorps VISTAs. My message is always the same: see what you can do to change the world. Social justice is no longer an explicit focus of VISTA, so my message is a bit subversive. But it is the same message that I would give anybody who undertakes service, as a volunteer or for a living.

26

Profits through Principles

ROBERT D. HAAS

By the time I graduated from the University of California at Berkeley in 1964, young people nationwide were galvanized to serve. It was a golden age of service, prompted in part by President Kennedy's well-known call to action in his 1961 inaugural address.

Like many others, I joined the Peace Corps and then headed to the rural village of Adzope in the Ivory Coast of Africa. My experience there teaching English and getting a public health project off the ground taught me to make the most out of opportunities to bring about positive change, a lesson I have carried with me throughout my business life. It reinforced a commitment to community involvement that goes back through generations of my family.

My great-great-granduncle, Levi Strauss, was a merchant and a philanthropist, a civic-minded business leader who believed deeply in community service. In fact, throughout our company's 149-year history, business and corporate citizenship have been linked as one. This principle of "responsible commercial success" has endured in good times and bad and continues to anchor our beliefs and behaviors today. It is one of the reasons consumers trust our brands and company.

Today, American business faces a crisis of trust. Consumers have been barraged with news accounts of egregious corporate misconduct. Allegations of dishonesty, subterfuge, and executive greed have triggered government investigations, indictments, and company bankruptcies. Public trust of business has collapsed to levels not seen since the early 1900s.

Increasingly, consumers are holding corporations accountable not only for their products and services but also for how they are made and marketed. Consumers want more than growth in shareholder value from business; they also expect good corporate citizenship. Great brands and businesses are built through a combination of two things: continuously providing superior products and services and earning the trust of consumers, employees, and the communities in which they operate. This is the formula for sustained business success.

Since September 11, Americans have expressed more interest in civic involvement and trust in one another and their government. As Robert Putnam, the chronicler of trends in U.S. civic engagement, mentions elsewhere in this book, "In the aftermath of September's tragedy, a window of opportunity has opened for a sort of civic renewal that occurs only once or twice a century." This upswing in civic attitudes does not include greater trust of business. Knowing this, business has a timely opportunity—as well as a responsibility—to help shape society by modeling ethical conduct and civic engagement. Integrity means more than mere compliance with the law. It means "doing the right thing" through a range of responsible business practices, including increased transparency, outstanding workplace practices, exemplary environmental stewardship, generous philanthropic support, and more.

On a local level, businesses can help their workers become more engaged in the community. Employees want to do this but are often hamstrung by the demands of their time-starved lives. To further this goal, therefore, companies can conduct volunteer days, when teams of employees work together on community improvement projects; provide matching grants to employee contributions; and create a culture where senior leadership demonstrates the importance of community service. In return, businesses can attract and hold superior talent, improve employee morale, and generate community goodwill.

Internationally, U.S. multinational companies can play a progressive role as well. Business and communities prosper in America because of free markets and a democratic society. In diverse marketplaces around the world, business leaders can model the best of what America stands for—

freedom, opportunity, and compassion. Corporate leaders must stand up for human rights and freedom of association; encourage responsible open trade and environmental stewardship; and support educational and employment opportunities for underserved populations, especially women and local minorities.

Of course, corporate citizenship is not uniquely American. Companies throughout the world have pioneered progressive practices and used their resources to help people, not just sell to them. We must build coalitions and create common frameworks for policies and programs that serve the public good.

My commitment to corporate social responsibility and community involvement stems from a family tradition and a national call to service that took me to a remote African village. Many ideals of Peace Corps service apply equally to the success of a global enterprise. A profits-through-principles approach to business is good for business and good for society.

27

A New Citizenship
for a New Century

ALAN KHAZEI

HISTORIANS WILL LIKELY say that the twenty-first century began on September 11, 2001. We have reached a turning point in the history not only of our country, but also of democracy and of our increasingly global community. It is time to make real a new and deeper citizenship for this new century, as the actions we take now will shape our nation and our world for decades to come.

At a time of such momentous change, we look back nostalgically sixty years and rightly revere the "Greatest Generation" for fighting a depression and a world war for freedom and democracy. Today, as we fight a war against terrorists, we must also fight against the terrible injustice we see all around us. Every night in America, 750,000 people sleep on the streets. Every day, 11.6 million children—20 percent of our kids—wake up in poverty. Worldwide, 40 million people are living with AIDS, and a quarter of the world's population lives on no more than $1.08 a day.

Since September 11, another great generation has been growing in America. Our nation's civic spirit has been renewed, and we must tap that spirit by creating a comprehensive system through which Americans can serve their communities, country, and world. President Bush has challenged all Americans to dedicate at least two years of their lives to service.

That goal should become our north star, and we must not rest until we reach it.

To do that, we must dramatically expand the opportunities for Americans to serve full time, and we must leverage those full-time servers to inspire millions of Americans to serve part time. Our nation's greatest untapped resource is its 25 million young people between the ages of eighteen and twenty-five. We should enable one million of them to enter full-time civilian service each year by 2020. To do so, we must expand America's current national service system, engaging all sectors of society. The president took several crucial first steps by creating the USA Freedom Corps, by proposing to increase AmeriCorps by 50 percent, and by doubling the Peace Corps. But more can be done.

—Universities and employers can publicly adopt a year of service as a key criterion in admissions and hiring.

—Universities can match AmeriCorps awards as part of their college financial aid programs.

—The president can host an annual White House summit on the state of national and community service in America and issue an annual State of Service report.

—All major American business companies can give each employee a week of paid time off to do community service.

—Congress can amend the Family and Medical Leave Act to allow all employees to take up to two weeks' unpaid leave each year to serve.

—Congress can set a goal of at least $1 billion a year in federal challenge grants (to be matched one-to-one with nonfederal funding) to expand model national service programs.

—High schools can create "community service coach" positions and enable hundreds of thousands of students to do service learning.

—Communities can provide opportunities for tens of thousands of high school students to commit a "summer of service," spending summer break serving full time while earning educational awards for college.

—Several communities can bring leading model national service programs to scale to demonstrate the transformative power of a critical mass of service opportunities.

—AmeriCorps should permit some members to do some service

abroad and allow programs to enroll people from other countries to serve here. The exchange would promote freedom and democracy worldwide.

—A new Global Service Corps can unite young people from many different countries to serve together all over the world.

By implementing these ideas and others, we can build a system of national service that will engage each and every generation in confronting the challenges of its time. Once all Americans commit themselves to service, the Greatest Generation will become the rule rather than the exception, and our grand experiment in democracy and citizen responsibility will truly inspire the world.

28

First Vote

JANE EISNER

IF DEMOCRACY IS America's civic religion, then voting is communion on Easter Sunday, the lighting of Hanukah candles, and the fast of Ramadan rolled into one. It is the ritual we all can share. When my children were younger, I'd insist they partake in this ceremony of civic life and accompany me when I voted, but it became harder to corral them the older they grew. Then, on a Tuesday this past May, my oldest daughter was eligible to vote for the first time, and I had a powerful, disturbing revelation. Almost no one made a fuss.

Oh, the poll workers, bless them, clapped when they learned this was her initial venture. But society did nothing else to encourage her to vote or to mark the occasion. This induction into the central act of citizenship that millions have died to achieve and maintain was greeted by a collective yawn.

Other rites of passage are met by great fanfare. We capture a child's first step with documentary-sized videos. We spend hundreds on prom dresses, thousands on bar mitzvah parties. We all but break a bottle of champagne over the first car.

Yet the first vote is welcomed as enthusiastically as a chemistry test on a rainy Monday. No wonder that in the cliffhanger 2000 presidential election, only 26.7 percent of eighteen-year-olds reported voting.

This generation, which is gravitating toward national service in record numbers, has still not made the connection between service to the community and participation in the very process that governs community life. The link is essential. As the national service movement strengthens and matures, it must produce more than individual fulfillment for those involved and temporary assistance for communities in need.

Why else serve? John Bridgeland, executive director of the new USA Freedom Corps, tried to answer the question last June in Philadelphia, at City Year's annual convention. "Service is a duty associated with living in free society," he said.[1] Service is a way to show love of country and, in the aftermath of the terrorist attacks, to protect the homeland. All true. It is even part of a happy life—and studies prove it.

But national service must be more than that. It must lead to an appetite for substantive change, a commitment to address the social problems that have created the need for service in the first place. As Ira Harkavy, a University of Pennsylvania professor who has long championed community partnerships, said recently: "It's not enough to serve soup in a soup kitchen. We have to work toward ending the conditions that make people hungry."[2]

National service is a means to an end—a point too often lost, sadly, in the dreamy exhortations of this newly popular crusade. It ought not to stand above or away from the political arena; at its best, it can lead to a mass movement for active citizenship and structural reform.

So, bravo to all who volunteer in overcrowded, understaffed public schools; but when the volunteers go home, the debilitating conditions remain. National service will truly be service to the nation if it produces a cadre of informed leaders committed to improving the nation's schools— or at the very least to voting in the next school board election.

I can think of no better way to forge that link than to promote the "First Vote," to indeed celebrate what we value. Between now and the next election day, I urge parents, teachers, coaches, and other caring adults to create their own First Vote ritual for newly minted voters, to publicly acknowledge this civic coming-of-age. I imagine something with the feel of an Aaron Copland symphony, a Frank Capra film, a poem by Maya Angelou.

If an eighteen-year-old is in the army or away at college, send a celebratory package. If she's home, take her out for coffee, buy her flowers or a keepsake book.

High schools should laud students who vote. Employers should offer them time to participate. Neighbors should shake their hands. Those blustery radio stations my kids listen to incessantly should read off the names of first-time voters. Applause, attention—all that is due them.

"I hear America singing," Walt Whitman wrote in the slim volume of poetry I gave my daughter to commemorate her First Vote. Touched as she was, I don't pretend that she'll run home every day to read it. I don't pretend, either, that fifteen minutes in a voting booth on a brisk Tuesday morning will mark a turning point in a young life. I'm just glad she was awake. But I do believe that one day she'll open the pages of Whitman's extraordinary celebration of American life and understand the connection. When Whitman heard the "varied carols" of America singing—the mechanics and masons, shoemakers and sewers, "singing with open mouths their strong melodious songs"—I am certain he heard the sounds of a people who cared enough about their destiny to spend a few minutes once or twice a year in a voting booth. A people who understood that it is not enough to feel good, but to do good; to serve, but also to vote; to fix, but also to change.

PART FIVE
Service and the Challenges of Civic Participation

29

Can Civic Knowledge
Motivate the Next Generation?

WILLIAM GALSTON

THE EVENTS OF September 11 evoked an outpouring of patriotism, not least among young Americans. Scholars, pundits, and young people themselves wondered whether the attacks on the Pentagon and World Trade Center would represent a defining event for this new generation, much as Vietnam did for their parents and Pearl Harbor did for their grandparents. Skeptics (among whom I counted myself) asked whether September 11 could be a real turning point if young Americans were not asked to change their lives meaningfully, to do something to give substance to their patriotic sentiments. Would Pearl Harbor have been a defining event if it had not been followed by a national mobilization and four years of war that altered the lives of soldiers and civilians alike? In the immediate wake of September 11, the administration's failure to call for any real sacrifice from citizens fortified my belief that the terrorist attack would be the functional equivalent of Pearl Harbor without World War II, intensifying insecurity without altering civic behavior.

An Institute of Politics survey of college students released in November 2002 sheds some light on this issue.[1] It shows that intense patriotism and trust in government and other key institutions have declined from their post–September 11 spike. While students overwhelmingly believed that politics is relevant to their lives, 80 percent remained wholly disengaged from political activities. And while they strongly supported action against Iraq in concert with our allies, they did not wish to be involved personally in the conflict. Two-thirds opposed reinstating the draft, and a plurality would seek alternatives if called upon to join the military. The evidence of this and other recent surveys hardly suggests that September 11 has sparked a resurgence of civic engagement among young Americans.

To be sure, anxiety about the civic attitudes and activities of young U.S. adults is nothing new. As far back as solid evidence can be found, it appears that young adults have been less attached to civic life than their parents and grandparents. Civic attachment is linked to factors such as professional interests, stable residential location, leaving one's parents' home, educational attainment, and parenthood, all of which are statistically less characteristic of younger adults. In every generation, not surprisingly, the simple passage of time has brought maturing young adults more fully into the circle of civic life.

Against this backdrop, were today's young adults at all distinctive on the eve of the terrorists' attack? The answer, I believe, is yes. The key is to be found in the demographic distinction between cohort effects and generational effects. Cohorts represent a snapshot of different age groups at the same historical moment, while generations represent the same age groups at different historical moments. If we compare generations rather than cohorts—that is, if we compare today's young adults not with today's older adults, but with young adults of the past, we find evidence of diminished civic attachment.

Some of the basic facts are well known. In the early 1970s, about half of those aged eighteen to twenty-nine voted in presidential elections. By 2000 less than one-third did. The same pattern holds for congressional elections: about one-third voted in the 1970s, compared to less than one-fifth in 1998 (and as far as we can tell, in 2002 as well).

Less well known are the trends charted by the remarkable UCLA study involving 250,000 matriculating college freshmen each year, conducted since the mid-1960s.[2] Over this period, every significant indicator of political engagement fell by at least half. By 2000 only 26 percent of freshmen felt that keeping up with politics was important, down from 58 percent in 1966. Only 14 percent said they frequently discussed politics, down from 30 percent. The UCLA studies for 2001 and 2002 suggest modest improvements in these measures, perhaps in response to international events and domestic tensions, which have increased the perceived salience of government and public issues. Not surprisingly, acquisition of political knowledge from traditional media sources is way down, and relatively few young people are using the Internet to replace newspapers and network TV news as sources of political information.

Freshmen did report significantly increased levels of volunteering in their last year of high school, a trend that seems to be carrying over to their early college years. But only a third of today's young volunteers thought that they would continue this practice once they entered the paid workforce. And there is no evidence that it was leading to wider civic engagement. On the contrary, young people characterized their volunteering as an alternative to politics, which they saw as corrupt, untrustworthy, and unrelated to their deeper ideals. They had limited knowledge of government's impact, either on themselves or on those they seek to assist. They understood why it matters to feed a hungry person at a soup kitchen; they did not understand why it matters where government sets eligibility levels for food stamps or payment levels for the earned income tax credit. They displayed confidence in personalized acts with consequences they could see for themselves; they had no such confidence in collective actions (especially those undertaken through public institutions), whose consequences they saw as remote, opaque, and impossible to control.

There are many reasons why the civic detachment of the young should not be regarded with equanimity. Let me begin with a truism about representative democracy: political engagement is not sufficient for political effectiveness, but it is necessary. If today's young people have legitimate generational interests that do not wholly coincide with the interests of their elders, those interests cannot help shape public decisions unless they are forcefully articulated. The withdrawal of a cohort of citizens from public affairs disturbs the balance of public deliberation, to the detriment of those who withdraw (and the rest of us as well).

Second, political scientists have found that civic attitudes and patterns of behavior formed when young tend to persist throughout adult life. The young Americans who banded together to battle the Great Depression and fight in World War II became what Robert Putnam has called the civic generation—unabashedly patriotic and pervasively participatory. The young Americans who came of age during Vietnam and Watergate cannot shed their deep suspicion of politicians and political power. If today's young Americans continue to regard civic affairs as irrelevant, they are likely to abstain from political involvement throughout their lives.

Third is the relation between citizenship and self-development, much debated of late among political theorists. Even if we agree (and we may not) on the activities that constitute good citizenship, one may still wonder why it is good to be a good citizen. It is possible, I believe, for many individuals to realize their good in ways that do not involve the active exercise of citizenship. A private life is not necessarily an impoverished life.

Still, there is something to the proposition that under appropriate circumstances, political engagement helps develop important human capacities. I have in mind the sorts of intellectual and moral qualities that Alexis de Tocqueville and John Stuart Mill emphasized, among them

—enlarged interests,

—a wider human sympathy,

—a sense of active responsibility for oneself,

—the skills needed to work with others towards goods that can only be obtained or created through collective action, and

—the powers of sympathetic understanding needed to build bridges of persuasive words to those with whom one must act.

It may well be that even as civic engagement has declined, the development of these human capacities has become even more necessary. Underlying this conjecture is the suspicion that as the market has become more pervasive during the past generation, both as organizing metaphor and as daily experience, the range of opportunities to develop nonmarket skills and dispositions has narrowed. For various reasons, the solidaristic organizations that dominated the U.S. landscape from the 1930s through the early 1960s have weakened, and the principle of individual choice has emerged as our central value. Indeed, citizenship itself has become optional, as the sense of civic obligation (to vote, or for that matter to do anything else of civic consequence) has faded and as the military draft has been replaced by all-volunteer armed forces. When the chips are down, we prefer exit to voice, and any sense of loyalty to something larger than ourselves has all but disappeared. In this context, the experience of collective action directed toward common purposes is one of the few conceivable counterweights to today's hyperextended principle of individual choice.

Finally, I would offer an old-fashioned argument from obligation. Most young Americans derive great benefits from their membership in a stable, prosperous, and free society. These goods do not fall like manna from heaven; they must be produced, and renewed, by each generation. When all the subtleties are stripped away, there remains the injunction to do one's fair share to uphold the institutions that help secure these advantages. Absent this principle of reciprocity, young people are likely to live not only selfishly but also heedlessly. It is hard to see how they can build good and satisfying lives on this basis.

If civic engagement is more necessary than ever, our failure to encourage it among young adults looms all the larger. We have allowed our politics to degenerate into an unedifying spectator sport that breeds cynicism, especially among the young. We have presided over the dismantling of institutions, such as political parties, that once invited young people into civic life. We have abolished the civic experiences shared by previous generations of young Americans, such as the military draft, without putting anything much in their place.

Although we should get to work right away on these sources of civic disengagement, they will be hard to fix, at least in the short run. Another problem would be easier to solve, if we put our minds to it: namely, our failure to transmit basic civic knowledge and skills to the next generation of citizens. The evidence is now incontrovertible. In our decentralized system of public education, the closest thing we have to a national examination is the National Assessment of Educational Progress (NAEP). The results of the most recent NAEP assessment of civic knowledge, administered in 1998, were discouraging.[3] About three-quarters of all students scored below the level of proficiency. Thirty-five percent of high school seniors tested below basic level, indicating near-total civic ignorance. Another 39 percent were only at the basic level, a state of working knowledge below what they need to function competently as citizens.

When we combine these results with other data from the past decade of survey research, we are driven to a gloomy conclusion: whether we are concerned with the rules of the political game, political players, domestic policy, foreign policy, or political geography, student mastery is startlingly low. This poses a conundrum: although the level of formal schooling in the United States is much higher than it was fifty years ago, the civic knowledge of today's students is at best no higher than that of their parents and grandparents. We have made a major investment in formal education without any discernible payoff in increased civic knowledge.

It is easy to dismiss these findings as irrelevant. Who cares whether young people master the boring content of civics courses? Why does it matter whether they can identify their congressman or name the branches of government? Surprisingly, recent research documents important links between basic civic information and the civic attributes that we have good reason to care about.[4] Other things being equal, civic knowledge enhances support for democratic values, promotes political participation, helps citizens better understand the impact of public policy on their interests, gives citizens the framework they need to learn more about civic affairs, and reduces generalized mistrust and fear of public life.

Policies to promote school-based civic education enjoy wide support, not only among the citizenry as a whole but also among young people. A January 2002 survey cosponsored by the Center for Information and Research on Civic Learning and Engagement (CIRCLE) and the Council for Excellence in Government showed that two-thirds of Americans aged fifteen to twenty-five support making successful completion of coursework in civics and government a requirement for high school graduation.[5]

This survey also points toward another promising possibility for public policy: fully 81 percent of young people favor having the opportunity to serve their country full-time for a year while earning money for college or advanced training. Today, roughly 50,000 young Americans are able to do so each year, just a bit more than 1 percent of each high school graduating class. The administration has called for expanding this to 75,000—a good start, but not nearly enough either to meet urgent national needs or to rebuild citizenship. By contrast, proposals by Senators John McCain and Evan Bayh and others to quintuple annual full-time service opportunities to 250,000 while relinking civilian and military service are far more likely to weave a new thread of meaningful citizenship into the fabric of our civic life.

The terrible events of September 11 created a surge of patriotism and a new sense of connection between young Americans and their public institutions. For many, it was their first experience of public service as meaningful; of national leaders, local leaders, police, firemen, and their fellow citizens as virtuous, even heroic. But no civic invisible hand guarantees that these effects will endure. At best, we have an opportunity, which may prove fleeting, to solidify this new civic sense. If we clean up our politics, rebuild the institutions that ask citizens to participate, multiply opportunities for national and community service, and restore the civic mission of our educational institutions, we have a chance to reverse the cynicism evoked by the politics of the past three decades. If we squander this opportunity, the civic impact of the terrorist attacks will continue to fade, leaving young Americans with only a dim memory of what might have been.

COMMENT

Learning Service
at Ground Zero

MASON ANDERSON AND
KAYLA MELTZER DROGOSZ

On September 14, 2001, Ohio University student Bryan Randolph decided he could no longer watch footage of the September 11 attacks on the World Trade Center from his campus in Athens. Wanting to assist the victims directly, he called his mother and said he was thinking of dropping his classes and going to help. "I think you should go," she replied.

Later that week Randolph headed for New York City where he joined the American Red Cross at Ground Zero. Realizing that much more help was needed, he returned to Athens to recruit more student volunteers. He contacted the Athens County chapter of the Red Cross and, together with several friends, enrolled in disaster relief courses. With donations received from passing out candles, Randolph and his friends organized the Ohio Students United for New York relief group. They left for New York City on October 5.

The students immediately began working in Red Cross operations throughout Ground Zero. Some worked in kitchens; others drove emergency response vehicles (ERVs) to distribute food and water.

By the time the group returned to Ohio a few weeks later, word had spread of their accomplishments. "When I got back, there were e-mails and phone calls like you wouldn't believe from people who wanted to help," said Randolph. The original small group quickly grew into a statewide relief effort. Ohio University president Robert Glidden personally paid for a charter bus to transport the students back to New York.

On its fourth trip, the group operated a respite center at Ground Zero where they worked tirelessly to provide everything from hot meals to sleeping quarters for exhausted firemen and construction crews. Randolph recalled, "It's hard work but it's incredibly rewarding. I will never forget one day, September 23. I was working on an ERV with some friends when a fireman came up to one of us. He just hugged her and started crying."

Bryan Randolph remained in New York City as a Red Cross volunteer for almost a year. After helping sustain the recovery crews working both Ground Zero and the Staten Island dumping ground, he helped set up facilities for the Red Cross's long-term recovery effort. On August 31, 2002, he left New York to return to Ohio University, where he is teaching a course that will certify fellow students as Red Cross disaster volunteers. He hopes to pursue a career in disaster relief.

30

Service and the State
Should We Politicize Social Bonds?

TOD LINDBERG

In April 1998, Al Gore suffered an embarrassment. As usual, he released his income tax return for the previous year. Total taxable income on the joint return for 1997 was $197,729, most of which came from his vice presidential salary of $171,500. The Gores paid a total of $47,662 in federal taxes. But Schedule A, for itemized deductions, listed charitable contributions for the year at a grand total of $353.

Critics pounced: Gore was a charity cheapskate. The Republican National Committee issued a press release. Conservative columnists snickered. Nor was the furor confined to conservative media. In *USA Today,* Stacy Palmer of the *Chronicle of Philanthropy* commented that "certainly a lot of other Americans in that income bracket have found ways to dig deeper in their pockets."[1] The *New York Times* noted that the Gores' charitable contributions for 1997 amounted to "less than two-tenths of 1 percent of their income."[2] Ouch.

Now, surely, anyone who had thought politically about the release of Gore's tax return would have told the vice president that charitable giving in such a small amount would provoke a response. Not giving more would be imprudent, at best. But let us set aside political considerations for a moment. Let us ask, instead, a moral question: shouldn't Al Gore—or, for that matter, anyone with taxable income of $197,729 for the year—give more than $353 to charity?

Before you reach the "obvious" conclusion, may I offer a little context? Household income is not the same as great wealth. Gore's May 1998 financial disclosure form listed assets between $770,000 and $870,000, all highly illiquid: a house and farm in Carthage, Tennessee; a house in Arlington, Virginia; and leasing rights to zinc mined on the Carthage property. Uncharacteristically for a person with Gore's income, the vice president reported no investments in stocks or mutual funds. The strong bull market of the 1990s roared all around the vice president without really touching him.

As for that sizable income, it is true that the Gores were well-off compared with most other Americans, but they also had some considerable expenses in 1997. The vice president incurred some $100,000 in legal bills in connection with the Justice Department investigation into Democratic campaign finance irregularities in 1996.[3] To pay part of them, he borrowed money from a Carthage bank. Also, three of the Gore children were attending expensive schools. I do not know whether the Gores received financial aid, but tuition and fees for the year would have approached $70,000. In addition, in July 1997, Gore's oldest daughter, Karenna, married Andrew Schiff in a ceremony followed by a reception for 300 guests at the vice president's residence. The cost of such an event could approximate one of the private school tuitions. In short, if I take an after-tax income of $150,000 and start subtracting, I can arrive at a negative number for the year in a hurry.

It is also worth noting that 1997 was an aberration. The previous year, the Gores donated to charity some $35,000 in royalties from a book by Tipper. And I think one would be hard-pressed to state that either Al or Tipper Gore was somehow derelict in their contribution to public life, broadly construed. For example, in 1997 Tipper won the Hubert H. Humphrey Civil Rights Award for "selfless and devoted service to the cause of equality" as a result of her advocacy for the homeless and the mentally ill.

Thus I cannot support the conclusion that the Gores should have given more to charity in 1997 than they did—except on the grounds of political prudence. What this case shows, and the reason I have belabored it, is that the real-world circumstances of individuals or families do not always fit neatly with generalizations, even valid ones, about what people "should" do.

Is It Bad Not to Serve?

The question of national service invites the same scrutiny. Is service good? The answer must be yes. As President Bush noted in a speech at Ohio State University in June 2002, "Service is important to your neighbors; service is important to your character; and service is important to your country."[4]

As for neighbors, he observed rightly that "in the shadow of our nation's prosperity, too many children grow up without love and guidance, too many women are abandoned and abused, too many men are addicted and illiterate, and too many elderly Americans live in loneliness. These Americans are not strangers, they are fellow citizens; not problems, but priorities. They are as much a part of the American community as you and I, and they deserve better from this country." As for each individual doing service, "Everyone needs some cause larger than his or her own profit." As for country, "We serve others because we're Americans, and we want to do something for the country we love."[5]

Who would disagree? Certainly not former president Clinton, who noted in a *USA Today* op-ed around the same time, "We must take full advantage of the current convergence of political support for national service and the deep desire of so many Americans to serve."[6] But now that we have established our moral generalization—service is good—it seems to me we are obliged to invert it and particularize it: is the failure to serve always bad? Looking at the Gores' circumstances in the closely related case of charitable contributions—donating one's labor versus the product of one's labor, money— I don't see how one can answer simply and always yes. To increase his tithe, should Gore have pulled one of his children out of private school, stiffed his lawyers or skimped on legal representation, and encouraged Karenna and her beau to elope?

Well, surely he should have done something—for the sake of his political career? Yes, he should have. That question was put aside earlier, but in fact, it is of the essence. How much you or I give to charity is nobody's business but our own. How much the Gores gave in 1997 turns out to be everybody's business solely and precisely because he was a holder of high public office. Thus being publicly accountable for one's contributions breaks the connection between giving and an underlying charitable intention. If we are going to be graded on our giving, and the grades posted, and our future depends to some degree on whether people think we pass, we are going to give first and foremost to pass. Another way of putting this is that in the instance of Al Gore, his charitable giving was politicized.

Do we run the risk of a similar politicization in the case of a government role in promoting service? I think the answer must be yes. It is already evident in the nation's largest voluntary national service program, the U.S. military.

There are many good reasons to join the Marine Corps—and also many reasons not to. Those who make the latter decision have a price to pay (admittedly, typically small): a deficiency in comparison with those who have worn the uniform and therefore presumably have been willing to risk their lives in service to their country. It is not quite "bad" not to have served in uniform, but neither is it quite as "good" as having done so. I occasionally receive e-mail in response to my writing on foreign affairs from correspondents demanding to know whether I ever served in the military and telling me to shut up if I didn't. I reply that foreign affairs analysis deserves to be considered on the merits, not dismissed with ad hominem attacks. But this response isn't entirely adequate; something is missing: a uniform.

But, really, is one a better writer on foreign affairs for having served in the military? Not necessarily. Military service might be desirable, but everything has an opportunity cost. The two years spent in the army are two years spent not doing something else, and it is not obvious that the "something else" is valueless in shaping the person who will go on to write about foreign affairs. And if one joins the army in order to credential oneself for a career, there is nothing of an impulse to serve motivating that decision. Again, one does so to forestall future public opprobrium: the decision is politicized.

A more extreme case would be that of President Clinton. As a young man during the Vietnam War, he wrote a letter to the head of his local draft board explaining that his sympathies did not lie with the U.S. military but that he wanted to maintain his "political viability within the system" and so wasn't willing to consider actions too drastic in avoiding service. Decades later, as commander-in-chief, he suffered for his nonservice. His political opponents made hay of his lack of military experience and what they took to be the contemptuous tone of his letter. Worse, a palpable anti-Clinton sentiment took hold within the military itself. Many thought him unworthy to be their commander.

Would Clinton have been a better commander-in-chief had he served? The case is surprisingly hard to make convincingly. Serving in the military does not cause some certain, distinct effect on the person who has served—an effect measurably missing in those who have not served. It seems more accurate to say that the character of the person has a constitutive effect on the meaning of the military service. People's responses to the experience of combat, for example, can range from superhawkish to hyperdovish.

The Clinton nonservice took place in the context of a draft during wartime; mine, in the context of the all-volunteer force during peacetime. But note that the voluntariness is not dispositive. One cannot say that the compulsory system politicizes but that the voluntary system manages not to. Both politicize, in that they set a state standard for good service that implicitly invites the judgment that those who do not serve are wanting.

Serving Because We Have To?

We cannot do without a military; therefore, we must live with the problem of the distinction between those who served in it and those who did not. But we do not need a civilian service program administered by the state. We do not need to create a world in which the state says, "Service is good"—thereby implying that a failure to perform it, according to the fashion prescribed by the state, is bad.

Of course service is good. Americans obviously think so. Everett Carll Ladd in *The Ladd Report* demonstrated that the United States has "an unusually expansive and demanding sense of citizenship" whereby "the citizen has responsibilities for the health and well-being of his society that extend far beyond his relationship with the state."[7] Hence, Americans volunteer in large numbers and give substantial sums to charitable causes—and have always done so. This is not because their tax returns will be scrutinized to make sure their contributions measure up but because they want to. The individualism of the American polity has always been grounded in a dense social fabric. We are not monads; we need connections with others to be fully ourselves.

Furthermore, I do not know to whom President Bush was referring when he spoke of someone with no "cause larger than his or her own profit." I suppose the unreconstructed Silas Marner would do. But the point of that story would seem to be that Marner starts out lacking something that no amount of gold will satisfy. Even tech stock analysts and lawyers get married, have kids, coach soccer, and contribute to the United Way.

The circumstances of different lives, or of a single life over the course of time, call forth different solutions to the problem of social connection, which is the impulse underlying both service and charitable giving. There is no political solution to this problem, only the possibility of its politicization by the state, transforming something that we do to fulfill our heartfelt desires into something we do to avoid the sanction that follows from not doing so. To the extent we are acting only to avoid sanction, we will not satisfy that longing anyway.

In the name of promoting social connection—"these Americans are not strangers, they are fellow citizens"—proponents of national service propose, in effect, to colonize a part of the social field—the impulse to serve and give—that is constituted precisely by the felt need for social connection. I doubt that the state is up to the task. It is possible the result will be benign. It is also possible that young people (and others) will begin to approach service through the state in the same way that some children approach eating the vegetables on their plate: they do it because they think they have to.

I am not inclined to think that national service will spoil anyone's impulse to serve and give by making the failure to do so within the format of national service a matter of implicit social sanction. I think the human need for social connection is far, far stronger than that. And for many, no doubt, national service will be fulfilling. But as more and more high school guidance counselors ask their charges whether they have considered a stint in the program—service being, after all, a good thing—the more they will also convey the message that not serving is a bad thing. You may, under those circumstances, get a work force of some utility, but you will be adding little to the fulfillment of the human need for social connection. The notion that service administered through the state will strengthen the ties that bind us into a society, or create new ties, strikes me therefore as mistaken.

31

Civic Innovation and Public Policy for Democracy

CARMEN SIRIANNI

I BEGAN MY own civic career in the early 1960s at a Catholic high school in New York City. Each week our Legion of Mary group, under the guidance of Brother Gabriel, met to discuss service and faith, and every Sunday for several years I went to Welfare Island (since renamed Roosevelt Island) to take mass to impoverished people in long-term care at Goldwater Memorial Hospital. I visited with them, asked how they had been feeling, and shared stories of their lives. They wanted to know how we were doing in school and in our extracurricular activities.

My regular buddy on those Sundays was Mr. Clarence Chambers, who was confined to a rickety old wooden wheelchair and rarely had family visitors. Every Sunday when I walked through the swinging doors of the bleak long hallway, Mr. Chambers welcomed me as a son. He always wanted to know how my track meets had gone, and he was especially pleased when, in the spring of my sophomore year, I brought him my gold medal from the Penn Relays and asked him to keep it for me. Every now and then I have a twinge of regret about not having that medal to show my own son. But it was a small sacrifice for a volunteer to make. And Mr. Chambers gave me much more than I could ever have given him.

Hampton, Virginia, 2002: Youth Civic Engagement

Today, some four decades later, I sit in my home office wearing a T-shirt, emblazoned "Volunteer Superstar," that was given to me earlier this year by Alicia Tundidor, a tenth-grade African American "youth commissioner" from Hampton, Virginia. She made the gift during a city council meeting that was packed to overflowing with young people to proclaim Youth Service Day and recognize the city's efforts to build what she described as "a youth civic engagement system."

For the past ten years, Hampton, a city of 146,000 with a modest economic base and a population roughly split between black and white, has been building this system. Many of the young people undoubtedly have motives much like mine when I was a volunteer at their age. But what is going on in Hampton is considerably more sophisticated than anything I knew as a young person, even considering the student government and mock political conventions in which I was also involved. Civic engagement of young people has become a core value of the local political scene in Hampton, including its administrative, educational, and service systems.

Terry O'Neill, Hampton's director of planning, sees the engagement of young people as an essential component in reinventing government. He has two paid high school "youth planners" on staff, each for fifteen hours a week, and says he could use "four times that number if we had the resources." He and his staff provide mentoring and technical assistance to the youth planners, who work with young people citywide to develop youth-friendly space and transportation for the city's comprehensive plan. Laurine Press, director of parks and recreation, engages youth, asking them to envision the kinds of recreation they will want, not just now but when they have young families of their own. Shellae Blackwell draws young people into the work of the Neighborhood Commission to collaborate with adults on community improvement. Dr. Allen Davis and Johnny Pauls, superintendent of schools and director of secondary education, respectively, convene student representatives of the Superintendent's Advisory Group to discuss issues such as curricular requirements and state standards. Students in advisory groups meet regularly in each of the city's four public high schools. Hampton has "youth community policing" in schools and neighborhoods. And every month Hampton's twenty-two youth commissioners convene in open session in the city council chambers, sitting in the raised seats of the city councilors.

System Change, Culture Change

Assistant city manager Mike Monteith recalls that Hampton set out not just to have more youth "programs" but to "create a learning community" among a broad range of professionals and stakeholder groups. The goal was to build a system that progressively expanded leadership opportunities for sustained impact and began to treat youth "as assets, not deficits."

Once Hampton decided to invest in youth development, it established a city office, the Coalition for Youth, to be a catalyst for change. A multiyear federal community partnership grant from the Department of Health and Human Services provided early critical support to enable the city to do the planning that brought so many stakeholders on board.

Early on, Hampton's leading nonprofit youth services agency, Alternatives, Inc., had to reinvent itself from a substance abuse agency to one that developed youth leadership. Hampton's young people objected to its deficits approach. They did not want to be "fixed" by professionals or even "prevented" from needing to be fixed. They wanted opportunities to contribute in real and visible ways to the community, and they wanted the respect that comes with doing public work of genuine value.

Over the years, the key adult catalysts of change at both the Coalition for Youth and Alternatives, Inc., especially Cindy Carlson and Richard Goll, have approached their work as long-term organizing, mentoring, and relationship building. They have identified adult and youth leaders and worked to build lasting collaboration around a vision of engaged youth.

Volunteer superstars? Yes! But the real story in Hampton is one of organizing for civic democracy, of a formal role for youth in governance, of transforming organizational and professional norms to support the work of citizens. It is a story of public policy that can support sustained civic innovation.

Hampton's youth civic engagement movement has channeled individual volunteerism—volunteerism that would otherwise be big-hearted yet episodic and divorced from power—into sustained institutional work. Unlike my own volunteer experience, it has changed the way that citizens in all their roles—volunteers, social service and educational professionals, public officials, members of stakeholder groups—do the work of the public. This is not volunteerism but civic democracy woven throughout core institutional systems and designed to tackle the complex problems of the twenty-first century.

Civic Innovation

Over the past eight years, Lewis Friedland and I, with our research teams at Brandeis University and the University of Wisconsin, have interviewed more than 700 civic innovators like those in Hampton—youth and adults, community activists and heads of major networks, local officials and federal agency staff.

Some have reinvented congregation-based community organizing in national networks, such as the Industrial Areas Foundation, so that low-income communities can share in power and help build sustainable partnerships for job training, housing development, and school reform. Others have reinvigorated urban democracy in cities like Portland, Oregon, where neighborhood and civic associations have become more inclusive and more capable of sustained problem solving, and where their work is complemented by community policing, neighborhood district attorneys, environmental and community planning, watershed associations, greenspace partnerships, and a Portland State University curriculum devoted to generating community leadership.

"Civic environmentalists" have developed watershed, forest, and estuary restoration strategies for partnerships among community and environmental groups, farmers and ranchers, and government officials. "Healthy community" innovators have engaged community organizations, congregations, parish nurses' associations, hospitals, public health agencies, and some managed care systems to develop community-based health improvement strategies. More and more universities have begun to rethink their mission and practices in terms of civic engagement. As Robert Bruininks, provost and vice president for academic affairs at the University of Minnesota, put it, these universities are making big changes in how undergraduates learn, how faculty are rewarded, how they partner with communities—even how researchers map the human genome by making them responsible for leading discussions on the ethical and public policy implications of their work.

Public Policy for Democracy

At all levels of the federal system, public policy can support such civic innovation. There are many models of policy design on which to build.

In environmental policy, for instance, the federal Chesapeake Bay Program has helped build the capacity of local partnerships among watershed associations, school-based water quality monitoring groups, fishing and boating clubs, and farm and business groups. It has also helped local governments catalyze civic partnerships for ecosystem restoration. The Environmental Education Act of 1990 and the Environmental Protection Agency's Office of Environmental Education have not only supported service learning in schools and communities but also helped build capacity among national and state environmental education associations to support community action. The Office of Environmental Justice and the Office of Pollution Prevention and Toxics have each helped support innovative civic strategies. The Estuary Restoration Act of 2000, designed in part by a national coalition of eleven restoration groups, has spurred further community-based restoration partnerships. States like Massachusetts, California, and Washington have made collaborative watershed restoration a centerpiece of environmental protection. And more and more local governments are working in "sustainable communities" partnerships.

One could catalog and analyze a whole range of program and policy designs that build youth civic capacity for public problem solving. The Office of University Partnerships at the Department of Housing and Urban Development (HUD) has helped support universities working with local groups on a wide array of community development issues. HUD's YouthBuild supports leadership development as part of its job training and education programs for young adults from inner-city neighborhoods. The Corporation for National and Community Service supports service learning, local capacity building, and volunteering in numerous local and national projects. The Department of Agriculture supported the 4-H National Conversation on Youth Development for the Twenty-First Century, which engaged some 50,000 people in 2002 in helping reorient the 4-H movement around a vision of "empowering youth as equal partners." The Justice Department's Office of Juvenile Justice and Delinquency Prevention has supported innovative teen courts where youth assume responsible roles in adjudication.

There are also examples of innovative public policy on a more local level. Massachusetts offers peer leadership programs for young people in health promotion. San Francisco now includes a youth commission as part of its charter. And New York City has its Beacon centers in every school district, offering community service, problem solving, and leadership development opportunities.

Needed: Strong Political Leadership at the Top

Over the past decade, we have reached the point where we, as a nation, can set the goal of reinventing government to catalyze robust civic problem solving across the land. Doing so will take political leadership at the highest levels.

The Clinton administration, despite its support for many of these programs and its 1995 State of the Union theme of "reinventing citizenship," was unable to focus its efforts or capture the public imagination. A proposal for a White House office that would systematically catalyze civic initiatives across federal agencies was dropped in 1994. The Gore campaign of 2000 ignored these themes almost entirely, leaving the field of community and citizenship to Ralph Nader's anticorporate populism on the left and George W. Bush's compassionate conservatism on the right.

In the wake of September 11, President Bush has raised the ideal of active citizenship to a new level of public discourse. Yet his approach has major shortcomings. First, the Office of Faith-Based and Community Initiatives, designed narrowly from the start, has never had the capacity to support community-based and civic problem-solving strategies across the full range of federal agencies and programmatic areas. The work of the Corporation for National and Community Service is essential, but its scope is also limited. Second, the frame of volunteerism and service is simply not muscular enough to do the heavy lifting required for reinvigorating civic democracy and institutional change. And, third, public support for innovative civic strategies, which often require new ways of thinking about regulation and service delivery, will weaken if accompanied by one-sided corporate versions of deregulation or social service cutbacks.

Looking Ahead

The service I did as a volunteer was formative in my teenage years, and it is a hopeful sign that service is on the rise among today's youth. Yet volunteerism, service, and compassion, however laudable, too easily slide into individual good works, ignore core institutional practices, sidestep questions of power, and often reinforce paternalism and dependency.

To reinvent democracy, we will need to go beyond volunteerism to build civic engagement.[1] We can—and must—revitalize democratic problem solving to draw in poor, working-class, and minority communities that have drifted away or been driven away from civic and political participation in recent decades. They are not populations to be "served" by big-hearted volunteers. Nor are they simply constituencies to be mobilized for more "services." They are communities to be fully engaged in problem solving and public work in partnership with the full spectrum of our government, business, and civic institutions.

32

The Volunteering Decision
What Prompts It? What Sustains It?

PAUL C. LIGHT

GEORGE W. BUSH is not the first president to ask Americans to give more of themselves to volunteering. Except for Gerald Ford, every president since John F. Kennedy has called for greater volunteerism. Some calls have been resonant, others barely audible. Some have produced new federal agencies; others, private initiatives. But whatever the form, volunteering has been a staple of presidential agendas since 1961.

The Presidential Call to Service

Kennedy's call to service was the most eloquent and famous. Like George W. Bush, Kennedy viewed volunteerism as essential to defending the nation in a time of great risk.

> In the long history of the world, only a few generations have been granted the role of defending freedom in its hour of maximum danger. . . . The energy, the faith, the devotion which we bring to this endeavor will light our country and all who serve it—and the glow from that fire can truly light the world. And so, my fellow Americans: ask not what your country can do for you—ask what you can do for your country.[1]

Kennedy's Peace Corps was the first in a long list of federal programs to promote volunteerism. Lyndon Johnson followed Kennedy's lead in 1964 when he signed the Economic Opportunity Act creating Volunteers in Service to America (VISTA). He also helped create the Retired and Senior Volunteer Program (RSVP), the Foster Grandparents Program, the Senior Companion Program, and the Small Business Administration's Service Corps of Retired Executives (SCORE). But Johnson never issued a stirring national call to volunteerism; rather, he rooted his volunteerism in a handful of important, but small, federal initiatives. Ironically, of all Johnson's efforts to draw young Americans into civic life, the Vietnam War probably did the most—albeit through marches, rallies, flag burnings, and demonstrations.

Richard Nixon may have boosted volunteerism more than any other president in modern history. Just four months into his administration, Nixon had created the Cabinet Committee on Voluntary Action and the Office of Voluntary Action within the Department of Housing and Urban Development and appointed a special consultant to the president on voluntary action. In November 1969, he announced his National Program on Voluntary Action, and then in 1971 he established the National Center for Voluntary Action, a nonprofit, nonpartisan private group, to pursue its goals. Nixon also created an entirely new federal bureaucracy to administer the government's growing collection of voluntary programs. That same year, he placed the Peace Corps, VISTA, the Foster Grandparents Program, SCORE, all the volunteer programs in the Office of Economic Opportunity, and the Office of Voluntary Action within a new agency called ACTION. In late 1973, he signed the Domestic Volunteer Service Act, giving ACTION greater authority to design and implement new programs aimed at a wider range of audiences.

Jimmy Carter—perhaps surprisingly, given his own recent work promoting Habitat for Humanity—did not make voluntary service a centerpiece of his presidency, although he did reorganize ACTION halfway through his term to give the Peace Corps greater autonomy.

Ronald Reagan established the White House Office of Private-Sector Initiatives in 1981 in the belief that such initiatives would "accomplish far, far more than government programs ever could."[2] He said little more about volunteerism until 1986, when his May 24 radio address focused on the rising tide of volunteerism—"a reassertion of good, old-fashioned neighborliness now that our country has regained its self-confidence."[3] The next day he joined in the first "Hands Across America" antihunger rally, which stretched across the nation.

George H. W. Bush was more Nixonian in his approach to volunteerism. He launched his "Points of Light" volunteering initiative in 1989 to call all Americans and institutions such as corporations, schools, and places of worship to claim society's problems as their own and to help solve them. His call led directly to the creation of the private nonprofit Points of Light Foundation, which merged with Nixon's National Center for Voluntary Action in 1991 and is alive and active today. Together with other nonprofits, the Points of Light Foundation connects citizens to volunteer opportunities and dispenses advice and research on best practices to make those opportunities as meaningful as possible.

Bill Clinton also did his share to promote federally sponsored volunteer service, placing his National and Community Service Trust Act at the top of his first-year agenda. The resulting Corporation for National and Community Service administers the AmeriCorps volunteer service program, the Senior Corps, and Learn and Serve America; it also absorbed all the programs of ACTION. And in April 1997, Clinton joined former presidents Bush, Carter, and Ford—not to mention Oprah Winfrey—in the Presidents' Summit for America's Future in Philadelphia. The summit produced a new nonprofit organization called America's Promise to help children and youth.

Evaluations of Impact

George W. Bush's recent call for volunteerism fits comfortably within the tradition established by Nixon, Reagan, and his father. His focus is on the traditional notion that individuals should give to their communities out of the goodness of their hearts, not because of government inducements, although he acknowledges that inducements through programs such as AmeriCorps have their place in the volunteering regime.

Bush's call was unique in its specificity. He asked not just for community spirit but for 4,000 hours of it. He set a measurable goal that every

American can track by creating his or her own electronic journal on the Corporation for National and Community Service website. But Bush does not want just 4,000 hours of service. He wants Americans to get into the volunteering habit. Once past the first 4,000 hours, he hopes that volunteers will not stop.

Much as one can applaud the goal, however, little data suggest that presidents, past or present, have much weight when it comes to Americans' decisions to volunteer. For example, according to the Higher Education Research Institute at the University of California, Los Angeles, the number of freshmen who reported any type of volunteering has been going up 1 to 3 percent a year since 1989, with little variation that might be attributed to presidential activism.[4]

None of this means that presidents should stop talking about volunteering or supporting federal programs such as AmeriCorps. The Corporation for National and Community Service reported a dramatic surge in website visits following the president's State of the Union address. Online applications to AmeriCorps increased 50 percent in the month after the address, while the number of visits to the Senior Corps website jumped more than 130 percent.

But the research does suggest that something other than presidential goal setting may be at work in prompting someone to decide to volunteer. Most important, it turns out, is making sure that volunteers are engaged by people they know and that their service allows them to make a difference.

The Service-Learning Effect

Ongoing research by the Higher Education Research Institute suggests that service learning—those classes and educational programs that incorporate volunteer service—has a powerful effect on volunteering. According to a January 2000 research-in-progress report, college students who enrolled in a service-learning course were particularly aware of the benefits of community service—probably, the authors surmise, because they discussed their service with each other and received emotional support from faculty.[5] The study is based on a random sample of more than 22,000 undergraduates, most of whom entered college in the fall of 1994.

Compared with students who did traditional community service, students in service-learning courses were more likely to develop a heightened sense of civic responsibility and personal effectiveness through their work.

All Volunteering Is Local

Parents, teachers, rabbis, and pastors may all have far greater sway over the decision to volunteer than presidents do. Presidents can certainly light the match, but others must fan the flame. The influence starts at home. A 2002 random-sample survey of 1,500 youths aged fifteen to twenty-five, conducted on behalf of the University of Maryland's Center for Information and Research in Civic Learning and Engagement (CIRCLE), found that young Americans who discuss politics at home are much more likely to register to vote, trust government, believe politicians pay attention to their concerns, and say they can make a difference solving community problems.[6] In fact, dinner table conversations about politics are more strongly related to volunteering than are traditional demographic variables such as race, sex, education, and income. As CIRCLE concludes, "Parental socialization affects both whether young adults volunteer, and how often."

The personal influence continues in connecting a diffuse readiness to volunteer with real opportunities. According to a 1997 random-sample survey of 1,002 youths aged fifteen to twenty-nine conducted for DoSomething, a national nonprofit that encourages community organizing, young Americans hear about volunteer opportunities with a community organization from a host of sources—advertisements (66 percent), friends or family members (59 percent), teachers (54 percent), posters or flyers at school (48 percent), specific organizations (48 percent), places of worship (42 percent), jobs (38 percent), coaches, scout leaders or other local leaders (33 percent), and groups to which they belong (30 percent).[7] Obviously, there is plenty of chatter out there on volunteering.

But not all sources produce results equally. Forty-two percent of young Americans who heard about a volunteering opportunity from a direct source (friend, family member, coach, scout leader, teacher, or the organization itself) volunteered versus only 14 percent of those who heard from an indirect source (place of worship, job or employer, posters or fly- ers, and advertisements).

And the more contacts from direct sources, the greater the results. Just 14 percent of students who never heard from a direct source said they vol- unteered, compared with 25 percent who heard from one source, 41 per- cent who heard from two, 47 percent from three, and 62 percent from four. Just as in the CIRCLE study, volunteering is clearly related to social networks. Having a parent who is, or was, involved in community activ- ity, as well as being a young person who attends religious services regularly, also increases volunteer experience.

All volunteering, it seems, is local. Presidents can opine all they wish about the need for greater engagement, but parents, friends, and the vol- unteer organizations themselves get the results.

The Chance to Make a Difference

To get Americans into the volunteering habit, though, it will not be enough to ask them to volunteer—or even to get them to show up for a first experience. The service itself must be meaningful, or the volunteers will not come back.

According to the DoSomething survey, young Americans respond to programs that make good use of their time. Volunteers want to make a dif- ference—make key decisions, see the effects of their work, gain valuable experience, skills, or contacts. Half of the DoSomething respondents who made key decisions rated their volunteer experience as excellent, compared with just 29 percent of those who did not; 46 percent who could see the impact of their work also rated their experience as excellent versus just 15 percent who could not.[8]

Although a lack of time is by far the most important reason cited by most young Americans for a decision to stop volunteering, frustration and a lack of meaning may also diminish future engagements. Without ques- tion, for example, the quality of their volunteer experiences affects the way students view future jobs in charitable organizations. According to a

May 2002 random-sample survey of 1,015 college seniors, students who volunteered and rated their experience as very positive and found their skills and talents very well used were more likely than others to consider seriously a career in the nonprofit sector.[9] For example, 23 percent of students who felt their skills and talents were very well used said they had seriously thought about a job in the nonprofit sector, compared with 10 percent of those whose skills and talents were not used well at all, and 0 percent who never volunteered at all. To the extent that interest in work in the nonprofit sector can be used as a surrogate for future interest in volunteering, these data suggest that the quality of the volunteer experience matters.

Strengthening the President's Call

If President Bush wants Americans, especially young Americans, to meet his 4,000-hour goal, he might broaden his agenda to include three provisions related to this research. First, he should ask Congress for more funding to promote more service-learning opportunities at the primary, secondary, and college levels. The federal Learn and Serve America program should be highlighted for the largest increase in funding possible. Congress would be well advised to change the AmeriCorps job description to include an explicit commitment to recruiting and connecting volunteers at the local level.

Second, the president might encourage his Corporation for Community and National Service to enlist parents, peers, and organizations to help advertise and promote volunteering. Although young Americans do pay attention to flyers and conventional advertising for volunteering, they respond best to direct appeals from the people and organizations they already know.

Third, and perhaps most important, the president should ask Congress to provide limited grants to make sure that volunteers are wisely used by the organizations they serve. According to Leslie Lenkowsky, the chief executive of the Corporation for National and Community Service, the success of any call to service "needs to go beyond massing forces to figuring out how to deploy them most effectively."[10] One might add "and making sure they are wisely used." The federal budget includes no money to build capacity in the nonprofit sector or within faith-based organizations. President Bush may well encourage more volunteers to show up, but it is up to the organizations they serve to provide the work needed for a longer engagement.

PART SIX
Serving God and Country

33

Civil Society, Religion, and the Formation of Citizens

JEAN BETHKE ELSHTAIN

WHAT SUSTAINS A civil society? I propose to zero in on one theme—authority—as the prelude to a consideration of moral formation and education.

Legitimate, accountable authority is implicit in every discussion of civil society. Democratic institutions require robust yet resilient authority, and our present confusion over the meaning of authority in all spheres of civil and moral life is surely one reason civil society is in trouble. There is, for example, a modern tendency (exemplified most tellingly, perhaps, by John Stuart Mill in his classic tract *On Liberty*) to contrast liberty with authority. Rather than posing liberty against tyranny or domination or authoritarianism, Mill sets up liberty and authority as opposites.

Mill got things entirely wrong. We require authority to sustain decent, other-regarding liberty. Authority—from the notion "to authorize," to help generate and even to bring into being—secures that which is generated. It sustains social institutions. It derives from the fact that we see people as responsible and can hold them accountable.

If we are incapable of distinguishing authority from unacceptable forms of coercion and even violence, we fall into a deep conceptual and ethical abyss. This was the argument of the political theorist Hannah Arendt in a famous essay on authority. Minus authority, claimed Arendt,

we lose a sense of the past and of tradition, as "the permanence and durability" of the world seems to melt away. This loss is "tantamount to the loss
of the groundwork of the world, which indeed . . . has begun to shift, to
change and transform itself with ever-increasing rapidity from one shape
to another, as though we were living and struggling with a protean universe
where everything at any moment can become almost anything else."[1]

Arendt singles out for critical fire arguments deeply implicated in the
conflation of coercion and authority. She reminds us that, historically, the
legitimate authoritative figure—whether parent, teacher, or legislator—
was bound by law, tradition, and the force of past example and experience.
Being bound in particular ways guaranteed a framework for action and
created particular public spaces—whether of church, polity, or other institutions of social life. Bounded freedom, constituted by authority, is the
only way human beings have to guarantee creation of those spaces of public freedom and civil society that Arendt so cherished, spaces within which
our action is both nurtured and yet constrained.

The point of a decent civil society and polity, after all, is about realizing some vision of a good life. This good life plays a formative role even
as it depends in the first instance on formed, civically educated citizens. It
inducts each generation into a way of being in the world made possible
only when people submit to authority mutually and thereby hold one
another accountable. Without such an authoritative framework, there is
only violence or rampant antinomianism.

Tocqueville suggested that, over time, the horizon of democratic civil
societies might recede as complex, authoritative traditions eroded or collapsed.[2] The upshot would be the triumph of the cynical notion that the
past had been nothing but a story of chicanery and arbitrariness. But we
err in presuming that in order to be free, we must escape binding institutions altogether. This condition would be one not of freedom, but of a
kind of license in a civil universe stripped of its moral texture.

In such a world, we would grow more and more apart from one
another. We would likely repudiate even the possibility of a rough-and-
ready sharing of moral norms and aspirations of the sort that helped us
treat one another decently and work together in the first place. Even the
procedural norms of democratic governmental institutions might be

called into question. Our confidence in the possibility of sustaining claims of shared truth would wane. We would come to believe that all that exists is self-interested and self-serving opinion. This is indeed worrisome for, as Hannah Arendt also insisted in *The Origins of Totalitarianism*, "The ideal subject of totalitarian rule is not the convinced Nazi or the convinced Communist, but people for whom the distinction between fact and fiction . . . and the distinction between true and false . . . no longer exist."[3] Here education in and for democracy is crucial, for education and religion are two great formative institutions, each of which has as its aim—or at least once did—the discovery and embrace of truth and the honing of our ability to discern the truth.

Defining Education Up

The aims of education in a democratic civil society have always been rather lofty, moving beyond questions of adaptation and functional skills to an appreciation of the moral wages of democracy itself and its deep reliance on citizens formed for civic life. Because a democratic culture is one in which freedom and responsibility go hand in hand, human beings must be taught how to sort out the important from the less important, the vital from the trivial, the worthy from the unworthy, the excellent from the mediocre, the false from the true. This is an enormous challenge, one that is undermined rather than strengthened if we accept John Locke's famous distinction, in his classic "Letter Concerning Toleration" (1689), between soulcraft and statecraft.[4]

Locke insisted, as a precondition for civil government, that religion and government had to be distinguished sharply. In his civic map, religion was in one sphere (the private), and it dealt with soulcraft, the forming of souls to and for the truths of religion. But statecraft was properly public and had to do with the civil realm, where God and religion no longer figure directly. Religion becomes irrelevant in a public sense.

In practice, however, religion and politics in America have always been entangled, and nowhere more so than in the formation of citizens as persons with developed ethical sensibilities and civic attachments. But in recent decades, the formation of souls and citizens has once again been theoretically severed in the United States by those who construe church-state separation to mean the bifurcation of religion and civil society.

But the logic of the one—church-state separation—need not extend to the other—religion and civil society. There has always been considerable overlap in practice, in part because religion and politics touch unavoidably on one another's turf. Each embraces some normative vision of what is fair or decent or just. Each offers criteria for distinguishing truth from falsehood. Each calls human beings to service, to a good that goes beyond self-interest. If one falters, so does the other. Any attempt to take the soul out of statecraft and the state (or civic life) out of soulcraft must fail and will harm each enterprise, inviting the possibility that politics becomes soul-less, and the formation of souls becomes privatized and stripped of any civic dimension.

To bring statecraft and soulcraft together is not to call for the blatant politicization of education. That danger comes from other directions. For example, we are all aware that at present in our culture, education is increasingly defined with reference to diversity or, as it is usually put, multiculturalism. We are asked to become sensitive to group exclusivities and grievances. Too often, however, rather than making us aware of the wondrous variety of idioms and voices in a plural civic world, such concentration results in an inappropriate politicization of education and the triumph of a discourse of victimization.

Of course, education is never outside a world of which politics—how human beings order a way of life in common—is a necessary feature. Education is always cast as the means whereby citizens of a particular society get their bearings and learn to live with one another. Education always reflects a society's view of what is excellent, worthy, and necessary, and this ongoing reflection is refracted and reshaped as definitions, meanings, and purposes change through contestation. In this sense, education is political, but this is different from being directly and blatantly politicized.

Education is neither the family nor the state nor a church. It is not the primary locus of child rearing nor an arm of governance nor the source of knowledge about understandings of God in relation to the human person and vice versa. Schools are, in many ways, somewhat apart, or should be. They are places of refuge—a kind of civically sacred space, at their best, where young people come together and learn (among the many things they learn) how to live with one another by respecting distinctions and eschewing destructive divisions.

But the underlying moral impetus for civic brotherhood and sister-hood cannot come from a civic life that has been stripped of its sustaining moral markers as embodied in religious institutions. Religion should help us tap the "better angels of our nature," in Lincoln's memorable phrase, and it cannot do that if it is segregated to a private realm of soulcraft, stripped of civil significance and legitimacy. When our civil society works well, it helps us to see the sturdy interplay of our basic formative institu-tions as they engage in the process of creating loving parents and friends, decent colleagues, fair-minded citizens. Thus those among us who seek a thoroughly secularized society, devoid of any and all public markers and reminders of religion because religion must be invisible to public life, wind up, however inadvertently, weakening our civic life.

In light of the fact that we live in a skeptical if not disillusioned era and, on the best available evidence, those most cynical about our civic prospects are the young, it is a task of critical importance to civil society that we do all we can to form sturdy, caring, involved young people in and through the overlapping—not separated—institutions assigned that task. Here religion and education can and should walk together, not in lockstep but in the direction of a shared recognition that forming souls and form-ing citizens are tasks that go together. Our democratic country depends on responsibility and self-limiting freedom. If we drain education of its nor-mative, character-forming tasks, we open children up to more, not less, manipulation by powerful forces in our culture such as technology and the media; in effect, we cede responsibility to whatever constitutes a culture's overriding *Weltanschauung* at any given moment.

This can have tragic consequences. Once a world of personal respon-sibility, with its characteristic virtues and marks of decency (justice, honor, friendship, fidelity), is ruptured or emptied, what rushes in to take its place is politics as a "technology of power," in Czech president Vaclav Havel's phrase.[5]

Responsibility, according to Havel, flows from our plurality and capacity for independent self-constitution, in contrast to the conformity, uniformity, and stultifying dogmas of ideologues (whether of the left or the right) who abandon the complexities of moral development and civic ordering in favor of abstract chimeras.

Our malaise over how to define education within our democracy stems in part from a culturally sanctioned abdication by adults of their responsible authority as parents and educators. What Hannah Arendt, writing in the 1960s, already referred to as a "crisis in education" has come about not because a few self-interested groups have hijacked the system.[6] It is far more plausible to argue that education in America is in its present straits because of a general withering away of authoritative meanings and institutions and an undermining of authoritative persons (teachers, parents, politicians). Only the bringing together of what we too often separate, including the forces of religion and education, can stem the tide that seems to rush in the direction of civic withdrawal and depletion, and the generation of widespread cynicism about our human capacity for thinking about a good in common that we cannot know alone.

One troubling sign of our times is growing evidence that those most cynical about our prospects, particularly about politics and government, are the young, with high school students the most "turned off" of all. This is a complex phenomenon, no doubt. But one factor in the triumph of cynicism is that young people are too often fed stories that represent U.S. history as nothing but a tale of failed promises. In an attempt to be more critical and not to instill in our young people a simplistic and too-benign view of the past, some have gone overboard in the other direction. Because our civic story is so intertwined with narratives about American religious history, a sour sense of civic life is surely one by-product of accounts that stress only the marginalization of this sect or the maltreatment of some other, losing sight along the way of the millions of Americans whose commitment to their faith lifted them up, sustained hope and faithfulness, and helped to form them as good stewards and responsible members of their communities.

Before September 11, many of us had forgotten what it means to be a neighbor and a citizen. For years we had seen ourselves as little sovereigns in our own domains. Sovereign selves neither need nor solicit help, but no one was sovereign on September 11. We were confronted with the horror of last moments, when men and women faced, in many cases, an agonizing final choice of how to die (not whether or not to die) as they plummeted to earth like broken birds, knowing that rescue would never come. We bore witness as our fellow citizens, our neighbors, rushed into the inferno to try to spare others, at sure and certain risk of their own lives. We were aghast and we were astonished; we were horrified and we were grateful. A truth was revealed to us—the truth of citizenship and the civic affections that bind us one to another.

Given our widely shared conviction before September 11 that politics was either sordid or boring or both, perhaps it made good, self-interested sense to ignore it and adopt a cynical attitude toward any notion of civic duty or responsibility. We paid scant attention to those charged with the public responsibility of keeping us safe and secure in our homes, our schools, our places of worship and work, our neighborhoods. But now that awareness is seared into our collective consciousness. The result may be a realization that we are indeed our brothers' and sisters' keepers, and that politics, however imperfectly, is forged in part on the anvil of that recognition.

We are not called to be heroes every day, but some may be called; September 11 demonstrated that. We are, however, called to honor our bonds of civic affection. A terrible tragedy effaces distinctions of race, religion, ethnicity, and economic status. On September 11, the window washer and stockbroker found themselves in the same boat. They were terrified, they were threatened, and they leaned on one another. Does this mean that we will henceforth put our shoulders to the civic wheel, that we will insist that school curriculums take up what used to be called civics and teach us the importance of forging bonds of civic affection? We will see. But we cannot pretend that the stakes are so low it scarcely matters. None of the goods human beings cherish can flourish, absent a measure of civic peace and security.

Civically and religiously, we have too often failed to live up to our promises and premises. But the staccato repetition of the dark side of our history, if that becomes the dominant motif, fuels cynicism rather than active participation. It is worth considering several contrasting models of how to treat the history of religion, education, and civic life in America.

Model One: The Traditional Story

Our then-five-year-old granddaughter told me her vision of the traditional story shortly before Thanksgiving Day 1999:

> We learned about Thanksgiving and why we have turkeys. The Pilgrims got on a boat called the *Mayflower* because the king wouldn't let them be free. They couldn't pray free. So they got on the *Mayflower* and then they sailed for a long time across the ocean to come to America. Some Pilgrims got sick and died. The Pilgrim children had to sleep on the hard wood floors on the ship. They thought they'd never get there. But they did! It was cold, and they were hungry. They got to be friends with the Indians, and they shared some turkeys and some corn, and that's why we eat turkey and have Thanksgiving, because the Pilgrims could pray free.

This is not a bad story, and it is essentially the one many of us were taught. It is a hopeful baseline from which to work. The story gets more complex over time. The encounter with indigenous people is, we know, one with many layers of suspicion, violence, failed and occasionally successful attempts at communication, and pathos aplenty. We are familiar with how this proceeds, and how, indeed, it should proceed as education continues and a child's capacities for critical interpretation are engaged. But jump-starting the civic formation of children with a strong, decent story seems appropriate. One could not—and no responsible parent or teacher would—offer a benign version of the coming of slavery in America. But one could tell even this horrific tale in a way that emphasized the strength of the African slaves and their determination to try to hold on to their dignity even under conditions of slavery; their valiant efforts to sustain families; their cultural contributions even while enslaved.

The traditional story becomes a problem if it gets reified and frozen— the teacher who turns the story of the Founding Fathers into an exercise in hagiography and the Constitution into a nigh-miraculous distillation of the essence of the wisdom of the ages, good for all times and places. If uncritical adulation triumphs, the dialogic, deliberative, and critical dimensions of civic engagement (an encounter that is always both retro-spective and prospective) are lost. A traditional story of the reified sort about American religion and civic life would present it as a cheery tale of beleaguered folks seeking to "pray free" (true enough) but then go on to envelop the entirety of our religious history in a kind of roseate haze that overlooks the vituperation meted out against religious dissenters; the often violent exclusions; the organized attacks (the Know-Nothings or the Ku Klux Klan, who were anti-Catholic and anti-Jewish as well as anti-black); the pretense that the common or public schools were solely a generous and benign effort to educate all American young people, thus sanitizing the effort and neglecting the explicit anti-immigrant, anti-Catholic thrust of the common schools; and so on. The good, the bad, and the ugly must be part of the story without any single element dominating, for that would be to distort through oversimplification. Thus there is a traditional model narrative that illuminates, another that narrows and distorts.

Model Two: The Hermeneutics of Suspicion Ascendant

The hagiographer's mirror image is offered by the teacher who, if the American founding and the beginning of our civic story is the reference point, declares that nothing good ever came from the hand of that abstract, all-purpose villain, the "dead, white European male." The words and deeds of the Founders were nefarious because they were hypocritical racists and patriarchal. It follows that their creations, including the Con-stitution, are tainted.

The key words in this negative scenario are "nothing good," for these two little words always signify a reductionist agenda. Within the rigidities of this model, debate simply ends or is discouraged. To express a different point of view, to say that perhaps some courageous, brilliant, good things emerged from the hands of the complex and quite various men who made up so much of our early history, is to betray one's own "false conscious-ness" or class or race privilege. If a hermeneutics of suspicion goes all the way down, that is surely one of the strands inviting cynicism, especially among students.

Turned against religion, a harsh hermeneutics of suspicion sees only patriarchy, horror, and hypocrisy at work. But here, too, there is much to be gleaned and learned and appropriated for a generous civic education. There is a mode of critical interpretation that is vital and necessary in offering up a complex, nuanced, rich tapestry that affords ways for us to ask questions such as this: are there resources internal to this religious tradition or that one that enable its adherents to criticize followers of the religions who are acting (so they say) on their religious beliefs, but who are, in fact, betraying those beliefs in some fundamental way?

One can ask what textual distortions, elisions, excisions, and selective use or abuse of history are required, for example, to draw upon the New Testament for a defense of chattel slavery, even as other Christians declared slavery a sin. Looking closely at such examples, one can readily see that this is by no means a case of two equally valid interpretations between which one just opts arbitrarily. Rather, those who found support for race-based chattel slavery in the New Testament systematically distorted the message of Jesus of Nazareth to make that message fit the institution they sought to defend. The best response to such claims is to go to the text itself and show how such distortions occurred.

This is a complex enterprise that relies on the well-educated, robustly and ethically formed intelligence. It is far simpler to debunk cynically than to criticize intelligently. Does our education today prepare children for intelligent criticism or push them toward cynical debunking?

Model Three: Civic and Hopeful

The civic and hopeful approach to education and formation draws upon elements from the traditional and critical interpretive models, then intermingles them with a strong civic philosophy to which a faith community brings its own beliefs that may well challenge or put pressure upon an extant civic scheme of things. Within the Christian tradition with which I am most familiar, for example, believers are called not to conform to the world but to be formed in such a way that they can transform the world: active citizenship and membership is a good. This model begins with a presupposition that each and every person is dignified and that the religious dimension is obliged to honor and lift up their dignity. Other traditions would have their own starting points. The critical-hopeful model promotes a dialogue between faith and culture and civic life, striving to prevent the triumph of any and all philosophies that isolate us from one another, invite us to mistrust one another, or construe us as always in competition with one another. In this model, schools would play the central role in educating in hopeful civic ways; churches, synagogues, and mosques, in hopeful faith-based ways. But each overlaps with the other, and each dimension of formation conjoins to encourage young people to develop an orientation toward a common good.

Hope is a great theological virtue, but it is also a civic virtue, one tied to coming to grips with the reality one faces and responding appropriately, without excessive sentimentality on the one hand or excessive pessimism on the other. In the wake of the attacks of September 11, we must stop those who would harm us. But we must also meet and greet one another, love one another, and hope that the affections that bind us to one another will also help to make our world less brutal and more just.

The Future Of Civil Society

The stakes, it seems, couldn't be higher. We have entered the twenty-first century with many of our fellow citizens perplexed and deeply skeptical about the fate of all our basic institutions. The most penetrating observers of Western culture, whether in developed democracies like our own or in developing democracies, like the Czech Republic, fear that democratic civics is either withering or not developing in the first place. Thus Vaclav Havel commented critically on the state of Czech culture in an address delivered on December 9, 1997, to that nation's parliament and senate:

> I am talking about what is usually called a civil society. That means a society that makes room for the richest possible self-structuring and the richest possible participation in public life. In this sense civil society is important for two reasons: in the first

place, it enables people to be themselves in all their dimensions, which include being social creatures who desire, in thousands of ways, to participate in the life of the community in which they live. In the second place, it functions as a genuine guarantee of political stability. The more developed all the organs, institutions, and instruments of civil society are, the more resistant that society will be to political upheavals and reversals.[7]

Havel's words conjure up the concept of subsidiarity, a powerful theoretical framework for explaining a civil society and what it does that cannot be done by other, more centralized and top-heavy institutions and forces. Subsidiarity is a direct contribution by a tradition of religious thought—Catholic social thought—to our self-understanding as a democratic society. In the modern social encyclicals, culminating with the extraordinary contributions of Pope John Paul II, we find an affirmation that human rights should be seen not in individualistic but in social terms. Working from the principle of subsidiarity, John Paul and others find a violation of a right order of things in assigning to greater or higher associations what smaller associations can do.[8] The purpose of larger associations, including the state, is to help members of a body politic and society rather than to erode or absorb its many plural associations. Subsidiarity, then, is a theory of and for civil society. It keeps alive alternatives between individualism, on the one hand, and collectivism, on the other. It helps us to understand why families, schools, and churches are all vital and must remain vibrant and healthy if a "more perfect union" is ever to be realized.

But who knows about subsidiarity—or Alexis de Tocqueville, for that matter? No doubt parochial schools do a better job including Tocqueville than public schools do evoking the concept of subsidiarity (at an appropriate grade level) in courses of civic education, to the extent that civics is even taught any longer. Perhaps what has happened is something like this: our very success as a vibrant, energetic democracy went to our heads, and we began to take for granted what we depend on—families, schools, religious institutions. We thought they would always be there and always be strong. Even if we were not engaged in one or more of these areas, others were bound to be.

It turns out this was far too optimistic a view. It seems that a democratic civil society requires the efforts of all of us. Does it require institutionalizing some form of national service? Possibly, although the devil, as usual, is in the details.

Americans have always been deeply ambivalent about conscription because it seems at odds with our abiding commitment to liberty, both political and personal. More important by far is the development of character such that, when the country and its communities are in need, young people feel called to service. Liberty, if it isn't forged on the anvil of recognition of our shared humanity and neighborliness, disintegrates into narrow individualism. Service to community, if it is coerced and part of a view that puts loyalty to nation above all other loyalties, whatever the circumstance, is not the stuff out of which pluralistic societies committed to liberty are made.

American civil society at its best forms a middle way between these extremes. We must make our way to the middle, not as a tepid compromise but as a solid and worthy achievement.

34

The Impact of Religious
Involvement on Civic Life

ROBERT WUTHNOW

THROUGHOUT AMERICAN HISTORY, civic involvement has been deeply
influenced by the commitment of the nation's people to their religious
organizations. When Alexis de Tocqueville visited the United States in the
1830s, new denominations were moving westward with the rapidly
expanding population, helping to promote a sense of obligation to fellow
citizens as much as to God. The benevolent and temperance societies born
in that era, the craft guilds and ladies' auxiliaries that so often met in
church basements, and subsequent waves of labor organizations, women's
clubs, and Masonic orders all depended on the leadership skills and social
networks people developed at their places of worship.[1]

But what about religion's capacity to mobilize civic involvement
today? One way to begin answering that question is to look at two men
who exemplify contemporary American religious commitment (both were
interviewed as part of a research project I conducted in 1997).

Edward Nelson, age sixty, is a certified public accountant in rural
Pennsylvania. Ed and his wife have been members of the local Presbyterian church for more than thirty years. He attends Sunday services at least
twice a month (less often during tax season) and has served on the church's
executive council, its search committee, and several denominational committees. His church involvement is a way of keeping in touch with people

in the community. He became closely acquainted with the Kiwanis president while working on a church search committee. Through his church contacts, he was invited to join Rotary and became active on the YMCA board. Ed has his doubts about some of the stories in the Bible, but he believes he has an obligation to serve other people as much as he can.

Gary Rush manages a bookstore a few blocks from Ed Nelson's accounting office. Gary and his wife, both in their late thirties, attend Faith Fellowship, an independent evangelical church. Gary likes the biblical preaching and the way people care for one another. "We're the body of Christ," he explains, "that's why we call ourselves a fellowship." He faithfully attends Sunday school and the worship service each Sunday morning, a Bible study group on Sunday evening, and prayer meeting on Wednesday. In recent years he has taught Sunday school, served as a deacon, and been on the board of elders. Because of growing needs in the community, he helped set up a benevolence committee. He wants the church to be a "resting place" where people in need can "find hope." Like Ed Nelson, he believes God wants him to care about others.

Both men illustrate how religious commitment can encourage civic engagement, though one uses his church as a springboard to community involvement while the other devotes himself more exclusively to service to this church community.

The following discussion reviews recent trends in American religion and then examines the relationships between participation in religious organizations and involvement in other kinds of civic activity. The evidence suggests the importance of recognizing the divergent forms of religious commitment exemplified by Edward Nelson and Gary Rush, as well as the need to consider new ways for religious organizations to stimulate civic involvement.

The Religion Factor

Research has documented the continuing link between religious participation and civic engagement in the United States. Surveys conducted by the Gallup Organization for Independent Sector since the late 1980s consistently show that those who actively attend church are more likely to give

money and time to voluntary organizations, including ones that have no
evident church connection.[2] The work of Sidney Verba and his coauthors
on political mobilization demonstrates that churches are one of the most
important places in which people learn transferable civic skills.[3] Some
comparative research also suggests that higher levels of volunteering in the
United States than in other advanced industrial societies may be the result
of Americans' more active religious participation.[4] People like Edward
Nelson and Gary Rush exemplify the reasons for these connections. Active
church members are likely to be exposed to religious teachings about loving their neighbor and being responsible citizens; they are more likely to
have social capital in the form of ties to fellow congregants that can be
used to mobilize their energies; and they are more likely to be aware of
needs and opportunities in their communities as a result of attending services in their congregations.[5]

Religious participation appears to have remained relatively constant
over the past several decades or, if anything, to have declined modestly
compared to many forms of community involvement.[6] In Gallup surveys,
approximately four Americans in ten currently say they have attended religious services in the past week, just as they did in surveys in the early
1970s, while the General Social Surveys conducted by the University of
Chicago show that the proportion of Americans who say they attend religious services "nearly every week" edged downward from 36 percent in
1973 to 30 percent in 2000.[7]

Certain changes in the composition of religious participation over the
past four decades, however, have important implications for the precise
form of civic involvement by American churchgoers. The most significant
change has been the decline of so-called mainline Protestant denominations and the relative rise of some evangelical and independent churches.
The mainline denominations' relative decline is rooted in demographic
change more than in public rejection of teachings or practices: sharply
falling birth rates and later marriage and age at first birth have resulted in
fewer potential members. In contrast, the large numbers of working-class
families that populated evangelical churches tended to have more children. Evangelical churches also placed higher expectations on children
about retaining their parents' religious loyalties, and some of these

churches benefited from growing numbers of new immigrants after 1965.[8] Although the relative shift from mainline to evangelical Protestantism should not be exaggerated, its importance to civic engagement lies in the different religious traditions represented by the two.

Mainline denominations grew out of the Protestant Reformation and were territorial churches deeply implicated in civic affairs from the start. In North America they formed regional and national federations that kept local congregations in contact with one another and that encouraged the formation of benevolent associations, Bible societies, and temperance unions. Evangelical churches emphasized greater local congregational autonomy. Mainline churches participated in progressive social betterment programs during the first half of the twentieth century, while evangelical churches focused more on individual piety.

During the 1980s many evangelical Protestants became interested in political issues, especially in response to *Roe* v. *Wade* and earlier court rulings on school prayer. Under the leadership of Jerry Falwell, Pat Robertson, and others, evangelicals forged what was known as the Religious Right, and through organizations such as the Moral Majority and the Christian Coalition became more active in partisan politics. At the local level, many evangelicals nevertheless continued to focus on personal piety and involvement in local church activities. Denominational affiliations remained intact, but evangelical pastors found that congregational growth was often associated with appeals other than to denominational background.

Membership in Associations

Does the level of civic engagement differ among evangelicals, mainline Protestants, and Catholics? One way of answering this question is simply to compare how likely they are to be members of any nonreligious voluntary association. The 1974 and 1991 General Social Survey data show that the odds of being a member of any such organization if one is an evangelical are approximately 20 percent lower than if one is a Catholic. If one is a mainline Protestant, these odds are about 30 percent higher than if one is a Catholic.[9]

A better answer comes from considering the effect of church attendance on civic engagement within the different religious communities. Among all evangelicals, church attendance was not significantly associated with being a member of some other civic group in either 1974 or 1991. Mainline Protestants, by contrast, showed a consistent and strong relationship between church attendance and membership in other civic organizations. In both surveys, the odds of being a member of a civic organization were almost 50 percent greater among those who attended church regularly than among those who did not. The specific kinds of civic organizations that showed the strongest relationships with mainline Protestants' church attendance were service groups, youth organizations, and school service groups.

Catholics fell in between. In both years those who attended regularly were about 20 percent more likely to be members of some civic organization than those who attended less frequently. But this effect was present only for women. Indeed, women who attended religious services regularly were about 40 percent more likely to be members of civic organizations than women who attended less regularly. These results are consistent with child-rearing practice in many traditional Catholic families: mothers are more likely to attend church than fathers and to take responsibility for the children's religious upbringing. By implication, these mothers may also be more active in school, youth, or study groups that benefit their children.

But while evangelicals who attend church are less likely than mainline Protestants and Catholics to join other civic groups, they participate heavily in church volunteer work. In one national survey, evangelicals who attended church regularly were more than six times as likely as evangelicals who did not to be involved exclusively in church volunteer work; in comparison, mainline Protestants who attended regularly were only about twice as likely as those who did not to be involved in this way.[10] One reason for the difference is that evangelical churches offer more internal activities. They are more likely to have adult Sunday school programs and small group ministries, and their members are more likely to have friends within the church. As evangelical churches have grown larger, they appear to be even more capable of dominating their members' activities. Many evangelical churches emphasize separation from "the world" or distinctive beliefs that may discourage mingling with outsiders. Among biblical literalists there is a significantly stronger relationship between church attendance and exclusive church volunteering than among people who rejected biblical literalism.[11]

The research of Robert Putnam and others shows that church membership is positively related to trust, voting, and other measures of community involvement. Most church members, surveys show, say they give time to church organizations. Volunteering and philanthropy are more common among them. The differences between evangelicals and mainline Protestants also pertain to some of these other activities. For instance, mainline Protestants are more likely to say they are currently involved in charity or social service activities, have donated time in the past year to a voluntary organization, and have worked on a community service project.[12]

In short, mainline Protestant churches encourage civic engagement in the wider community, whereas evangelical churches apparently do not. This is not to suggest that evangelical churches are ineffective at generating social capital. Indeed, they do better than mainline churches in getting members to attend services, creating friendships among these members, and mobilizing them for Bible studies and other church meetings. But their social capital is more likely to remain within their own organizations.

To the extent that social capital is a way of creating the volunteer labor to get important tasks done, evangelical churches may be growing because they do a better job of guarding their own social capital. To the extent that they grow, they may also contribute to the depletion of the society's wider stock of social capital.

Civic Skills

Apart from membership itself, participation in civic organizations is often thought to be beneficial to American democracy because it generates civic skills. People learn to work together on committees, lead meetings, and serve as officers; they may also develop networks or be encouraged to write news stories or contact public officials. Many of these skills can be learned in churches and then used in other settings. Churches, in fact, generate such skills, perhaps especially among Protestants and perhaps with greater benefit to lower-income people than is often the case in other civic organizations.[13]

Among evangelicals, church attendance is not statistically related to a greater likelihood of activity in nonreligious organizations. Among mainline Protestants, regular church attendees are more likely to have worked in nonreligious organizations than irregular attendees, and among Catholics, the relationship is about like that among mainline Protestants. In contrast, active work in church-affiliated groups is significantly more likely among regular attendees than among irregular attendees in evangelical churches, just as it is in mainline Protestant and Catholic churches.

Among evangelicals, regular church attendees were significantly more likely than irregular attendees to have engaged in four particular activities: serving on committees or as an officer, attending conferences or workshops, and giving money. For two activities—writing to newspapers or contacting government officials—there were no differences. Results were similar among mainline Protestants, with two exceptions: there is a marginally significant relationship between attendance and having written to newspapers, and all of the other relationships were stronger than they were among evangelicals. Among Catholics, attendance was largely unrelated to these specific activities; only serving on committees was significantly more likely among regular attendees than among irregular attendees.

These results are consistent with the conclusions of Verba and colleagues regarding the differences between Protestants and Catholics in generating civic skills.[14] Protestants are more likely to be drawn into laity-led activities. Catholics may attend large parishes in which there is little lay activity other than participating in weekly mass. Evangelicals learn certain skills, such as working together on committees and serving as officers, but they are less likely to hold memberships in nonreligious organizations to which they can transfer these skills.

Volunteering

The most detailed data for assessing the impact of religious involvement on volunteering is the 1994 Giving and Volunteering Survey, a nationally representative study conducted among approximately 1,500 respondents by the Gallup Organization for Independent Sector.[15] It asks respondents about volunteering for specific kinds of organizations, including religious organizations; organizations that benefit society and the public; human services organizations; health care institutions and organizations; formal and informal educational and instructional associations; youth development organizations; arts, culture, and humanities organizations; and informal, ad hoc volunteering that is not part of an organized group.

Not surprisingly, there is a strong relationship between church attendance and volunteering for religious organizations, especially for evangelicals. Regular evangelical church attendees are almost four times as likely as irregular attendees to have volunteered within the past year for a religious organization. In comparison, regular mainline Protestant church attendees are about three times as likely as irregular attendees to have done so, and the comparable ratio among Catholics is between two and three times.

Again, nonreligious volunteering tends to follow the same pattern as membership in civic associations. Among evangelicals, the only significant relationship between church attendance and volunteering was with youth development organizations. In contrast, mainline Protestants show significant relationships between church attendance and the following kinds of volunteering: public and society benefit, health, education, the arts, and informal volunteering. In each instance, the odds of regular church attendees volunteering were between 30 and 60 percent higher than the odds of irregular church attendees volunteering. Among Catholics, only two kinds of volunteering were significantly related to church attendance: volunteering for education-related activities and for informal activities (health activity was marginally related).

Statistical relationships between church attendance and volunteering do not necessarily mean that the rate of volunteering is always higher among mainline Protestants than evangelicals (especially when differences in education and race are taken into account). Nevertheless, mainline Protestants were significantly more likely to volunteer in all of the following areas: public and society benefit, human services, education, environment, and informally. Nearly 60 percent of evangelical volunteering was concerned with maintaining the religious life of the congregation itself, such as teaching Sunday school, assisting the pastor, singing in the choir, serving as a deacon, or ushering at worship services. As for wider connections between church attendance and volunteering in other kinds of agencies, mainline Protestants (followed by Catholics) are considerably more likely than evangelicals to mobilize such links.

Political Participation

A number of political participation measures, such as voting, were included in the 1987 General Social Survey. But the data also make it possible to compare participation in local activities with participation in national politics and to see what else people did besides show up at the polls.

Among evangelicals there was a significant relationship between church attendance and having voted in two presidential elections (1980 and 1984), having voted regularly in local elections, and having worked to solve local community problems. Among mainline Protestants the pattern was virtually identical. Regular attendees were more likely to have voted in presidential and local elections and to have worked on community problems; they were also marginally more likely to have worked for parties or candidates. Among Catholics, too, the results were similar. Attendance was significantly related to having voted in presidential and local elections; it was not associated with having worked on community problems, but it was related to having contacted local officials.

These results can be interpreted to indicate that evangelicals are just as likely as mainline Protestants or Catholics to be mobilized by religious involvement to participate in politics. Or they can mean that mainline Protestants are no more likely to exhibit a relationship between church attendance and political participation than evangelicals. In either case, the differences among evangelicals, mainline Protestants, and Catholics in civic engagement are not evident here. But these findings suggest an important qualification to the literature that has stressed the political mobilization of conservative Christians. To the extent that one would expect this mobilization to be more characteristic of evangelicals than of mainline Protestants, the difference does not appear to be particularly profound. To be sure, evangelicals are more likely to register and vote than they were before the early 1970s, partly because their church participation encourages them to vote and partly because more of them have social characteristics (such as higher education or living in suburbs) associated with voting. But these data do not support the idea that church attendance among evangelicals has also mobilized them to attend political rallies, lobby, and work to sway elections.

Of course, some of those activities became more pronounced after 1987, especially with the 1988 presidential candidacy of Pat Robertson and the subsequent formation of the Christian Coalition. But the Moral Majority, Religious Roundtable, and other conservative Christian movements that emerged between 1978 and 1980 appear in retrospect to have mobilized more attention in the media than they did energy among evangelicals. And no other studies in which specific questions were asked about membership in, active work for, or volunteering for political groups showed any relationship between church attendance and political activity among evangelicals.

Changing Modes of Organization

For many people, church participation facilitates civic involvement in strictly informal ways. In our interviews, for example, one woman recalled going to the Presbyterian church with her husband when they first moved to suburban Sacramento, meeting other women there, and through them becoming involved in the PTA. A Methodist woman talked about becoming active in an environmental organization and said her church's teachings about stewardship had motivated her involvement. Some activities would be missed in volunteering surveys. For instance, a Mennonite chiropractor says he often charges patients less than insurance companies would permit as a kind of "statement" that reflects his church's stance against greed and materialism.[16]

Beyond these informal connections, many people took part in congregational activities meant to benefit the wider community. At an evangelical church in New Jersey, for instance, a lay leader told us she was a member of a committee that supervised a special congregational collection each Sunday to purchase food and clothing for needy people who might come to the pastor.

One national study of congregations suggests that formal and informal charitable activities within local churches are common.[17] Even the most conservative estimates suggest that at least half of all congregations offer some kind of social service program to their communities.[18] In addition, we found churches teaming up with other religious organizations to mobilize their members more effectively for civic activities. Eastside Ministries in Cleveland, for example, a coalition of mainly white Protestant and Catholic congregations, provides social services in a largely Hispanic, low-income section of the city.

Then there were a number of temporary alliances between churches and secular nonprofit agencies.[19] In East Harlem, New York, a citizens' advocacy group has been working with local churches to hold public meetings to educate young people in the community about police brutality, access to legal assistance, and mobilizing voters during elections. In Allentown, Pennsylvania, a woman concerned about caring for people with AIDS received free church office space until she was able to organize a separate nonprofit agency with space of its own.

Finally, we found an increasing variety of complex, formal partnerships between religious and nonreligious organizations. Among the most common are partnerships with community development corporations (CDCs). One CDC in inner-city Philadelphia, for instance, coordinates the efforts of a number of other entities to provide low-income housing, including individual committees of local suburban congregations and denominations, municipal officials, representatives from HUD in Washington and its state-level counterpart, and local nonprofit organizations. A suburban church representative told us that his congregation's financial contribution to the CDC gave it a stake in the wider community and that he had significantly extended his personal network of community contacts.

Looking Ahead

None of the research discussed here suggests that religion has a negative effect on civic engagement. Despite an apparent emphasis on work within the congregation, evangelical religious involvement does not discourage participation in other voluntary associations; with the exception of voting, it just does not encourage it.

Evidence that religious involvement among Catholics encourages civic participation is also limited. The clearest relationships between religious involvement and civic engagement are among mainline Protestants. The decline of mainline Protestant churches in recent decades means that civic engagement is probably not as strong as it would be if this were not the case. Other research generally shows that mainline Protestant congregations are more likely than evangelical congregations to sponsor social service activities.[20]

Evangelicalism, mainline Protestantism, and Catholicism are all well institutionalized forms of religious expression in the United States, and they are likely to remain important to the well-being of civil society. Nevertheless, they are also subject in distinctive ways to social forces that influence their members and bear on their established modes of organization.

Evangelicals are perhaps in the strongest position to resist broader social influences, and yet the success of their churches has in many ways come at the price of cultural accommodation. Today most evangelicals live in suburbs, and a growing proportion has been exposed to higher education. Their concerns about work, layoffs, career changes, burnout, and conflicts between work and family life are indistinguishable from those of mainline Protestants and Catholics. More of them are remaining single, experiencing divorce, or postponing marriage and child rearing. The large minority of African American evangelicals is especially subject to racial discrimination, poverty, and unemployment. In all these ways, evangelicals confront the same influences as the American population in general.

Evangelicals have faced these challenges by devoting large shares of time and energy to their local congregations. These congregations have grown, expanded to new locations, and enlarged their share of the overall churched population. Higher levels of education among their members and a focus on family issues have helped to enlarge the resources needed to administer attractive church programs. But studies of better educated evangelicals also show that they become more like nonevangelicals in their willingness to engage in "cognitive bargaining" with the wider society, and they may find it harder in the future to shield themselves from cultural influences.

On the one hand, evangelicals' accommodation to the wider culture will probably result in their civic participation becoming more like that of mainline Protestants and Catholics—dispersed among social agencies rather than concentrated in churches themselves. On the other hand, this same accommodation may result in slower growth among evangelical churches and more sporadic connections to other civic organizations. Declining growth rates have already been observed in some evangelical fellowships, and many evangelical churches are facing hard times financially. In the short term, clergy may place greater emphasis on congregational loyalties. In the longer term, such loyalties may diminish relative to activities that are of greater interest to evangelicals. But evangelical families will also have to work around busy schedules, volunteering for a few hours here or there rather than devoting themselves fully to an organization over a long period of time. Insofar as they have national leaders to play symbolic roles in the political arena, they may also limit their political participation to voting or giving vocal support to a few selected issues rather than becoming seriously involved in grassroots political movements.

The likelihood of cultural accommodation is also enhanced by the fact that evangelical Protestants are compelled by their beliefs to draw connections between themselves and the outside world. Many to whom we talked expressed ambivalence about the fact that their churches seemed to be doing so little in the wider community.

The wild card in all this for evangelicals is government-sponsored faith-based social service initiatives. Many evangelical congregations are too small to sponsor formal service programs on their own, and they may not be in a competitive position to apply for government funding. But large evangelical churches and parachurch ministries may do more service work in their communities now that government restrictions on displaying religious symbols and combining service with evangelism have been lifted. Efforts to assist small congregations in applying for government funds may also facilitate greater community involvement among evangelical churches.

The influence of the same social forces on mainline Protestants means declining loyalties to particular denominations, some emphasis on the local experience of "community" that attracts evangelicals, and diminishing resources for the broad social programs mainline denominations sponsored a few decades ago. That mainline church attendance continues to facilitate civic involvement is encouraging for future civic engagement. At least critics who charge that mainline Protestantism has become too privatized to have any discernible consequences appear to be wrong; only the declining number of mainline Protestants gives cause for a pessimistic assessment of civic engagement's future, and even this decline does not appear to be as serious a concern as it was a few decades ago.

But mainline Protestants are exposed to all the social forces that undermine long-term memberships in hierarchical civic organizations and encourage more short-term involvement. A person like Edward Nelson, who stays involved in Rotary for decades as a way of fulfilling his responsibilities as a Christian citizen, may become rarer while those who spend an hour helping Habitat for Humanity, who do no volunteer work at the peak of their professional careers, and who then participate in volunteer activities as retirees may become more typical. Many nonprofit organizations have come into being over the past half-century, often with strong backing from Protestant clergy and laity. Mainline churches are likely to work increasingly with these secular agencies, forming short-term partnerships rather than encouraging members to join traditional civic groups on their own.

In the past, mainline Protestant churches inspired civic engagement by locating near the town square and attracting prominent citizens predisposed to civic activities. But mainline churches have had to work harder in cities and suburbs where their memberships were more geographically dispersed. In case after case, we found that mainline members involved in outside civic activities had also been a part of deliberate efforts within the church to cultivate those connections. One woman had served on her church's "Church and Society" committee for several years before she initiated a violence prevention program in the community. Another went from directing her church's Christian education committee to serving on a learning task force in the local schools. These examples show that the health of church programs themselves is an important factor in mobilizing future civic engagement. As many mainline churches shrink in membership and experience financial difficulties, it is unclear whether they will be able to nurture other civic activities.

Mainline Protestants do have local, national, and international resources at their disposal. They remain well connected with influential members of their communities. Congregations remain federated with regional and national judicatories and through their denominations sponsor effective activities in areas such as environmental justice and corporate responsibility. Being part of international religious organizations also gives them opportunities to work for international debt relief, human rights, and peace.

What about the future of civic engagement among Catholics? To the extent that they are more diverse than mainline Protestants or evangelicals, they are likely to mirror the wider population. Critics appear to be correct when they charge that U.S. Catholicism has accommodated itself to the dominant Protestant culture by encouraging privatized convictions; attendance at Catholic churches does not encourage civic participation to the same extent that attendance at mainline Protestant churches does. Still, Catholic parishes in the past have worked through a wide variety of Catholic institutions, such as parochial schools and church-related colleges and hospitals, thereby having an effect on the wider society that depended little on lay volunteering.

In personal interviews a number of Catholics described a spirituality that offers some perspective on the statistics. It increasingly expressed itself in personal explorations and deeds of service. Volunteering emanated from their worldview, not church participation or the lack thereof. As a Catholic man who volunteers three hours each week at a shelter for runaway teenagers told us, "I strive at every moment to be true to my spirituality, and volunteering is just a part of what I do." For people like this, service to others may be mobilized more by their work or their involvement in social movements than by church participation.

The Catholic population is also becoming more diverse as a result of immigration, suggesting that its role as an agent of assimilation in civil society may be especially important in the future. Whereas Protestant congregations recruit members voluntarily and thus divide readily along racial and ethnic lines, the territorial basis of Catholic parishes means that direct interaction among racial and ethnic groups cannot be as easily avoided.

Religion may have a salutary effect on civil society by encouraging its members to worship, spend time with their families, and learn the moral lessons embedded in religious traditions. But it is likely to have a diminished impact on society if that is the only role it plays. What interested Tocqueville about voluntary organizations was not just their ability to provide friendships or teach people civic skills; it was their ability to forge connections across large segments of the population, spanning communities and regions and drawing together people from different ethnic backgrounds and occupations. The denominational structures and benevolent associations that grew out of religious impulses in Tocqueville's time were such organizations. In the twenty-first century, as many of these traditional civic organizations decline, the ability of religious people to create innovative partnerships with nonreligious community agencies, volunteer centers, and nonprofit corporations may be the greatest test of their role in mobilizing civic engagement.

35

Challenging America's Faithful

STEVEN WALDMAN

GEORGE BUSH'S PET idea probably owes its life to Bill Clinton's pet idea. By the spring of 2001, an unusual alliance of conservative Baptists and liberal civil libertarians had torpedoed President Bush's original faith-based initiative—especially the plan to give government grants to religiously oriented charities. His proposal to change the tax code to make it easier for people to give to charity had been hobbled by his early decision to spend most of his tax-cut chits on repealing the estate tax. But Bush still had one card up his sleeve: he made Clinton's AmeriCorps program (and community service) a key element of his faith-based initiative.

The link forged by Bush between AmeriCorps and the faith-based initiative is a welcome one for those interested in national service, for it broadens service's political base and its pool of leadership talent. But just as important, it is good for religion. On a practical level, there is a very compelling case for religious institutions to embrace national service. Even before Bush came along, about 15 percent of AmeriCorps members—some 6,000 strong—were working in faith-based groups counseling drug addicts, teaching reading to city kids, and handing out peanut-butter-and-jelly sandwiches to the homeless.

Faith-based groups love full-time service workers. Leaders of religious charities routinely report that they have no shortage of unpaid, "occasional" volunteers; what they're missing is the people to help recruit, train, and manage these volunteers. John DiIulio, the first head of Bush's office of faith-based action, noted that the "missing link" is a group of full-time, energetic people who show up every day and supervise the volunteers. A typical AmeriCorps member recruits or manages twelve additional unpaid volunteers.

For years, Habitat for Humanity managers complained that they had to turn away volunteers because they did not have enough reliable crew leaders. Along came AmeriCorps. At first, Habitat's founder, Millard Fuller, turned down AmeriCorps, fearing government entanglement. But he was (as he now reports gladly) overruled by his board. Today Habitat is one of the largest AmeriCorps programs, and Fuller estimates that the AmeriCorps members have significantly increased their flock of volunteers. In all, the 600 Habitat AmeriCorps members have directly supervised 241,000 Habitat volunteers, who have built more than 2,000 houses that otherwise would never have been built.

National service helped the faith-based initiative by aiding small religious groups without adding huge bureaucratic burdens. In supporting service, the government is usually funding a person rather than a program; as a result, it requires less intrusive monitoring of the religious group. Mostly the government wants to know what the AmeriCorps member is doing, rather than what the group as a whole is doing. It doesn't matter how much of Habitat's budget goes to administrative overhead or overseas missions or salaries. What matters is that the AmeriCorps member attached to the program is working hard and accomplishing something.

Consequently, national service solves some of the tricky church-state dilemmas of the faith-based initiative. Instead of worrying about whether consumers of the charity are getting a dose of illegal religion, the government can view its aid as akin to Pell Grants or student loans. It is perfectly constitutional for a twenty-year-old to use a Pell Grant to go to Catholic seminary. The aid is going to the student, not the school (even though the school clearly benefits).

Pressing Churches to Do More

The government's current approach both to service and to religious groups, however, cannot be described as Kennedyesque. It emphasizes what your country can do for you (and your church), not what you (or your church) can do for your country.

Most of Clinton's senior staff never quite bought into the sacrifice-for-the-country part of the service initiative and instead primarily pitched AmeriCorps as a way of paying for college. When Clinton introduced his plan for AmeriCorps in New Orleans in April 1993, the banner behind him read, "National Service Means Equal Opportunity." The pitch often was altruistic bribery: do good work and you'll get helped in return.

Likewise, George Bush's faith-based rhetoric is all about helping religion and very little about challenging the faithful. Without implying that these cash-strapped, noble institutions are anything other than angelic, it must nevertheless be said that religious groups do need to be challenged.

Americans are more generous with their time and money than almost any other culture. They give $190 billion to charity and volunteer 20 billion hours a year. Those statistics, however, are deeply misleading, in a way few people want to discuss. The $190 billion figure is less a sign of America's generosity than its religiosity. Sixty percent of Americans' contributions go to religious institutions—more than go to youth development, human services, education, health, and foreign crises combined.

The money is essential for the functioning of religion in America. It is why pluralism flourishes here without the need for (and risks of) massive government funding. But while all this charitable activity is valuable, it should not be confused with help for the poor—or with solving social problems. Most religious charity and volunteerism is directed inward— toward the congregation, the building, the Sunday school, the organ— rather than outward toward the community as a whole. In 1997 a typical congregant of a Protestant church gave an average of $497. But $418 of that went to upkeep of the church and only $79 to "benevolences," according to a survey by Empty Tomb, a Christian research firm.[1]

How about volunteering? Here again, much of the service done with the church is done for the church. According to Lester Salamon, director of the Institute for Policy Studies at Johns Hopkins University, only 7 to 15 percent of volunteering done through churches helps the larger community.[2]

There are religiously based service corps, such as the Jesuit Volunteer Corps, that operate independently of AmeriCorps. Yet all of these religious corps together field only a few thousand volunteers. Few religious faiths make full-time national service an important part of their mission, and few donors to these faiths focus their money on such an effort. If every house of worship in America sponsored one person a year to do full-time service, it would generate roughly 350,000 corps members.

Those religious groups that do emphasize missionary work—like the Mormons—are among the fastest-growing religions in the world. To be sure, that's partly because their missionary work involves proselytizing, but it is mostly because they are helping the needy. In other words, it is most likely that religions that increase their emphasis on community service will be improving their image and appealing to a new generation of young people—exactly the sort they struggle most to attract into their pews right now.

One of the few things on which all the world's religions agree is the need to do good works. A national service effort enlisting the nation's houses of worship would not only revitalize service, it could well revitalize religion.

PART SEVEN
Making Good Citizens

36

Citizenship without Politics?
A Critique of Pure Service

KAYLA MELTZER DROGOSZ

> Politics not only brings many associations into being, it also cre-
> ates extensive ones. The common interests of civic life seldom
> naturally induce great numbers to act together. . . . But in poli-
> tics. . . it is only large associations which make the general value
> of this method plain. . . . A political association draws a lot of
> people at the same time out of their circle; however much differ-
> ences in age, intelligence, or wealth may naturally keep them
> apart. . . . Once they have met, they always know how to meet
> again. . . . So one may think of political associations as great free
> schools to which all citizens come to be taught the general theory
> of association.
>
> Alexis de Tocqueville, *Democracy in America*

CONSERVATIVES AND LIBERALS both claim to be heirs to the true Tocqueville. To conservatives, his caution against "too much democracy" and the
"tyranny of the majority" put sensible limits on mob rule. To progressives,
his emphasis on freedom and the vibrancy of associations serves as a basis
for reinvigorating grassroots democracy. It is, however, undisputed that
Tocqueville serves as the central inspiration for the present revival of

interest in civil society, even though little turns on whether current scholars are faithful interpreters of his life's work. Two brilliant thinkers have
shown that his conception of civil society is inextricably linked to strong
national government and politically engaged citizenship.

In *Diminished Democracy,* Theda Skocpol laments what she considers
to be an impoverished debate about what is wrong with American civic life.
She describes successful associations as those that "expressed broadly shared
identities and values, engaged in raucous conflict with one another, and
linked local people to state, regional, and national centers of power. Voluntary federations also sought to influence government and in many cases
worked closely with it."[1] Skocpol shows that while association-building is
far from dead, the associations that now flourish appear less likely than
those of the past to foster civic involvement and political participation.

Sheldon Wolin's magisterial study of Tocqueville's life and ideas also
seeks to revive the political within democracy. Tocqueville's elevation of
the political and the making of the "public self" were deliberate gestures
of his opposition to the "privatizing tendencies" in the communities he
studied. Wolin writes, "The abiding concern of Tocqueville's thinking, the
referent point by which he tried to define his life as well as the task before
his generation, was the revival of the political, in his phrase: *la chose
publique.*"[2] The web of relationships and networks of associational life—
much of what later came to be called social capital—grew from the inter-
section of the heroic and the mundane in politics. So, ultimately, the
strength and vibrancy of responsive national institutions and participatory
citizenship arise, in part, from the everyday activities of community life.
But these are also inextricably linked to *la chose publique,* a preoccupation
with public obligations and political choices that resist the privatizing tendencies of some forms of community life.

About a century ago, the American L. Judson Hanifan came to the
same conclusion and articulated what may be the earliest formulation of
the phrase "social capital." Hanifan was a social reformer—"Presbyterian,
Rotarian and Republican"—who returned to his home in Appalachia to
work in its crumbling rural school system. Hanifan struggled to understand
why his community had lost its vitality and neighborliness. He concluded
that its serious economic and political problems could only be resolved by

strengthening community ties, which had weakened over time. In 1916 Hanifan urged the importance of community involvement in sustaining the economically downtrodden communities. "If he comes into contact with his neighbor, and they with other neighbors, there will be an accumulation of social capital." The "good will, fellowship, sympathy, and social intercourse" that result because of stronger community bonds would be the key to "substantial improvement of living conditions in the whole community."[3] From the perspective of democracy, communities, including the networks and associations they create, depend on the stability, continuity, and economic well-being of real places where real people work. And how do good will, fellowship, and sympathy transform the public realm? They can do so only through politics.

What Would Tocqueville Do?

A powerful tradition of social thought has insisted that stable democracies must be grounded in strong communities—the sort that so captivated Tocqueville—which are themselves firmly rooted in civil society and its many mediating institutions. In recent decades, there has been what Bill Schambra calls a "political eclipse of national community." The challenges facing democracy have been captured by the president's call to build "communities of character" and by such phrases as "the decline of social capital" and "the erosion of trust" in nearly all things public.

This explains the outpouring of books describing the need to focus on establishing cultural standards that encourage virtue or integrity. Their titles reflect sought-after virtues: "Civility," "Integrity," "Trust," and "Making Men Moral." All seek to uncover what is deeply uncivil about us. There is a pervasive sense that our most important civic institutions are unraveling and that we are not in control of the forces that have the greatest effect on our lives. We also know that many forms of political participation, such as working for a political party, are at a forty-year low.[4] And targeting what people do not know about civics remains a favorite pastime not only of David Letterman but also of professors, pundits, and politicians.

Liberal and conservative communitarians continue to remind us that individuals are more than autonomous actors with bundles of rights. They are embedded in families, faith communities, associations, ethnic groups, and political parties, and these flourish only as the larger communities to which they belong are prosperous in the widest sense of that word.[5]

There is little doubt that sociological and communitarian analysis has gained ground, but too often the perspectives of political economy have been eclipsed or disaggregated from the public conversation. Whether because of Marxism's fall from grace with the collapse of the Soviet empire or what Benjamin Barber has called the "rising hegemony of neoliberal theory," it is certain that far less thought has been given in recent years to how economic and political inequality define the very "civility" of civil society.[6] Some of the political dimensions of citzenship have also been denigrated and what is at stake is the vibrancy of both community and democracy.

Others have voiced important critiques of communities based on racial or class homogeneity, especially in the context of highly diverse populations. This has led scholars to specify that truly desirable communities must be places in which citizens recognize their mutual obligations and inclusive relationships, but also be places that preserve the norms of toleration and nonexclusion.[7] Several others, whose ideas have not been taken seriously enough, have argued that well-functioning state institutions are necessary to contain social conflict and turn aside the tendencies of civil society that encourage disengagement from or ambivalence towards politics and economic reform.[8] And Benjamin Barber has called attention to the often overlooked fact that, "Given these new realities, democracy clearly depends not only on local social capital but also on local economic capital." It depends, he continues, "not only on the kinds of social trust engendered by civic relations but also on the kinds of economic loyalty spurned by global corporatism, not only on enunciating a market rationale for civics but also on developing a civic rationale for markets."[9]

Social Capital and Inequality: Toward "Municipal Citizenship"

The ideas of fostering national service and strengthening the mediating institutions of civil society seem contradictory in their respective emphasis on the national and the local. But both are part of the quest for what Michael Sandel calls a "new public philosophy," one he hopes will resurrect a vision of civic republicanism. This tradition, Sandel says, "reminds us that politics is not only about the size and distribution of the national product. It is also about bringing economic power to democratic account and equipping men and women with the habits and dispositions that suit them to self-rule."[10] This view emphasizes not only revitalizing but also altering political arrangements and economic policies that directly contradict the goal of community-building.[11]

Stephen Goldsmith, former mayor of Indianapolis, current chair of the Corporation for National Service and special advisor to President Bush's Office of Faith-Based and Community Initiatives, knows this well. In *Putting Faith in Neighborhoods*, Goldsmith explains how Indianapolis invented a national model for creating vibrant cities by encouraging citizenship and engaging community organizations. He argues that social pathologies are best confronted by productive partnerships between citizens and public officials. He also claims that community engagement for its own sake may well miss the point if it focuses, as Robert Nisbet wrote, only on "principal moral ends and psychological gratification" without recognizing the crucial need for these associations to have a direct influence on government institutions.[12]

The implication of Goldsmith's argument is bold. When localized civic engagement encourages only "bonding" social capital—which strengthens social solidarity within one group—then it can fail in its public purpose. If, however, it reinforces the ties *between groups* that may have different motivations but a common purpose, it can create a workable partnership with public agencies and strengthen what Goldsmith calls "municipal citizenship."

Like others before him, Goldsmith describes the importance of self-governance and personal responsibility. But he also insists that public agencies must create responsive partnerships in which "each member is stronger as a result of the partnership." He writes: "It is a challenge to involve citizens in a way that mediates between differing views and results in effective, practical solutions—especially if indigenous participation is to be real and not after-the-fact window dressing."[13]

Municipal citizens work to develop habits of democracy, strengthen civic virtues, and cultivate personal responsibility. They are oriented to solution-focused thinking and open to broader civic obligations beyond their own personal interests. Goldsmith recognizes that many groups have a stake in the way government does its business, and that these groups may have very different motivations. Nevertheless, he remains committed to the idea that citizen and public official are mutually obligated to foster arrangements that leave both parties better off for their engagement with each other.

As some authors in this book have argued, we cannot strengthen the ties that bind us as a nation unless our civic duty is fostered by "bridging" social capital that helps us create links across groups. There is a "strength in weak ties" that stretch across lines of race, class, and religion since these weak ties allow us to recognize our dependence on one another so we can become more than communities of strangers.[14] In Putnam's book *Democracies in Flux,* he examined the condition of social capital in several countries. The trends he finds are toward narrower forms of social participation and mounting discontent over political institutions. Yet he also finds evidence that the welfare state and "big government" have sustained rather than eroded social capital. Why? Putnam's most striking observation is that the unequal distribution of social capital remains a major problem. This unequal distribution of social power appears strongly connected to the shrinking membership and political power of traditional large membership organizations, such as unions, that once organized the working class. With the breakdown of these institutions, the welfare state is often the only remaining force fostering even a modicum of social equality.[15] Unless the decline of American *political* institutions is reversed, our problems and conflicts will not be adequately addressed, no matter how many bird-watching groups and church picnics we attend. Self-government is not just a social venture; it is a political venture.

Bringing Politics Back In: Service and Citizenship

That is why citizenship will not be strengthened if service is entirely divorced from politics. Yes, service is essential to civil society and it is part of what makes us citizens. But do not mistake it for politics. In his chapter here, Harry Boyte shows us that while service is about helping the disadvantaged, politics is about managing competing interests and finding structural changes that can break the cycles of disadvantage. It is about developing solutions, even with people you do not like and may not agree with. And democracy functions well only if everyone is, in a sense, a politician plodding through the muck of compromise and negotiation.

No one disagrees about the merits of community service. Service can, indeed, demonstrate that citizens can be efficacious on matters of public concern. It is a discrete, tangible form of human bonding and "public work." It is straightforwardly good to build a house for someone without one or to volunteer in a soup kitchen and provide a meal to someone who is hungry.

Politics is always more complicated than such acts of mercy. It is often unpleasant and adversarial. It tries to get at the sources of poverty, hunger, and homelessness by connecting these problems to national policy and seeking systematic solutions.[16] If service is positioned as a morally superior alternative to politics, it could thus weaken rather than strengthen democratic citizenship. Service can so focus on individual acts of compassion and character building that it ignores the demands and satisfactions of politics. "Service," Kevin Mattson argues, "became just another commodity to be bought and sold."[17]

Yet legislators expressly prohibited AmeriCorps programs from "engaging in political advocacy."[18] An early newsletter from the Corporation for National Service, describing why AmeriCorps participants were prohibited from attending the Stand for Children rally in Washington, D.C., explained the decision this way: "National service has to be nonpartisan. What's more, it should be about bringing communities together by getting things done. Strikes, demonstrations and political activities can have the opposite effect. They polarize and divide."[19] Yet all these are activities at the heart of democratic politics.[20]

The ban on political activity within AmeriCorps was understandable as a means of ensuring congressional support. But it has the effect of denigrating politics altogether and of depriving AmeriCorps members of opportunities to learn, as Tobi Walker has put it, "about how politics works, about the kinds of compromises and choices that are necessary in a representative, pluralistic democracy."[21] Rhetoric about service that is divorced from institutional change and political engagement will not, by itself, reinvigorate democratic citizenship. Civic engagement increases during and after national crisis, as the experience of the great civic generation demonstrated after World War II. But that generation had already been conditioned to the importance of democratic engagement by the tumultuous years of the Great Depression and the New Deal. The great civic generation learned the importance of service in wartime. But it learned the necessity of politics when the nation was at peace.

President Bush has said that creating a "culture of service, citizenship and responsibility" could turn the Unites States into a "land of justice, liberty, and tolerance."[22] It is a worthy thought. Yet justice, liberty, and tolerance are themselves the creation of politics. Service divorced from politics will never live up to its promise. Service harnessed to political and social reform could transform a nation.

37

Public Work and the Dignity of Politics

HARRY C. BOYTE

TODAY, POLITICS IN America has become like the Cheshire cat in Alice in Wonderland, disappearing until only a grimace remains. As E. J. Dionne observed in *Why Americans Hate Politics*, people tolerate *contentiousness* in politics if they see politics as *productive*. But increasingly, partisanship substitutes for productive action. Today's problems—whether corporate scandals or global warming or growing numbers of citizens lacking health coverage—quickly become yesterday's forgotten headlines.[1]

National service as conventionally conceived—as altruistic voluntarism—does not address the decay of politics. In contrast, "national service" in the vein of the public work initiatives of the New Deal, or elements of the Peace Corps and AmeriCorps with a "public work" orientation, can help if their political dimensions are understood.

President Bush used the idea of altruistic citizen service from the beginning of his run for the presidency. Our nation's greatness, he argued, is to be found in "small, unnumbered acts of caring and courage and self-denial." On November 8, 2001, outlining the nation's course in facing the "terrorist threat," Bush described "a nation awakened to service and citizenship and compassion" to define "American civilization" itself, at war with a ruthless enemy. "We value life," Bush declared. "The terrorists ruthlessly destroy it." He called for "all of us [to] become a September 11 volunteer, by making a commitment to service in our communities."[2]

President Bush is not alone in constructing the world as a clash between the virtuous and evildoers. Citizen groups on the left, as on the right, demonize their opponents and proclaim their blamelessness.

What is missing from both the left and right is the concept of the citizen as a "political" agent, in the deepest meaning of the word: someone able to negotiate diverse interests for the sake of accomplishing some public task. The formal political system is reactive here. As Representative Lindsey Graham (R-S.C.) observed after the impeachment debate, polarized constituencies made it hard for the House to return to collaborative work. For better and worse, the people shape the nation's agenda.

The language of altruistic service reflects the ways in which America has become professionalized in the recent years. Service *substitutes* for politics. Mediating institutions such as political parties, schools, congregations, settlements, unions, and universities once taught a practical politics including the skills of dealing with others with whom we may sharply disagree. They were the nonpartisan root system for the life of democracy.

As the political, interactive qualities of everyday settings atrophied, governmental politics lost vitality. Today, Americans feel collectively powerless. The rubric of service covers many worthwhile activities. But to renew democracy and address the problems we face, we need to focus less on service and more on politics.

A Prophetic Populist

According to John Dewey, "Democracy must be reborn in each generation. Education is the midwife."[3] The decline of politics corresponds to what Hannah Arendt called replacement of "the public" with "the social."[4] To remedy the problem requires politics based on plurality, practiced by citizens and productive. This kind of politics differs from that of the left wing or the right wing, since it is focused not on ideology but on citizen empowerment, problem solving, and a broad philosophy of democracy. The work of John Dewey is useful as a take off point, both for its strengths and limits. Dewey believed that citizens create democracy. His mistake was to think of democracy as "social," not "political."

"It is scarcely an exaggeration to say that for a generation no major issue was clarified until Dewey had spoken," wrote Henry Steele Commager.[5] Dewey railed against liberals who thought ideas had no consequences, but his own life was the best refutation. In addition to his prolific academic career, Dewey was cofounder of such organizations as the NAACP and the American Association of University Professors and was an architect of progressive education. Many see him as the father of today's community service.

To return to the formative period in Dewey's intellectual life is to go back to young intellectuals involved in the "back to the people" movement of the late nineteenth century. Jane Addams, a leading voice of this generation, said, "[We were all motivated] by a desire to get back to the people, to be identified with the common lot."[6]

John Dewey's background, from family farming and small business life in Vermont, was emblematic of American populism as it emerged not only as the political party of the 1890s but also as a political approach.[7] Populism continued through the New Deal and beyond, as Lawrence Goodwyn, Lary May, and Fredrick Harris, among others, have shown.[8] This approach focuses on developing the power of the people and the productive work of democracy. As a political philosophy, it forms a democratic alternative to ideologies of left and right. It judges particular programs and policies by the query, "What do they contribute to civic power and the commonwealth?"

What made Dewey's populism prophetic is that he understood, better than many today, the dynamics of power in an information society. Knowledge power is not a scarce good that requires a bitter struggle, matching gains with losses on the other side. Rather, knowledge power is increased through sharing transactions, even if its democratization often is fiercely contested.

Dewey had great respect for ordinary people's values, work, and intelligence. He believed in what he called the "social" quality of knowledge. Truth only becomes free, he argued, when it "distributes itself to all so that it becomes the Commonwealth."[9]

Dewey's argument, profoundly democratic in its implications, is that all knowledge—academic no less than practical—is social knowledge, the product of an interplay of experience, testing and experiment, observation, reflection, and conversation. All people have the capacity and right to participate in knowledge creation. "Consider the development of the power of guiding ships across trackless wastes from the day when they hugged the shore," wrote Dewey. "The record would be an account of a vast multitude of cooperative efforts, in which one individual uses the results provided for him by a countless number of other individuals . . . so as to add to the common and public store. A survey of such facts brings home the actual social character of intelligence as it actually develops and makes its way."[10]

While Dewey's theory of knowledge is important, he thought of knowledge in social, not political, ways. As a result, his writings on democracy and education often were highly idealized. Dewey was also part of a generation of progressive intellectuals who narrowed the orbit of politics, removing it from community. To realize the democratic possibilities Dewey envisioned for education or for the world requires a look at how citizen politics disappeared—and how we can put it back in.

Shrinking Politics

Jane Addams warned about the emergence of a class of "experts" who saw themselves outside the life of the people: "Would it be dangerous to conclude that the corrupt politician himself, because he is democratic in method, is on a more ethical line of social development than the reformer who believes that the people must be made over by 'good citizens' and governed by 'experts'?"[11] Addams defined the expert class broadly to encompass not only political professionals but also educators, health providers, social workers, and many others. She challenged the expert's posture of innocence. "We are all involved in this political corruption," she argued. "None of us can stand aside; our feet are mired in the same soil, and our lungs breathe the same air."[12]

The irony is that Dewey, inspired by Addams's work with immigrants in Chicago's Hull House, nonetheless shared with most progressive thought a faulty distinction between politics and community. "I mean by 'society' the less definite and freer play of the forces of the community which goes on in the daily intercourse and contact of men in an endless variety of ways that have nothing to do with politics or government," he argued.[13] Dewey's apolitical community still haunts community service.

Continuing through the New Deal, many settings continued to have an everyday political quality, however intellectuals were defining politics. Hubert Humphrey traced his political career to roots in his father's drug store in Doland, S.D. "In his store there was eager talk about politics, town affairs, and religion," he said. "I've listened to some of the great parliamentary debates of our time, but have seldom heard better discussions of basic issues than I did as a boy standing on a wooden platform behind the soda fountain."[14]

Citizen politics was tied to a "public work" conception of citizenship. During the New Deal, productive citizenship was not the high-minded, virtuous, leisure-time activity of gentlemen. Rather it was the down-to-earth labor of ordinary people who created goods and undertook projects of public benefit.

Public work citizenship and politics emerged during the New Deal in programs that today would be called voluntarism and service but were then seen as work with public impact. ("Voluntarism," according to the *Oxford English Dictionary*, does not appear as a term until the 1950s.) For instance, the Civilian Conservation Corps (CCC) employed more than three million young men in conservation efforts between 1933 and 1942. They planted more than 2.3 billion trees, erected 3,470 fire towers, constructed 97,000 miles of roads, logged 4,135,500 days in fighting fires, and reclaimed 20 million acres of land from soil erosion. Over time, CCC participants realized they were helping to create a national treasure. As one observer put it, "The CCC enrollees feel a part-ownership as citizens in the forest that they have seen improve through the labor of their hands. These youths are interested because the woods, streams, and lakes are theirs in a new way. They have toiled in them, protected them, improved them, replenished them."[15]

The rise of the experts about whom Jane Addams warned shrunk politics everywhere. Thus, as Alan Ehrenhalt described in *The United States of*

Ambition, sixties activists often, ironically, furthered this process in electoral politics. They ran for office motivated by issues such as civil rights, feminism, and environmentalism, and they attacked local parties and backroom deals, but they ended up with little connecting them to the general citizenry other than television ads. The policymaking skills of politicians may be better than ever, but gridlock and isolation await many officeholders, like Rick Knobe, who won the Sioux Falls, South Dakota mayoral race against the establishment in 1983 only to find that "I was carrying the whole city on my back. I was an island unto myself."[16]

Today's civic theory has lost the insight that citizens help make democracy. Thus, in both communitarianism and liberalism—the leading schools of political theory—citizens are absent from politics except on the (relatively rare) occasions when citizens vote, protest, or otherwise interact with their government.[17]

Communitarian theorists such as Amitai Etzioni, founder of the Communitarian Caucus, or Don Eberly, a Bush advisor, have made helpful criticisms of the conception of the citizen as an individual bearer of rights. In communitarianism the citizen is a community member who expresses his or her citizenship through service. Yet the ideal of compassionate volunteers does not convey boldness, intelligence, gritty determination, courage in fighting injustice, or capacities for sustained engagement with others outside our "community."

An etymology of service, at the heart of communitarianism, illustrates the problem. Service is from the Latin *servus*, meaning slave, associated with "servile" and "serf." In one of its meanings, performing duties connected with a position, service is a useful bridge for re-connection with the world. Yet in all meanings, service is associated with other-directedness. The service giver, in focusing on the needs of those being served, adopts a stance of selflessness or disinterestedness. Service is the paradigmatic stance of the "outside expert." But interests are the elemental particles of politics.[18]

Liberals challenge communitarians and the Bush administration for substituting "service" for "justice." They are right: real politics is full of the struggle for justice. Yet like communitarians, liberals narrow the orbit of politics to government and see it as a zero-sum fight.[19] It is crucial to reclaim an expansive definition of politics if citizens are to be cocreators of democracy and if we are to address the challenges we face.

Bringing Back Citizen Politics

Politics is best understood as the interplay of diverse interests to accomplish public purposes. Politics, in this sense, is everywhere, every day.

Sometimes there is an intractable clash of interests and power. Yet sometimes politics can negotiate clashing interests for general benefit. This is politics as a productive, not simply distributive, activity. Politics is the way people with divergent values and views work together to solve problems and create common things.

This kind of politics can only be sustained if it is dispersed—not the property of professional politicians. Politics is from the Greek root *politikos*, meaning "of the citizen." Until modern times the word had no associations with the state at all. As the intellectual historian Giovanni Sartori has detailed, this meant horizontal civic relationships, not vertical, state-centered relationships.[20]

In his 1962 dissenting work *In Defense of Politics,* the British theorist Bernard Crick stressed politics as "a great and civilizing activity." He emphasized politics as negotiation of diverse views and interests. Drawing on Aristotle, Crick argued that politics is about plurality, not similarity. Crick defended politics against a list of "enemies" including nationalism, technology, and mass democracy, as well as overzealous partisans of conservative, liberal, and socialist ideologies.[21]

We have to spread the ownership of politics if we are to revive politics in this sense. Electoral politics alone emphasizes partisanship, not engagement with difference. Citizen politics does not *replace* representative government; it *enhances* the performance of politicians whose thinking is broad and long range. Recent research indicates that although there are inevitable tensions between strong, independent citizen groups and politicians, both sides can benefit considerably, and the electoral process is enlivened by nonpartisan politics.[22]

Service or Politics?

A variety of diagnoses are offered to explain the political disengagement of young people: the role of money, the unraveling of morality, the rise of individualism, and the pervasiveness of television. *But from a populist*

perspective, the elephant in the room is the widespread sense of powerlessness.
Young people invoke their feelings of powerlessness to explain their preference for service over politics.

The remedy for powerlessness is the experience of power, not service.
Power is built through citizen politics and public work. We have sought
for some years at the Humphrey Institute's Center for Democracy and
Citizenship (CDC) to understand the link.[23]

Thus, for instance, the civic education initiative called Public
Achievement has shown how civic education can help young people learn
skills of empowerment tied to public work. In Public Achievement, teams
of young people—ranging from elementary through high school students—work over the school year on public issues they choose. They are
coached by adults, teachers, college students, community members, and
others, who help them develop achievable goals and learn political skills
and political concepts.

In one school, St. Bernard's, several teams of ten- to thirteen-year-olds
worked for four years to build a playground, overcoming neighborhood
opposition, negotiating with the city, and raising more than $60,000 from
local businesses. In this case, young people had to learn how to interview
people, write letters, give speeches, call people they didn't know on the
phone, negotiate, make alliances, raise money, map power, and do
research. They also learned about power, public life, diverse interests, and
politics itself. Beyond skills, the young people learned to take themselves
seriously in a world that sentimentalizes them. "Citizenship is tackling
problems and taking things into your own hands," said Chou Yang, a
Hmong sixth grader. "It means not just sitting back and watching."[24]

Evaluations find that young people develop many political skills in
such work. Participants in Public Achievement develop a favorable view of
politics from their experiences.[25]

Democratic Professionalism

There is nothing inevitably apolitical about professional practice. Jane
Addams believed the educator's task was to "free the powers" of each person. In today's successful faith-based community organizations, the
clergy's work has changed, expanding beyond pastoral service into tasks

that are far more energizing and politically educating. The CDC and our colleagues translate this precedent into other professions.

For instance, on the West Side of St. Paul, professionals learn citizen politics at the Jane Addams School for Democracy (JAS), a learning and public work partnership with Hmong, Latino, and Somali immigrants and community and educational institutions. At the JAS, immigrants teach college students as well as get help with the citizenship test. Teenagers learn journalism skills that they employ to make visible the stories of young people's public work. JAS also has created a working relationship with the regional Immigration and Naturalization Service (INS), which allows participants to bring their colearner to the test and involves INS staff in a variety of community projects. Throughout the learning community, public leadership training is vital. As Nan Skelton, one of the founders, put it, "Public leadership training [is essential] to help community leaders interact with and influence that world."[26]

If institutional contexts and democratic professions for civic education are emphasized, then there is the potential to develop far more effective and powerful citizens and to reinvigorate the public purposes of schools, colleges, and other educational institutions. In American higher education during the last several years, a large movement with a more political and civic approach has begun to appear, one that explicitly moves beyond traditional service and voluntarism and is tied to higher education's role in the revitalization of democracy. It is reflected in national statements like *The Wingspread Declaration: Renewing the Civic Mission of the American Research University* and *The Presidents' Declaration on the Civic Responsibilities of American Colleges and Universities,* now signed by more than 800 presidents.[27] On the ground, it is manifested in large-scale civic engagement efforts like that at the University of Minnesota, which aim to reinvigorate the public dimensions of every kind of professional work, including teaching and research.[28]

A Different Politics

Through the 1940s, democracy was something the people made. Citizenship as public work lent dynamism and an everyday "politicalness" to American democracy. It accorded honor and authority to those who were "builders of the commonwealth," whatever their birth, and this sense of public creation was generalized to the citizenry as a whole. Moreover, citizens had high regard for the commonwealths they helped to make: laws and litigation, schools and libraries, art fairs and holidays. Productive politics and citizenship created a counterweight to the unbridled market in the political culture. In contrast, today's view of citizens as government's "customers" has disastrous consequences. As Lawrence Sommers quipped, people never wash their rented car.[29]

National initiatives in the tradition of the Work Projects Administration (WPA) or the CCC, through which young people can learn skills and experience citizenship while building the commonwealth, can help renew democracy if such efforts incorporate an understanding of citizen politics. A summons for citizens to engage the larger world through expansion of the Peace Corps and other citizen efforts is also a potent alternative to Bush's expert approach, which seeks to "solve" the world's problems through military intervention. My Republican, southern relatives do not believe that President Bush and his technology will make the world safe. They are waiting for a call to citizenship.

We need to remember Jefferson's dictum: the only safe repository of the powers of the society are the people. To exercise power "with a wholesome discretion" requires that we educate ourselves in the political ways of the world.

38

How People Learn to Be Civic

MICHAEL SCHUDSON

A SENSE OF citizenship is passed on from one generation to the next, not only in formal education or through intentional efforts but indirectly or collaterally in the small details of everyday life. Lecturing in London a few years ago, I illustrated this point with a homely example. I said, "Take, for instance, those moments in your own family where you assert your parental authority and declare to your children, 'Eat your vegetables.'

'No'.

'Eat your vegetables, please.'

'No.'

'Eat your vegetables or there will be no dessert.'

'No.'

'Eat your vegetables or else!'

And one of those little wise guys retorts, 'You can't make me. It's a free country.'"

In the United States, audiences invariably acknowledge this illustration with knowing chuckles or smiles. In London, I looked out at a roomful of blank faces—not a soul cracked a smile. They had politely puzzled expressions. Only then did it dawn on me. Only then did I realize that no British child in all of history has ever said, "You can't make me, it's a free country." And suddenly I knew that democracy is not just one thing you have more or less of; it comes in an assortment of flavors. Democratic

263

citizenship is not just something one is more or less socialized into; there are different citizenships in different democracies, and each of them is renewed in its own subtle fashion.

What I had taken as an invariant expression of children in any democratic society is, in fact, peculiarly American. It is America, not Britain, that conceives of itself self-importantly and extravagantly and naively and tragically and wonderfully as a "free country." America's children pick that up early on.

But how? How is it American kids learn to say that it's a free country and British kids learn not to? How do people acquire their sense of civic life, and how does that sense become second nature? How do we learn the values we are supposed to learn as members of our national culture? I am not asking how to make people better citizens. Instead, I am asking how people learn to be the sort of citizen that society wants them to be. How do they come to know what good citizenship is?

I have no confidence that earnest efforts at teaching U.S. history or turning out the vote or getting more school children to pick up trash on the beach make us good citizens, admirable as these activities may be in their own right. Nor am I convinced that liberal education does the trick either, even though I believe in its values. Political theorist Richard Flathman writes that the greatest contribution liberal education can make to our common political life is to instill a "disposition . . . wary of politics and government."[1] That is not what you normally hear in circles of educators devoted to civics education. But I was reminded of it in the aftermath of September 11. One of the most noteworthy and, to my mind, admirable features of the American response in those first weeks was that many of our leaders, from the president on down, waved the flag proudly but at the same time cautioned citizens about the dangers of flag waving. The only precedent I know for this kind of chastened patriotism in other countries is contemporary Germany, where the Nazi past envelops even the most timid of patriotic demonstrations with a flood of second thoughts.[2] In the United States, I can think of no prior expression of this kind of proud but muted patriotism, a patriotism tempered by its own self-consciousness.

If citizenship is not learned primarily in school or in get-out-the-vote drives, and if college is as likely to induce skepticism about politics as it is

fervent devotion to it, where do people learn their sense of civic obligation? This is a question that civic educators themselves need to think about more clearly, deeply, and historically. What I offer here is a briefly sketched framework for doing so.

A citizen is a person who has full membership in a political community, especially a nation-state. In its common legal usage, citizenship means nationality, and its mark would be a passport, a birth certificate, or other citizenship papers. In its political usage, citizenship refers to rights of political participation, and its chief sign is that a person is eligible to vote. In its sociocultural sense, citizenship refers to emotional identification with a nation and its flag, history, and culture. Finally, citizenship has a broad moral meaning, as in the phrase "good citizen." It may refer to a person loyal to the state, and in this sense it is related to patriotism. Even more, it suggests a person who is informed about and takes an active role in civic affairs. Although all of these meanings of "citizen" have some relevance to my inquiry here, the broad moral meaning of civicness is my primary concern.

"How do people become civic?" is in part the question, "How do we come to understand or accept or take for granted what counts as civic?" That is, how do people develop a particular sense of the public good, a willingness to participate in its advancement, and a view of what repertoire of acts will engender a better public life? How do we come to understand or accept or take for granted what counts as civic in our own culture? Four different areas need our attention.

First, we become civic if and when the civic penetrates into everyday life. Second, we become civic by what we are called to attend to and what we are called to ignore. Third, we become civic by joining with others in common enterprise. Fourth, we become civic when a civic infrastructure allows, encourages, and supports individual civic engagement. I will say something about each of these points.

Everyday Life

First, we become civic when civic activities become a part of everyday life. Think of the recycling bins that, in many communities today, the city or municipality provides so that each household can separate its own recy-clables and get them recycled by putting them out at curbside when the city picks up the weekly trash.

Think of the Pledge of Allegiance that children say in school. More is learned in this act by ritual repetition than by the actual words. I would be skeptical that school children understand the Pledge of Allegiance. Take the word "indivisible," for instance. Children learn to pronounce it years before they study John C. Calhoun and the doctrine of nullification, or the Lincoln-Douglas debates, or the Civil War. But the presence of the term "indivisible" in the Pledge is incomprehensible without knowing it to be a reference to the Civil War. In the end, however, that is less the point than that the school day is connected in some vague but unifying way to flag and country.

Think about what kind of education happens in the widespread "red ribbon week" of drug education in our public schools. I remember when my daughter, then in first grade, came home from Drug-Free School Day and told us happily it was Free Drug Day at school. In a personal mem-oir, essayist Sarah Vowell recalls watching the Mickey Mouse Club on tel-evision and singing along with the theme song—but she never quite got the words of it. When the Mouseketeers sang, "forever let us hold our ban-ner high," Sarah thought they were saying, "for every little polar bear to hide."[3] Much more of education is like that than we would ever want to admit. Still, the ritual of something like saying the Pledge, the activity of it, the collective enterprise of it, leaves a residue.

The activity that enters into ordinary life need not be everyday activ-ity. We learn a great deal from ritual moments that come only on rare occasion—like Christmas once a year or voting every year or two. We do not really know how deeply these activities teach us until we imagine how they might be different. Think about what lessons eighteenth-century Vir-ginians learned when they voted or nineteenth-century Americans, in con-trast to us. An eighteenth-century Virginian, that is to say a white male who owned property, went to the polling place, spoke his vote out loud in front of the sheriff and in front of the candidates, and then went over to the candidate he had favored with his vote and shook hands. The whole activity was one of ritually reaffirming a hierarchical social order in which

each person knew his place. The whole experience reinforced an understanding of citizenship as appropriate deference to community leaders.
There was no campaigning, there were no issues, there were no bombas-
tic speeches. The whole point was to invest responsibility for decision-
making in trusted senior members of the community.[4]

The nineteenth century experience of voting taught different civic lessons. In the nineteenth century, political parties controlled the elections.
On election day, the parties hired tens of thousands of workers to get out
the vote and to stand near the polling place to hand out the "tickets" the
parties had printed. The voter approached the polling place, took a ticket
from one of these "ticket peddlers" from his own party, and went up to the
voting station to deposit his ticket in the ballot box. He did not need to
look at it. He did not need to mark it in any way. Clearly, he did not have
to be literate. He could cast his ballot free of charge, but it would not have
been surprising if he received payment for his effort. In New Jersey, as
many as one-third of the electorate in the 1880s expected payment for
voting on election day, usually in an amount between $1 and $3.[5]

What did a vote express? Not a strong conviction that the party
offered better public policies; parties tended to be more devoted to dis-
tributing offices than to advocating policies. Party was related more to
comradeship than to policy; it was more an attachment than a choice,
something like a contemporary loyalty to a high school or college and its
teams. Voting was not a matter of assent to ideas but a statement of affiliation with people, and the connection of voter to party ticket peddler
underscored that. So did the postelection visit to the party's favorite local
tavern. Drink, dollars, and drama brought people to the polls, and other
than that social connection, voting was rarely anything more elevated.

Reformers at the end of the nineteenth century saw little in the parties to recommend them. The Mugwumps sought to make elections "educational," and the Progressives tried to insulate the independent, rational
citizen from the distorting enthusiasms of party. It is to them that we owe
the ideal of the informed citizen, not to the Founding Fathers. In the
1880s, political campaigns began to shift from parades to pamphlets, and
so put a premium on literacy. In the 1890s, the Australian ballot swept the
nation, and so for the first time in American history, literacy was required

to cast a ballot. The novelty of the Australian ballot was that the state took responsibility for printing ballots that listed the candidates from all parties qualifying for the election. This meant that voters received their ballots from state election officials at the polling place, not from party workers en route to the polling place. It meant that the voter had to make a choice of candidates by marking the ballot; and it normally meant that provision was made for the voter to mark the ballot in secret. With this innovation, voting changed from a social and public duty to a private right, from a social obligation to party enforceable by social pressure to a civic obligation or abstract loyalty, enforceable only by private conscience.

In the early 1900s, nonpartisan municipal elections, presidential primaries, and the initiative and referendum imposed more challenging cognitive tasks on prospective voters than ever before. These changes enshrined "the informed citizenry," incidentally provided a new mechanism and a new rationale for disenfranchising African Americans and immigrants, and inaugurated an enduring tradition of hand-wringing over popular political ignorance.

Between 1880 and 1910, the most basic understandings of American politics were challenged. Reformers attacked the emotional enthusiasm of political participation, the corruption in campaign financing and campaign practices, and the role of the parties in usurping the direct connection between citizens and their government. They succeeded in inventing the language by which we still judge our politics: it stresses being informed while it dismisses or demeans parties and partisanship. To put this more pointedly, the political party, the single most important agency ever invented for mass political participation, is the institution that current civics talk and current civics education regularly abhor and that is rendered almost invisible in the way we conduct the actual act of voting. Insofar as the way we *do* vote is a set of enduring instructions to us about the way we *should* vote and the way we should think about voting, the civic lesson of election day as we have organized it for the past century recommends contempt for parties and partisanship.

We learn a standard of civic practice by practicing civics. We may not live up to it, but we know, at least implicitly and roughly speaking, what it is, what we are supposed to be held accountable for. We learn it in large part by experience—as political theorist Stephen Elkin writes, "Experience . . . must be the teacher of democratic citizens," and this leads him to an interest in the design of local governments, not the design of school curricula.[6] What we do not know or reflect on is that our present standard is only one of a number of possible standards. We learn it so well we do not even recognize what alternatives it excludes.

Structures of Attention

The second way we become civic is by what the public is called to attend to and what it is called to ignore. The media and, even more strenuously, political leaders make the decisions about what will be on the public's agenda. In the weeks after September 11, there were many stories in the media about the stifling of dissent as the country unified behind the president's war on terrorism. Why were we called to attend to this? How did we know, as we read these stories, that stifling dissent is a bad thing? We assuredly were expected to get that point.

Consider an important recent example of citizenship talk: "What you do is as important as anything government does. I ask you to seek a common good beyond your comfort, to defend needed reforms against easy attacks, to serve your nation, beginning with your neighbor. I ask you to be citizens. Citizens, not spectators. Citizens, not subjects. Responsible citizens, building communities of service and a nation of character."[7]

At first blush, it is hard to object to the concept of citizenship George W. Bush expressed in these words in his inaugural address. Citizenship, he said, is public spirited rather than self-centered, neighborly rather than self-seeking, active and participatory rather than passive and spectator-like. And yet, President Bush advanced a subtext here: do not expect too much from your government. "Americans are generous and strong and decent, not because we believe in ourselves but because we hold beliefs beyond ourselves. When this spirit of citizenship is missing, no government program can replace it. When this spirit is present, no wrong can stand against it." Government should not overreach, government should not overlegislate, government should not overreact. The president favors people who take care of themselves and their neighbors, not those who depend on government for aid and comfort.

Note a second subtext: people are citizens insofar as they do not seek their own comfort, insofar as they serve the nation, and insofar as they hold beliefs beyond themselves. True citizens do not ask, to paraphrase a president from a different party, what the country can do for them but what they can do for the country. There is no place in this vision of citizenship for individuals to sue for their rights or to invoke the law on behalf of their liberties or to initiate actions for damages against tobacco companies or tire manufacturers. There is no acknowledgment that democracy has been enlarged in our lifetimes when individuals have been driven not by a desire to serve but by an effort to overcome indignities they themselves have suffered. This is important. The most important extension of citizenship in this century was produced by the civil rights movement. Not Thomas Jefferson so much as people like Thurgood Marshall and Martin Luther King Jr. made rights a household term and a household experience. The civil rights movement brought on the extraordinary wave of social movements and rights-centered litigation that has opened doors and windows for African Americans, women, gays and lesbians, people with disabilities, and many others. Why, then, do we cling rhetorically to a vision of civic education and citizenship that excludes the raw power of self-interested action? Why is citizenship reduced to service rather than linked to justice?

There is also an entirely missing text in President Bush's inaugural address: in the idealized world he beckoned his fellow citizens to join, there are citizens, there are neighbors, there are also communities of faith, but there are no parties, and in the good citizen, no partisanship; there are no interest groups, and in the good citizen, no joining with others in organized self-interest; there are no experts, and in the good citizen, no considered judgment about when and how judgment should be delegated. Why are the organizations and individual actors that in fact are the most involved on a day-to-day basis with the operation of government omitted from his account of citizenship?

In times of national crisis, the citizen President Bush envisions is the soldier, who serves country, ignores personal discomfort, and believes in a patriotic ideal. In ordinary times, Bush's ideal is the Rotarian, moved by a sense of neighborliness, Christian charity, and social responsibility but untouched by any sense of having a personal stake in public justice.

Is this the kind of civicness we should be instilling in our children? I don't think so, but that is not my topic here. I am addressing only the question of how people learn to be civic. My point about the president's speech is that it offers one model of civicness, not the only model. It is a powerful model, nonetheless, because the president is the country's best-placed civic pedagogue. As Justice Felix Frankfurter said, "The Presidency is the most important educational system in the country."[8] The president calls us to attention, but in a particular way, not in the only way.

Shared Enterprise

The third way we become civic is by joining with others in common enterprise, common work, common prayer, or common struggle. I will speak about this only briefly because, in this instance, the same President George W. Bush, whom I have just criticized, has offered a very shrewd analysis. In his press conference a month after September 11, he observed that his administration before September 11 was planning an initiative to be called "Communities of Character." It was, he said, "designed to help parents develop good character in our children and to strengthen the spirit of citizenship and service in our communities." But, he remarked, "the acts of September 11 have prompted that initiative to occur on its own, in ways far greater than I could have ever imagined."[9] He was right. He cited the cases of Christian and Jewish women who went shopping with Muslim neighbors when the Muslim women were afraid to leave their homes alone. There was, indeed, a rekindling of communal feelings, a reaching out to friends, neighbors, and strangers, and a joining in common enterprises of blood drives, fund raising, prayer services, and community memorials all across the country.

People can feel connections with one another and a sense of public purpose at one remove, through the Internet or through a novel, a film, or a news story. I do not know anyone who died at the World Trade Centers, but like almost all Americans, I felt intimately linked to what happened there. That lasted beyond the moment not because citizens feel an intimate acquaintance with Peter Jennings, Tom Brokaw, and Dan Rather (although they may) but because the information and images the media conveyed in this case touched everyone who has ever visited New York or knows someone there, everyone who has ever traveled by air or who has loved ones who travel by air, everyone who has ever been in a high-rise office building. And the horror and anxiety the news evoked in those millions of people were reaffirmed and reinforced in almost every conversation and in almost every glance from person to person, family member to family member, and coworker to coworker in subsequent weeks and months. The experience of September 11 was a national Durkheimian moment, that is, a collective experience where a sense of both power and meaning beyond the personal emerged from face-to-face contact and collective work—collective action embodied, not at a distance.

There is a great deal of attention to that generation, now rapidly aging and dying, that fought World War II, and it has been lionized in the title of Tom Brokaw's book, as "the greatest generation." Brokaw is not modest about his claims for his parents' generation: "I think this is the greatest generation any society has ever produced."[10] I am not going to quibble over rankings here; surely this generation accomplished a great deal. And, as Robert Putnam has assiduously documented, this same generation continued to be doggedly civic by voting in large numbers, attending community meetings, getting to know neighbors, maintaining church membership and attendance, exceeding the marks of the generation before them and the generations that followed them.[11] All of this I acknowledge. What I do not accept is the implication that this generation was unusually endowed with moral virtue or community fervor. What it was endowed with was the Great Depression and World War II, great collective experiences that forged a generational spirit.

This is not to suggest that the experience of World War II was a spontaneous emotional upheaval undirected by government leadership and institutional transformation. On the contrary, the Roosevelt administration mobilized the power of the state in the national defense to—literally—enlist the nation in the war effort. If September 11 seems to be a fading memory already for many Americans, it may be because the federal government chose in the end not to take advantage of the emotional effervescence of the moment to call on Americans for sacrifice or service. An opportunity was lost to enlarge national service programs like AmeriCorps—or even to call attention to them.

Civic Infrastructure

Fourth, we cannot become civic if there is no infrastructure of civicness for people to enroll in. Civic life requires maintenance: it requires staff, investment, access. Democracy does not come cheap. Elections cost money, effective service programs cost money, and courts cost money. Justice requires dollars.[12] This is not very dramatic stuff. In fact, it is invisible to most of us most of the time. I saw some of it, however, in the 2000 election, as I watched the mounting of the electoral machinery in my home of San Diego, California. Let me just give you a little sense of it.

On November 7, in one sixteen-hour period, 100 million people broke from their daily routine and voted. It is a mammoth exercise. In California, there were about 100,000 volunteers spending fifteen-hour days manning the polling places. In San Diego County, running the election cost $3.5 million in taxpayer dollars to produce 552 separate ballots and 552 separate voter information guides mailed out to registered voters to prepare them to act as informed citizens. There were 100 training sessions for 6,000 poll workers at 1,500 polling places, 300 of which had special provision for Spanish-speaking voters and all of which were designed to be accessible for the disabled. This is a massive activity, and a great deal of meaning is still to be found in it, what Walt Whitman called this "ballot-shower from East to West, America's choosing day."

There are 552 different ballots because there are 120 political jurisdictions in San Diego County—hospital districts, water districts, community college districts, school districts, congressional districts, assembly and state senate districts, and so on. There were some 800 candidates on the ballot in November. Mikel Haas, then the registrar of voters, told me, "It's like a watch: there are a whole lot of moving parts. Any one of them can trip you up." The registrar's core staff of forty-eight employees was supplemented in the election season by about 300 temporary workers, not to mention the 6,000 poll workers on election day.

Several weeks before the election, I attended what the registrar's office had entitled "Midnight Madness." On the last day to register to vote in San Diego County, the registrar's office stays open till midnight for "drive-through" registration. I came by around 8 p.m. to take a look. In the dark and the drizzle, cars were lined up for most of a long block and then in a single-file line through half the length of the county building. The whole area, though, was lit by a set of four floodlights, illuminating not only the building and the proceedings outside it but also a newly anchored "Uncle Sam" roughly forty feet high—a vast, cheery, red-white-and-blue inflated Uncle Sam. Registrar of Voters Haas had seen it displayed at a Chevrolet dealer. He had driven by and thought, "I have to have that," and he worked out a rental deal to use the inflatable for Midnight Madness.

There must have been between fifteen and twenty registrar personnel in yellow slickers at Midnight Madness. A number of them were directing traffic. In three lines, three people handed registration affidavits on clipboards to the driver-voters in their cars, SUVs, and pick-ups. The drivers were then directed to park while they filled out the form. When completed, they started up their cars again and another yellow-slickered official would come over to the car, take the affidavit, check it to see that it was filled out properly, and then send the new registrant on his or her way.

One senior civil servant I spoke to began her career with court reporting school, then worked in the district attorney's office, then took the test for the position of registrar of voters senior clerk and assumed the job in 1977 at age 26. In 1980 she left and went to work with one of the vendors who mail the sample ballots. "But I missed it . . . I missed the excitement." "Not many people leave here. No one will quit." It is not just this office—from email with her counterparts in other counties, "it sounds the same way." There is a lot of stress in the job, but people love it. She is married to a political consultant who is as interested in politics as she is. "When our child was born," she told me, "our birth announcement said 'height' and 'weight' and 'eligible to vote in 2007.'"

Despite the high morale of workers at the registrar's office, not everyone loves every part of it. One of the least popular sections is candidate services, dealing with candidates and would-be candidates as they learn how to file their papers, as they write up their statements for the voter information guides that in California are sent out to all registered voters, as they submit required campaign finance disclosure forms. "The candidates . . ." my informant began, and then rolled her eyes. She talked about the people who walk in and say, "Here's where I live. What can I run for?" "Who *are* these people?" she asked. When someone wants to file who has no chance at all, who has never even turned up at a meeting of the body they are running for, the personnel in candidate services try to act on behalf of democracy without entering improperly into the process: "We try to politely, well, not talk them out of it, but explain what's involved."

I attended some training sessions for the poll workers, as well as the training session for the trainers. Registrar staff plus a motivational speaker ran this session. There was a strong emphasis on getting people to participate and have a good time in the training. As one of the trainers said, "Adult learning really can be fun, it doesn't have to be toothpicks-in-the-eyelid time."

The training sessions for the poll workers were centered on a "railroad" theme, and the trainers were equipped with train engineers' hats, red bandannas, a loud train whistle, and a small flashing light that mimicked the lights at a railroad crossing. The trainers I observed—two vigorous women in their sixties—blew their train whistles together to start the session, and then they sang a song they themselves had written: "We've been working on the election all the live long day. We've been working on the election, so the voters have their say." Trained to get people talking and involved from the beginning, they asked people to talk among themselves about why they were volunteering their time. After a few minutes, they blew the train whistles again and asked people to tell the whole group what they had found out. Some people talked about the free tacos poll workers would get from a local fast food chain; many others spoke of wanting to do their civic duty. Many volunteered election after election and spoke of it as a kind of addiction—"Once you do it, you're hooked."

Multiply these stories of one registrar's office in one county of one state by the seventy California counties; multiply it again by the fifty states. Multiply it by the journalists who write about politics, the teachers who teach history and civics, the preschool teachers and kindergarten teachers who instruct children about sharing, the counselors, clergy, clerks of court, and others who are all civics teachers on a full-time basis, and you can see that the possibility of civicness for individuals may have less to do with individual virtue than with social investment and collective maintenance.

Civicness requires both volunteers and professionals, both ordinary citizens and experts. The kind of populism one finds in universities that is distrustful of expertise, to the point of self-hatred; that prefers participatory democracy over representation or delegation, to the point of having nothing at all to say about the latter; and that prefers John Dewey to Walter Lippmann or, more generally, romantics to realists, to a degree that refuses engagement with the actual messiness of democratic politics, lies somewhere between dreaminess and irresponsibility.

In thinking through the matter of civic education, I look more to structures, contexts, and institutions within which and through which education happens than to specific psychological processes that succeed or fail to attach individuals to the messages about civic engagement they hear. There are multiple meanings of citizenship afloat in the land, and practices of civic life have changed more rapidly and more radically than our public rhetoric has yet figured out. Many people still learn to participate in politics through community-based, faith-based experience, as was so often the case with the civil rights movement, but many others today come to politics (as is often the case in the environmentalist movement) through what sociologist Paul Lichterman calls "personalist" motivation.[13] Some opportunities for civic engagement fade—like political party rallies—but others arise without social analysts even noticing: if there is a study of the proliferation of charity runs and charity walks, I have not yet seen it. Or consider the enormous changes in women's lives and the movement toward gender equality in the past fifty years, and how the feminization of political and civic life, if you will, has altered civic practices—and should have altered what counts as citizenship and civic engagement. Along with the civil rights movement and the many other rights-oriented struggles that borrowed from it, feminism has extended norms of equality and indignation over injustice into the home, the club, the workplace, and other domains once far removed from political consciousness.

Citizens learn citizenship in everyday life and especially in participating in common civic exercises; in structures of attention shaped by political leaders, the media, the schools, and other voices of authority; in experiences of community solidarity that forge attachments to people beyond us (it is a familiar observation that soldiers fight not so much for their flag as for their comrades); and in structures and institutions that are cultivated and cared for by full-time staff whose work is required to make citizenship possible. Meanwhile, the realm of the civic shifts and expands as the legitimate demands of once-excluded groups enter into play and reshape the basic understandings of civic life.

Notes

Notes to E. J. Dionne Jr. and Kayla Meltzer Drogosz

1. John Walters, "Clinton's AmeriCorps Values: How the President Misunderstands Citizenship," *Policy Review,* no. 75 (January–February 1996), and Kenneth R. Weinstein and August Stofferahn, "Time to End the Troubled *AmeriCorps,*" Government Integrity Project Report, no. 13 (Washington: Heritage Foundation, May 22, 1997).

2. Quote from the *MacNeil/Lehrer NewsHour,* transcript no. 4745, September 1, 1993. Armey is never shy about his views. He also said famously, and recently, "I do not understand why anybody would embrace AmeriCorps. I consider just the structural framework of AmeriCorps as obnoxious." As reported on CNN, February 6, 2002.

3. Michael J. Sandel, *Democracy's Discontent: America in Search of Public Philosophy* (Harvard University Press, 1996), p. 5.

4. Marc Magee and Steven J. Nider, "Expand National Service, Not Bureaucracy," *Blueprint Magazine,* vol. 17 (August/July 2002).

5. Leslie Lenkowsky, opening plenary remarks for the National Conference of Community Volunteering and National Service, June 9, 2002.

6. Harry C. Boyte and Nancy N. Kari, *Building America: The Democratic Promise of Public Work* (Temple University Press, 1996), p. 16.

Notes to Theda Skocpol

1. Stanley B. Greenberg, "'We'—Not 'Me': Public Opinion and the Return of Government," *The American Prospect*, vol. 12, no. 22 (2001), pp. 25–27.

2. Independent Sector, "A Survey of Charitable Giving after September 11, 2001," October 23, 2001 (www.independentsector.org/PDFs/Sept11_giving.pdf [December 2002]).

3. Andrew Jacobs, "Town Sheds Its Anonymity to Comfort the Bereaved," *New York Times*, October 14, 2001, p. B1.

4. William Risser and Sam Ward, "USA Today Snapshots: Stars and Stripes Flying High," *USA Today*, October 19, 2001, p. A1.

5. Dana Milbank and Richard Morin, "Poll: Americans' Trust in Government Grows," *Washington Post Online*, September 28, 2001 (www.washingtonpost.com/articles/A42864-2001Sep28.html).

6. Richard D. Brown, "The Emergence of Urban Society in Rural Massachusetts, 1760–1820," *Journal of American History*, vol. 61, no. 1 (1974), pp. 29–51.

7. James W. Geary, *We Need Men: The Union Draft in the Civil War* (Northern Illinois University, 1991).

8. For details and references, see Theda Skocpol, *Diminished Democracy: From Membership to Management in American Civic Life* (University of Oklahoma, 2003), chapter 2.

9. Theda Skocpol and others, "Patriotic Partnerships: Why Great Wars Nourished American Civic Voluntarism," in Ira Katznelson and Marin Shefter, eds., *Shaped by War and Trade: International Influences on American Political Development* (Princeton University, 2002), pp. 134–80.

10. See E. J. Dionne Jr., "Our New Spirit of Community," *Boston Globe*, December 26, 2001, p. A19; William A. Galston, "Can Patriotism Be Turned into Civic Engagement?" *Chronicle of Higher Education*, November 16, 2001, p. B16; and Robert Putnam, "Bowling Together: The United State of America," *The American Prospect*, vol. 13, no. 3 (2002), pp. 20–22.

11. Putnam, "Bowling Together," p. 22.

12. Alison Mitchell, "Asking for Volunteers, Government Tries to Determine What They Will Do," *New York Times*, November 10, 2001, p. B7.

13. Albert R. Hunt, "Waiting for the Call," *Wall Street Journal*, May 30, 2002, p. A15.

14. For further evidence and citations, see Skocpol, *Diminished Democracy*, chaps. 1–3.

15. For the full argument, see Skocpol, *Diminished Democracy*, chaps. 4 and 5.

16. See Jeffrey M. Berry, *Lobbying for the People: The Political Behavior of Public Interest Groups* (Princeton University, 1977); and Berry, *The New Liberalism: The Rising Power of Citizen Groups* (Brookings, 1999).

17. Pew Forum on Religion and Public Life and Pew Research Center for the People and the American Press, "Post 9-11 Attitudes: Religion More Prominent; Muslim-Americans More Accepted," December 6, 2001 [(http://people-press.org/reports/display.php3?PageID=5 [December 2002]).

18. Deborah Sontag, "Who Brought Bernadine Healy Down?" *New York Times Magazine*, December 23, 2001, pp. 32–40, 52–55.

19. Winnie Hu, "Outpouring for Sept. 11 Groups Means Less for Food Banks," *New York Times*, November 21, 2001, p. B8.

20. Abraham McLaughlin, "Public Feels Urge to Act—but How?" *Christian Science Monitor*, October 16, 2001, pp. 1 and 11.

Notes to Charles Moskos

1. Institute of Politics, *The Campus Attitudes towards Politics and Public Service (CAPPS) Survey* (Harvard University, 2001).

2. Survey Research Center, *Monitoring the Future: A Continuing Study of American Youth* (Institute for Social Research, University of Michigan, 2000).

3. Obtaining these figures was most difficult. I am indebted to Dr. Charles Johnson, a staff member of the U.S. Commission on National Security/21st Century, for his perseverance in assembling these personnel costs.

4. Department of Defense statistics.

5. Gary Sheftick, "Army Meets Recruiting Goal," *ArmyLINK News* (http://dtic.mil/armylink/news/sep2000/a20000928recruiting.html [March 20, 2001]).

6. Charles Moskos, unpublished survey of UCLA students, Spring 2001.

7. George H. Gallup International Institute, "Survey Finds Support for AmeriCorps Ideals," September 17, 1995.

8. Juri Toomepuu, *Effects of a National Service Program on Army Recruiting* (Fort Sheridan, Ill.: U.S. Army Recruit Command, 1989).

Notes to Harris Wofford

1. Will Marshall, *Citizenship and National Service* (Washington, D.C.: Democratic Leadership Council, 1988).

2. Proposal memorandum from George Romney, submitted to Harris Wofford (CEO, Corporation for National Service) and Robert Goodwin (president and CEO, Points of Light Foundation) in 1995 proposing what would become the Presidents' Summit for America's Future in Philadelphia in 1997.

3. Dan Coates, "Why I Changed My Mind on AmeriCorps," *The Hill*, June 21, 2000.

Notes to John M. Bridgeland, Stephen Goldsmith, and Leslie Lenkowsky

1. Robert D. Putnam, *Bowling Alone: The Collapse and Revival of American Community* (Simon and Schuster, 2000).

2. Richard C. Cornuelle, *Reclaiming the American Dream* (Random House, 1965).

3. Peter Berger and Richard John Neuhaus, *To Empower People: From State to Civil Society* (American Enterprise Institute Press, 1996).

4. See www.usafreedomcorps.gov (December 2002).

Notes to John McCain

1. William F. Buckley Jr., *Gratitude: Reflections on What We Owe to Our Country* (Random House, October 1990).

2. Abt Associates, *AmeriCorps Tutoring Outcomes Study* (Washington, D.C.: Corporation for National and Community Service, February 2001).

3. Aguirre International, *AmeriCorps*State/National Direct Five Year Evaluation Report: A Follow-Up* (Washington, D.C.: Corporation for National and Community Service, September 1999).

4. *Call to Service Act of 2001*, S.1792, sponsored by Sen. Evan Bayh (D-Ind.), was introduced December 10, 2001, to the 107th Congress. This specific portion refers to Sec. 201, "Bonus for Short-Term Enlistment in the Armed Forces."

Notes to Will Marshall and Marc Magee

1. William James, "The Moral Equivalent of War," in *Essays on Faith and Morals* (New York: Longman, Greens, 1943), pp. 311–28.

2. Charles C. Moskos, *A Call to Civic Service: National Service for Country and Community* (New York: Free Press, 1988); Will Marshall, *Citizenship and National Service: A Blueprint for Civic Enterprise* (Washington: Democratic Leadership Council, 1988).

3. Newt Gingrich quoted in Steven Waldman, *The Bill: How Legislation Really Becomes Law: A Case Study of the National Service Bill* (Penguin Books, 1996), p. 249. Dick Armey quoted in Carolyn Barta, "Value of AmeriCorps Debated as Funding Battle Nears," *Dallas Morning News*, July 13, 1997, p. A1. Rick Santorum quoted in Claude R. Marx, "AmeriCorps is 5 Years Old with Many Fans, Critics," Associated Press, October 3, 1999.

4. PR Newswire, "49 Governors Urge Congress to Extend AmeriCorps," September 20, 2000 (www.nationalservice.org/news/pr/92000.html [December 2002]).

5. John M. Bridgeland and others, "New Directions: Service and the Bush Administration's Civic Agenda," *Brookings Review*, vol. 20, no. 4 (2002), p. 19.

6. Juliet Eilperin, "Armey Blasts Bush's AmeriCorps Plan," *Washington Post*, February 6, 2002, p. A17.

7. Marc Magee and Steven Nider, *Citizen Soldiers and the War on Terror*, policy report (Washington: Progressive Policy Institute, December 12, 2002).

8. Barbara Mikulski, "A New Kind of National Service," *Washington Post*, July 17, 1988, C7.

9. George H. W. Bush, "Remarks Announcing the Youth Engaged in Service to America Initiative," June 21, 1989 (http://bushlibrary.tamu.edu/papers/1989/89062100.html [February 2003]).

10. Veterans Administration Information Service, *GI Bill of Rights Anniversary: Fact Sheet for Editors, Broadcasters, Writers*, 1969.

11. Marc Magee and Steven Nider, *Protecting the Homeland through National Service: A Comparative Analysis*, policy report (Washington, D.C.: Progressive Policy Institute, June 2002).

12. Alexander W. Asti and others, "How Service Learning Affects Students" (Higher Education Research Institute, University of California, Los Angeles, January 2000).

Note to Jeff Swartz

1. Marion Wright Edelman, *The Measure of Our Success* (Harper Collins, 1993), pp. 5–6.

Notes to David Winston

1. Winston Group, *State of the Nation Project* (Washington, D.C.: Ripon Society, March 20, 2002). A series of focus groups were held from January 24 through February 7, 2002, in four locations: Seattle, Washington; Lexington, Kentucky; Philadelphia, Pennsylvania; and Northern Virginia. A national survey of 1,200 registered voters conducted February 20–24, 2002, followed the focus groups. The margin of error for the survey is ±2.8 percent.

2. This survey was conducted August 29–30, 2001, by the Winston Group for GOP Conference Chair J.C. Watts's New Models organization. It surveyed 1,000 registered voters and had a margin of error of ±3 percent.

3. *New York Times*–CBS News poll was based on nationwide telephone interviews conducted October 25–28, 2001, with 1,024 respondents.

4. Winston Group, *State of the Nation Project*.

5. David Winston, "2002 Post-Election Democracy Corps Survey and Analysis," November 18, 2002 (www.winstongroup.net [February 2003]).

Notes to Peter D. Hart and Mario A. Brossard

1. Peter D. Hart Research Associates, *Optimistic, Tolerant, and Involved: Young Americans Speak Out on Service, Race Relations, and the Effects of September 11*, survey conducted for Public Allies, April 19–29, 2002 (Washington, June 2002). Of the of 814 randomly selected young Americans, there were 132 African Americans, 121 Hispanics, and 113 Asian Americans.

2. Lake Snell Perry and Associates and the Tarrance Group, *Short Term Impacts, Long Term Opportunities: The Political and Civic Engagement of Young Adults in America*, report for the Center for Information and Research on Civic Learning and Engagement, the Center for Democracy and Citizenship, and the Partnership for Trust in Government at the Council for Excellence in Government (Washington, March 2002). This survey was conducted January 6–17, 2002.

3. Hart, *Optimistic.*

4. Lake Snell Perry, *Short Term Impacts.*

5. Hart, *Optimistic.*

6. Lake Snell Perry, *Short Term Impacts.*

7. Hart, *Optimistic.*

8. Lake Snell Perry, *Short Term Impacts.*

9. This and all subsequent data cited are from the Public Allies survey. See Hart, *Optimistic.*

Notes to Robert E. Litan

1. Julie Rawe, "Young and Jobless," *Time*, June 10, 2002.

2. "A National Service Debate," *Wall Street Journal*, May 29, 1981, p. 24, from Yaakov Kop and Robert E. Litan, *Sticking Together: The Israeli Experiment in Pluralism* (Brookings, 2002) p. 130.

3. Robert D. Putnam, *Bowling Alone: The Collapse and Revival of American Community* (Simon and Schuster, 2000).

4. General Accounting Office, *Americorps*USA Benefit-Cost Study*, no. HEHS-95-255R (September 7, 1995).

5. Ibid. See also George R. Neumann and others, *The Benefits and Cost of National Service: Methods for Benefit Assessment with Application to Three AmeriCorps Programs* (Washington: Kormendi/Gardner Partners, 1995).

Notes to Bruce Chapman

1. Philip Gold, *Against All Terrors: This Nation's Next Defense* (Seattle, Wash.: Discovery Institute, 2002).

2. See AmeriCorps, "Who We Are" (www.americorps.org/whoweare.html [March 2003]).

3. General Accounting Office, *Americorps*USA Benefit-Cost Study*, no. HEHS 95-255R (September 7, 1995); George R. Neumann and others, *The Benefits and Cost of National Service: Methods for Benefit Assessment with Application to Three AmeriCorps Programs* (Washington: Kormendi/Gardner Partners, 1995).

4. Lake Snell Perry and Associates and the Tarrance Group, *Short Term Impacts, Long Term Opportunities: The Political and Civic Engagement of Young Adults in America*, report for the Center for Information and Research in Civic Learning and Engagement, the Center for Democracy and Citizenship, and the Partnership for Trust in Government at the Council for Excellence in Government (Washington, March 2002).

5. Ibid., p. 18.

Notes to Michael Lind

1. William F. Buckley Jr., *Gratitude: Reflections on What We Owe to Our Country* (New York: Random House, 1990). See also Donald Eberly, *National Service: A Promise to Keep* (Rochester, N.Y.: Alden Books, 1988).

2. John Stuart Mill, *Utilitarianism, On Liberty and Considerations on Representative Government* (1863; reprint, London: Everyman Edition, 1972), p. 45.

3. William James, "The Moral Equivalent of War," lecture 11 in *Memories and Studies* (New York: Longman Green, 1911), pp. 267–96.

4. James, "Moral Equivalent."

5. Edward Bellamy, *Looking Backward: 2000–1887* (1888; reprint, with an introduction by Walter James Miller, Signet, 2000).

6. See, generally, M. N. S. Sellers, *The Sacred Fire of Liberty: Republicanism, Liberalism, and the Law* (New York University Press, 1998); Maurizio Viroli, *Republicanism* (New York: Hill and Wang, 1999).

7. Richard Morin, "Split Views on Campus," *Washington Post*, December 1, 2002, p. B5.

Note to Mark Shields

1. Charles Moskos, phone interview by author conducted in preparation for the October 15, 2002, column in the *Washington Post*. See also Moskos's chapter in this book for a fuller exploration.

Note to Caspar W. Weinberger

1. Editorial, "Draft Dodge," *Wall Street Journal*, January 6, 2003, p. A18.

Note to Stephen Hess

1. Brent Scowcroft, ed., *Military Service in the United States* (Englewood Cliffs, N.J.: Prentice Hall, 1982).

Note to Louis Caldera

1. Charles B. Rangel, "Bring Back the Draft," *New York Times,* December 31, 2002.

Notes to Jane Eisner

1. John Bridgeland, remarks made at the City Year Annual Convention, "cyzygy '02: Building Democracy through National Service," Philadelphia, June 7, 2002.

2. Ira Harkavy quoted in Jane Eisner, "First Vote," *Philadelphia Inquirer*, May 30, 2002.

Notes to William Galston

1. Institute of Politics, *The Institute of Politics Survey of Student Attitudes: A National Survey of College Undergraduates* (John F. Kennedy School of Government, Harvard University, October 18–27, 2002), p. 1.

2. Linda J. Sax and others, *The American Freshman: National Norms for Fall 2002* (Higher Education Research Institute, University of California, Los Angeles, 2002).

3. National Center for Education Statistics, *The NAEP 1998 Civics Report Card Highlights*, NCES 2000-460 (Department of Education, Office of Educational Research and Improvement, 1999).

4. Michael X. Delli Carpini and Scott Keeter, *What Americans Know about Politics and Why It Matters* (Yale University Press, 1996), chapter 6; William A. Galston, "Political Knowledge, Political Engagement, and Civic Education," *Annual Review of Political Science,* vol. 4 (2001), pp. 217–34.

5. Lake Snell Perry and Associates and the Tarrance Group, *Short Term Impacts, Long Term Opportunities: The Political and Civic Engagement of Young Adults in America*, report for the Center for Information and Research on Civic Learning and Engagement, the Center for Democracy and Citizenship, and the Partnership for Trust in Government at the Council for Excellence in Government (Washington, D.C.: March 2002).

Notes to Tod Lindberg

1. Stacy Palmer quoted in Mimi Hall, "Gores' Charitable Spending Raises Some Eyebrows," *USA Today*, April 15, 1998, p. 5A.

2. David Cay Johnston, "Clinton Tax Returns Show Book Proceeds Were Given to Charity," *New York Times*, April 14, 1998, p. A16.

3. The attorney general concluded there was no basis for further investigation of Gore.

4. George W. Bush, commencement address at Ohio State University, Columbus, Ohio, June 14, 2002 (www.whitehouse.gov/news/releases/2002/06/20020614-1.html [January 2003]).

5. Ibid.

6. Bill Clinton, "Faith in the USA Flourishes as Citizen Service Grows," *USA Today*, June 20, 2002, p. 23A.

7. Everett Carll Ladd, *The Ladd Report* (Free Press, 1999, p. 148).

Note to Carmen Sirianni

1. Robert Bruininks and others, *Civic Engagement Task Force Report* (Council on Public Engagement, University of Minnesota, May 15, 2002).

Notes to Paul C. Light

1. John F. Kennedy Library and Museum, "Inaugural Address: President John F. Kennedy," January 20, 1961, Washington, D.C. (www.cs.umb.edu/ jfklibrary/j012061.htm [January 2003]).

2. Ronald Reagan, "Remarks at the Annual Meeting of the National Alliance of Business, October 5, 1981," *Public Papers of the Presidents of the United States: Ronald Reagan, 1981,* vol. 1 (Government Printing Office, 1982), p. 883.

3. Ronald Reagan, "Radio Address to the Nation on Voluntarism, May 24, 1986," *Public Papers of the Presidents of the United States: Ronald Reagan, 1986,* vol. 1 (GPO, 1987), p. 670.

4. James C. Kielsmeier, "A Time to Serve, A Time to Learn—Service Learning and the Promise of Democracy," *Phi Delta Kappan,* vol. 81, no. 9 (2000), p. 652.

5. Alexander W. Astin and others, *How Service Learning Affects Students* (Higher Education Research Institute, University of California–Los Angeles, January 2000).

6. Center for Information and Research in Civic Learning and Engagement (CIRCLE), "Short-Term Impacts, Long-Term Opportunities," March 2002 (http://www.pewtrusts.com/pdf/pp_circle_0302.pdf [January 2003]).

7. Princeton Survey Research Associates, *The Do Something, Inc. Young People's Community Involvement Survey* (New York: DoSomething, 1997).

8. Ibid.

9. Princeton Survey Research Associates, *College Seniors and the Caring Service* (Center for Public Service, Brookings, 2002).

10. Leslie Lenkowsky, "Report Belies Group's Ability to Keep Promises," *Chronicle of Philanthropy,* June 17, 1999, p. 51.

Notes to Jean Bethke Elshtain

1. Hannah Arendt, "What Is Authority?" in *Between Past and Future* (New York: Penguin, 1978), p. 95.

2. Alexis de Tocqueville, *Democracy in America,* trans. George Lawrence (New York: Harper Perennial, 1988).

3. Hannah Arendt, *The Origins of Totalitarianism* (Harcourt Brace Jovanovich, 1973), p. 474.

4. John Locke, "A Letter Concerning Toleration," trans. William Popple (www.constitution.org/jl/tolerati.htm [January 2003]).

5. Vaclav Havel, "Politics and Conscience," in Paul Wilson, ed., *Open Letters: Selected Letters 1965–1990* (Knopf, 1991), pp. 256 and 259.

6. Hannah Arendt, "The Crisis in Education," in *Between Past and Future,* p. 185.

7. Vaclav Havel, "The Sad State of the Republic," *New York Review of Books,* March 5, 1998, pp. 45–46.

8. For a helpful, theoretically rich summary of papal teaching, see Michel Schooyans, "Democracy in the Teaching of the Popes," *Miscellanea I, Proceedings of the Workshop on Democracy* (Vatican City: Pontifical Academy for Social Science, 1998).

Notes to Robert Wuthnow

1. Peter Dobkin Hall, *Inventing the Nonprofit Sector: Essays on Philanthropy, Voluntarism, and Nonprofit Organizations* (Johns Hopkins University Press, 1992); Nancy A. Hewitt, *Women's Activism and Social Change: Rochester, New York: 1822–1872* (Cornell University Press, 1984); Pamela M. Jolicoeur and Louis L. Knowles, "Fraternal Associations and Civil Religion: Scottish Rite Freemasonry," *Review of Religious Research*, vol. 20 (Fall 1978), pp. 3–22.

2. Virginia A. Hodgkinson and others, *Giving and Volunteering in the United States, 1994.* Vol. 2*: Trends in Giving and Volunteering by Type of Charity* (Washington, D.C.: Independent Sector, 1995).

3. Sidney Verba, Kay Lehman Schlozman, and Henry E. Brady, *Voice and Equality: Civic Voluntarism in American Politics* (Harvard University Press, 1995).

4. Ibid., p. 80; Andrew M. Greeley, "The Other Civic America: Religion and Social Capital," *American Prospect*, vol. 32 (May-June 1997), pp. 68–73.

5. Robert Wuthnow, *Acts of Compassion: Caring for Others and Helping Ourselves* (Princeton University Press, 1991).

6. Robert Putnam, "Bowling Alone: America's Declining Social Capital," *Journal of Democracy*, vol. 6 (January 1995), pp. 65–78.

7. Robert Wuthnow, *All In Sync: How Music and Art Are Revitalizing American Religion* (University of California Press, 2003).

8. Michael Hout and Andrew M. Greeley, "The Center Doesn't Hold:

Church Attendance in the United States, 1940–1984," *American Sociological Review*, vol. 52 (June 1987), pp. 325–45.

9. Results are from logit regression models in which being or not being a member of any nonreligious voluntary organization is the dependent variable, type of religion is the independent variable (with Catholics as the comparison category), and year and education are control variables. The odds ratio for evangelicals (versus Catholics) is 0.809 and for mainline Protestants, 1.299 (both significant at or beyond the .01 level of probability).

10. The results in this paragraph are from my Economic Values Survey; see Robert Wuthnow, *God and Mammon in America* (Free Press, 1994). Exclusive volunteering at church was operationalized as saying yes to a question asking about having "done volunteer work at your church" in the past year and saying no to a question asking about having "donated time to a volunteer organization." The odds ratio from a logit regression analysis relating this variable to church attendance was 6.459 among evangelical Protestants, 2.550 among mainline Protestants, and 2.357 among Catholics.

11. Among all Protestants, logit regression models for exclusive church volunteering as the dependent variable, church attendance as the independent variable, with evangelical versus mainline controlled, yielded an odds ratio of 4.195 among biblical literalists and 2.826 among nonliteralists.

12. The differences between evangelicals and mainline Protestants should not be exaggerated. Many mainline Protestant congregations are growing, while many evangelical congregations are experiencing stagnation. Some argue that evangelical churches will continue to grow because they offer more distinctive beliefs and require greater commitment. Others say that evangelicalism has adapted better to a commercial, entrepreneurial culture, whereas mainline denominations hark too strongly to the national traditions from which they originated.

13. Verba, Schlozman, and Brady, *Voice and Equality*.

14. Ibid.

15. See Hodgkinson and others, *Giving and Volunteering*.

16. A national survey I conducted in 1989 (Values Survey; see Wuthnow, *Acts of Compassion*) showed that church attendance also motivated certain kinds of individual volunteering. Specifically, with education, age, and gender controlled for, logit regression models show that those who attend church at least several times a month are 1.167 times more likely than those who attend less

often to have visited someone in the hospital in the past year, 1.166 times more likely to have taken care of an elderly relative in their homes, and 1.179 times more likely to have taken care of someone who was very sick. There were no significant relationships, however, between church attendance and loaning money to someone, helping someone through a personal crisis, or giving money to a beggar.

17. Virginia A. Hodgkinson and Murray S. Weitzman, *From Belief to Commitment: The Community Service Activities and Finances of Religious Congregations in the United States. 1993 Edition: Findings from a National Survey* (Washington, D.C.: Independent Sector, 1993).

18. Mark Chaves, *Congregations in America* (Harvard University Press, 2003).

19. These and the following examples are from my Civic Involvement Project; see Robert Wuthnow, *Loose Connections: Joining Together in America's Fragmented Communities* (Harvard University Press, 1998).

20. Two separate national studies of congregations documented these differences, even when factors such as congregational size and composition were taken into account. See Mark Chaves, Helen M. Giesel, and William Tsitsos, "Religious Variations in Public Presence: Evidence from the National Congregations Study," in Robert Wuthnow and John H. Evans, eds., *The Quiet Hand of God: Faith-Based Activism and the Public Role of Mainline Protestantism* (University of California Press, 2002), pp. 108–28, and Nancy T. Ammerman, "Connecting Mainline Protestant Churches with Public Life," in Robert Wuthnow and John H. Evans, eds., *The Quiet Hand of God: Faith-Based Activism and the Public Role of Mainline Protestantism* (University of California Press, 2002), pp. 129–58.

The one study that did not is an interesting exception but probably needs to be weighed less heavily because it was not based on a representative sample and did not include as carefully drawn a denominational classification as the other studies. See Ram A. Cnaan, *The Invisible Caring Hand: American Congregations and the Provision of Welfare* (New York University Press, 2002). The fact that mainline participation is more positively associated with wider community involvement than is evangelical participation does not mean that evangelicals are uninvolved, only that their involvement focuses more on the church itself.

Notes to Steven Waldman

1. John L. Ronsvalle and Sylvia Ronsvalle, *The State of Church Giving* (Champaign, Ill.: Empty Tomb, 2002).

2. Lester Salamon, *Handbook on Nonprofit Institutions in the System of National Accounts* (Johns Hopkins University Press, 2002).

Notes to Kayla Meltzer Drogosz

1. Theda Skocpol, *Diminished Democracy: From Membership to Management in American Civic Life* (University of Oklahoma Press, 2003), p. 256. I am grateful to Theda Skocpol for drawing my attention to the excerpted Tocqueville quote that appears at the beginning of this chapter, a more extended version of which appears in *Diminished Democracy.*

2. Sheldon S. Wolin, *Tocqueville between Two Worlds: The Making of a Political and Theoretical Life* (Princeton University Press, 2001), p. 5.

3. L. J. Hanifan, "The Rural School Community Center," *Annals of the American Academy of Political and Social Science,* vol. 67 (1916), pp. 130–38, quotation at p. 130, as cited in Robert D. Putnam, ed., *Democracies in Flux: The Evolution of Social Capital in Contemporary Society* (Oxford University Press, 2002), p. 4.

4. Saguaro Seminar, *Report of the Saguaro Seminar: Civic Engagement in America* (John F. Kennedy School of Government, Harvard University, 2000). For a thoughtful discussion of the challenges of building a national community, see William A. Schambra, "Is There Life Beyond the Great National Community?" working paper prepared for the Scholars Working Group for the National Commission on Civic Renewal (Hudson Institute, March 8, 1997), p. 22.

5. It was also necessary that democratic theory expanded, opening up to broader perspectives that included social theory as well as the powerful analysis of a handful of sociologists like Robert Bellah, Seymour Martin Lipset, Amitai Etzioni, Michael Schudson, Robert Wuthnow, and others.

6. Benjamin Barber, "Foreword," in Thad Williamson, David Imbroscio, and Gar Alperovitz, *Making a Place for Community: Local Democracy in a Global Era* (New York: Routledge, 2002), p. ix.

7. Iris Marion Young, Stephen Macedo, Nancy Rosenblum, Michael Walzer, William Galston, Seyla Benhabib, Ira Katznelson, and Robert Putnam have all made similar formulations, as have many others.

8. See Roberto Mangabeira Unger, *Democracy Realized: The Progressive Alternative* (London: Verso, 1998); Roberto Mangabeira Unger and Cornel West,

The Future of American Progressivism: An Initiative for Political and Economic Reform (Boston, Mass.: Beacon Press, 1998); Todd Gitlin, *The Twilight of Common Dreams: Why America is Wracked by Culture Wars* (New York: Metropolitan Books, 1995); Sidney Verba, Kay Lehman Schlozman, and Henry Brady, *Voice and Equality: Civic Voluntarism in American Politics* (Harvard University Press, 1995); Carmen Sirianni and Lewis Friedland, *Civic Innovation in America: Community Empowerment, Public Policy, and the Movement for Civic Renewal* (University of California Press, 2001); and Skocpol, *Diminished Democracy*. See also the thoughtful criticism by Jeffrey C. Isaac, *The Poverty of Progressivism: The Future of American Democracy in a Time of Liberal Decline* (Lanham, Md.: Rowman & Littlefield, 2003).

9. Barber, "Foreword," pp. x–xi.

10. Michael Sandel, "Reply to Critics," in Anita L. Allen and Michael C. Regan, eds., *Debating Democracy's Discontent* (Oxford University Press, 1999), p. 335. See also Michael Sandel, *Democracy's Discontent* (Harvard University Press, 1996) and "America's Search for a New Public Philosophy," *Atlantic Monthly*, March 1996, pp. 57–74.

11. Thad Williamson, David Imbroscio, and Gar Alperovitz. *Making a Place for Community: Local Democracy in a Global Era* (New York: Routledge, 2002); Margaret Weir and Marshall Ganz, "Reconnecting People and Politics," in Stanley B. Greenberg and Theda Skocpol, eds., *The New Majority: Toward a Popular Progressive Politics* (Yale University Press, 1997); Bob Edwards, Michael W. Foley, and Mario Diani, *Beyond Tocqueville: Civil Society and the Social Capital Debate* (University Press of New England, 2001).

12. See Robert Nisbet, *The Quest for Community* (Oxford University Press, 1971), p. 54, as quoted in Stephen Goldsmith, *Putting Faith in Neighborhoods: Making Cities Work through Grassroots Citizenship* (Noblesville, Ind.: Hudson Institute Publications, 2002), p. 9.

13. Stephen Goldsmith, *Putting Faith in Neighborhoods*, p. 21–23.

14. Or, as Mark Granovetter puts it, "Weak ties are more likely to link members of different small groups than are strong ones, which tend to be concentrated within particular groups." Mark S. Granovetter, "The Strength of Weak Ties," *American Journal of Sociology*, vol. 78, no. 6 (May 1973), pp. 1360–80; see pp. 1360 and 1376 in particular. See also Granovetter's "The Strength of Weak Ties: A Network Theory Revisited," *Sociological Theory*, vol. 1 (1983), pp. 2001–233; Stephen Macedo, "The Constitution, Civic Virtue, and Civil Society: Social

Capital as Substantive Morality," *Fordham Law Review,* vol. 69 (April 2001, p. 1573); Michael Ignatieff, *The Needs of Strangers* (New York: Picador, 1984); Amitai Etzioni, *Next: The Road to the Good Society* (Basic Books, 2002).

15. Robert D. Putnam, ed., *Democracies in Flux: The Evolution of Social Capital in Contemporary Society* (Oxford University Press, 2002), pp. 393–416; and *Bowling Alone: The Collapse and Revival of American Community* (Simon and Schuster, 2000). Prior to *Bowling Alone,* the Putnam articles that prompted much debate about social capital are "The Strange Disappearance of Civic America," *American Prospect,* vol. 24 (Winter 1996), pp. 34–48, and "Bowling Alone: America's Declining Social Capital," *Journal of Democracy,* vol. 6, no. 1 (1994), pp. 65–78.

16. Sara Mosle, "The Vanity of Volunteerism," *New York Times Magazine,* July 2, 2000, pp. 22–26.

17. Kevin Mattson, *A Century Foundation Report: Engaging Youth: Combating the Apathy of Young Americans toward Politics* (New York: Century Foundation Press, 2003). See also Benjamin R. Barber, *The Truth of Power: Intellectual Affairs in the Clinton White House* (W. W. Norton, 2001), ch. 6; and Steven Waldman, *The Bill: How the Adventures of Clinton's National Service Bill Reveal What is Corrupt, Comic, Cynical—and Noble—about Washington* (Viking, 1995).

18. Waldman, *The Bill,* p. 243.

19. The quote is attributed to the Corporation for National Service general counsel. See Corporation for National Service, *National Service News,* no. 4, June 17, 1996, p.1, as cited in Tobi Walker, "The Service/Politics Split: Rethinking Service to Teach Political Engagement," *PS: Political Science and Politics,* September 2000.

20. One example might be to provide government support to organizations, like the Industrial Areas Foundation (IAF), that provide instruction on how to develop popular leaders and group capacities to work together for a common purpose. Cultivating leadership, teaching kids about the political process, and assisting with voter registration should not be considered a politically partisan activity. In a thoughtful study of the IAF network in Texas, sociologist Mark Warren concludes, "IAF combines authority with participation to create a dynamic form of intervention in democratic politics. . . . Many well-grounded community groups remain weak and isolated in their localities. Most advocacy groups, on the other hand, are top-heavy, lobbying in Washington without an organized base. The IAF has found a way to balance the two sides, placing a relentless concentration on

local organizing while leveraging power at higher levels." Mark R. Warren, *Dry Bones Rattling: Community Building to Revitalize American Democracy* (Princeton University Press, 2001), pp. 35, 253. See also Ernesto Cortes Jr., "Mobilizing Communities to Improve Schools," in E.J. Dionne Jr. and Ming Hsu Chen, eds., *Sacred Places, Civic Purposes: Should Government Help Faith-Based Charity?* (Brookings, 2001), p. 202–04; and Dennis Shirley, *Valley Interfaith and School Reform: Organizing for Power in South Texas* (University of Texas Press, 2002).

21. Walker, "Service/Politics Split."

22. Office of the Press Secretary, *Presidential Message New Years Day, 2003*, released December 31, 2002 (www.whitehouse.gov/news/releases/2002/12/20021231-2.html [March 2003]).

Notes to Harry C. Boyte

1. E.J. Dionne, *Why Americans Hate Politics* (New York: Simon and Schuster, 1991).

2. Originally used November 8, 2001, in his speech to the nation outlining our future course, this phrase has become a stock formulation. Thus, for instance, in his introduction to the *Life Magazine* special issue, "The American Spirit: Meeting the Challenge of September 11" (*Time*, September 2002), President Bush posed the rhetorical question, "What can I do to help in our fight?" and declared, "The answer is simple. All of us can become a September 11 volunteer." For an excellent treatment of the public relations techniques and corporate mindset of the Bush administration, see Frank Rich, "Never Forget What?" *New York Times*, September 14, 2002, p. A15.

3. John Dewey, quoted from Richard Battistoni, *Civic Engagement across the Curriculum* (Providence, R.I.: Campus Compact, 2001), p. 18.

4. Hannah Arendt, *The Human Condition* (Chicago: University of Chicago Press, 1958).

5. Commager quoted from Brian A. Williams, *Thought and Action: John Dewey at the University of Michigan* (Ann Arbor, Mich.: Bentley Historical Library, 1998), p. 1.

6. Jane Addams, quoted in Lewis S. Feuer, "Dewey and Back-to-the-People Movement," *Journal of the History of Ideas*, vol. 20 (1959), p. 546.

7. This portrait is drawn from George Dykhuizen, "John Dewey: The Vermont Years," *Journal of the History of Ideas*, vol. 20 (1959), pp. 515–44.

8. On populism, see for instance, Lawrence Goodwyn, *The Populist Moment: A Short History of the Agrarian Revolt in America* (Oxford University Press, 1978), and Lary May, *The Big Tomorrow: Hollywood and the Politics of the American Way* (University of Chicago Press, 2000). These arguments are also developed in Harry Boyte, *Community Is Possible: Repairing America's Roots* (Harper and Row, 1984); *Commonwealth: Return to Citizen Politics* (Free Press, 1989); and with Nan Kari, *Building America: The Democratic Promise of Public Work* (Temple University Press, 1996).

Fredrick Harris and a new group of young black historians have described the more complex and political relationship of blacks to America's civic traditions. As Harris put it, "Black mainstream institutions—churches, social clubs, Masonic orders, community organizations, schools—have traditionally nurtured norms that both legitimized the civic order and subtly and at times overtly served as sources of opposition to white supremacist practice and discourse." See Fredrick Harris, *Will the Circle Be Unbroken? The Erosion and Transformation of African American Civic Life,* report prepared for the National Commission on Civic Renewal (College Park, Md.: Institute for Philosophy and Public Policy, 1999), p. 21. See also the web page on black populism, at http://kalamumagazine.com/black_populism_intro.htm (January 2003).

9. These accounts are from Feuer, "Dewey," pp. 550–53.

10. John McDermott, ed., *The Philosophy of John Dewey* (University of Chicago Press, 1981), pp. 351.

11. Jane Addams, *Democracy and Social Ethics* (New York: Macmillan, 1902), p. 270.

12. Ibid., p. 256.

13. John Dewey, "School as Social Centre," *Elementary School Teacher,* vol. 3 (1902), p. 86.

14. The Humphrey drug store is a window into a kind of vitality of everyday politics that has since substantially eroded. He continues: "In Doland, Dad was a Democrat among friends and neighbors who took their Republicanism—along with their religion—very seriously. . . . A druggist in a tiny town in the middle of the continent, American history and world affairs were as real to him as they were in Washington, D.C. . . . He subscribed to the *Christian Science Monitor,* the New

York *Herald Tribune,* the *Minneapolis Journal,* the St. Paul *Dispatch,* and the Watertown *Public Opinion.* Time after time, when he read about some political development . . . he'd say, 'You should know this, Hubert. It might affect your life someday. . . . My political training began in Doland. When most of the town wanted to sell the municipally owned power plant to a private utility, Dad was against it . . . he fought the idea tooth and nail. I was twelve years old, and he would take me to the evening meetings of the council, install me in a chair by a corner window, and then do battle, hour after hour." Hubert H. Humphrey, *The Education of a Public Man: My Life and Politics* (University of Minnesota Press, 1991), pp. 8–10.

15. For detailed discussion, see Boyte and Kari, *Building America.* Figures on CCC work, p.107. The observer quote is from C. H. Blanchard, "I Talk with My CCC Boys," *Phi Delta Kappan* (Special Edition on Education in the CCC Camps), vol. 19, no. 9 (1937), p. 354 (personal communication from Melissa Bass, Brandeis University, December 4, 2002).

16. Alan Ehrenhalt, *The United States of Ambition* (Times Books, 1991); Knobe quote, p. 73.

17. For communitarian perspectives, see Amitai Etzioni, *The Spirit of Community: Rights, Responsibilities, and the Communitarian Agenda* (Crown Publishers, 1993). A rich liberal tradition has challenged various exclusions and inequalities. For instance, in his new work (*Civic Ideals* [Yale University Press, 2001], p.30), Rogers M. Smith calls for an unromantic liberalism attentive to the political saliency and appeal of particularist identities that have justified such exclusions: "We need an . . . account that gives full weight to America's pervasive ideologies of ascriptive inequality." Yet Smith sees politics as simply revolving around the state and as a quintessentially distributive struggle. As he puts it, "Political decision-making is in reality almost always more a matter of elite bargaining than popular deliberation" (p. 36). In practice, such concepts shape the techniques of today's mass policy issue mobilizations, such as the door-to-door issue canvass, Internet lobbying efforts, and direct mail. In a context of an expanding number of competitive claims to rights and victim status, they often lend a Manichean, inflamed quality to political discourse.

For communitarians, "social capital" furnishes the context for democracy to work. Robert Putnam defines social capital as "networks, norms, and trust . . . that enable participants to act together more effectively to pursue shared objectives"

(*Bowling Alone* [Simon and Schuster, 2000], p. 19). It is generated through participation in groups such as religious congregations, voluntary associations, fraternal and professional groups, and service and recreational organizations. Democracy's woes, in this account, stem from eroding social integration. Yet for all the differences, communitarians, like liberals, see citizens as largely removed from politics and power. For instance, in an important recent article, Cynthia Estlund argued for attention to the workplace as a key arena for the integration of diverse racial, cultural, and ideological groups neglected in conventional civic theory ("Working Together: The Workplace, Civil Society, and the Law," *Georgetown Law Journal*, vol. 89, no. 1 [2000], pp. 1–96). Yet Estlund saw little likelihood that workplaces might become sites of democratic power. The workplace, for Estlund, is *apolitical*. "Other than by voting, the ordinary citizen rarely attempts to influence the political process," she argues. "She may write an occasional letter to the editor or participate in a political demonstration, or she may join—that is, in most cases, write a check to—an advocacy organization. But . . . as a descriptive matter, ordinary citizens are largely left out of the [political] picture" (p. 53). In correspondence, Estlund emphasized to me that in her essay she meant "politics" in its conventional meanings and agrees with the idea of "public work politics."

For more on this argument about the similarities of liberal and communitarian views of politics, see Harry C. Boyte, "Off the Playground of Civil Society," Symposium on Commonwealth, Civil Society, and Democratic Renewal, *A PEGS Journal: The Good Society*, vol. 9, no. 2, 1999; "Reconstructing Democracy: The Citizen Politics of Public Work," visiting scholars lecture, the Havens Center, University of Wisconsin-Madison, April 11, 2001 (www.ssc.wisc.edu/havens center/boyte.doc [January 2003]); and "A Different Kind of Politics," Dewey lecture, University of Michigan, November 1, 2002 (www.cpn.org/crm/contemporary/ different.html [January 2003]).

Campus Compact, the national organization of college and university presidents originally formed to advocate for community service and, subsequently, service learning, has in the last several years begun to advocate for a far more political, public-work oriented, and civic approach. See, for instance, Harry Boyte and Elizabeth Hollander, *The Wingspread Declaration: Renewing the Civic Mission of the American Research University* (Providence, R.I.: Campus Compact, 1999), and Tom Ehrlich and Elizabeth Hollander, *The Presidents' Declaration on the Civic*

Responsibilities of American Colleges and Universities (Providence, R.I.: Campus Compact, 1999).

18. For a brief etymology, see *New World Dictionary of the American Language* (New York: William Collins, 1972).

19. See Michael S. Schudson, "How People Learn to be Civic," B. Aubrey Fisher Memorial Lecture (University of Utah, October 18, 2001), p. 6. Theda Skocpol, Marshall Ganz, and Ziad Munson make a similar critique of recent communitarian writings in "A Nation of Organizers: The Institutional Origins of Civic Voluntarism in the United States," *APSR*, vol. 94, no. 3 (2000), pp. 527–46.

20. In his history of the word, Giovanni Sartori ("What is Politics," *Political Theory*, vol. 1, no. 1 [1973], pp. 1–36) details the horizontal relationships of equal citizens at the heart of the language of politics and associated ideas. Not until the nineteenth century did "politics" acquire its associations of "verticality" or relations to the state. For related arguments about politics, see also Sheldon S. Wolin, *The Presence of the Past: Essays on the State and the Constitution* (Johns Hopkins Press, 1989); Mary Dietz, *Turning Operations: Feminism, Arendt, and Politics* (New York: Routledge, 2002); David Mathews, *Politics for People* (University of Illinois, 1999); and Boyte, "A Different Kind of Politics."

21. Bernard Crick, *In Defense of Politics* (London and New York: Continuum, 1962), p. 15. Drawing on Aristotle, Crick stresses the irreducible *plurality* of politics as negotiation of diverse and particular interests. As Aristotle had put it in his second book of *Politics:* "The nature of the *polis* is to be a plurality. A *polis* is not made up only of so many men but of different kinds of men; for similars do not constitute a *polis*. It is not like a military alliance." See Stephen Everson, ed., *Aristotle: The Politics and the Constitution of Athens* (Cambridge University Press, 1996), p. 31. See also Arlene Saxonhouse's treatment of Aristotle in *Fear of Diversity: The Birth of Political Science in Ancient Greek Thought* (University of Chicago Press, 1992). Saxonhouse has an excellent contrast of Aristotle with Plato.

22. See for instance Carmen Sirianni and Lewis Friedland, *Civic Innovation in America* (Berkeley: University of California Press, 2001); and Richard L. Wood, *Faith in Action: Religion, Race, and Democratic Organizing in America* (University of Chicago Press, 2002).

23. See www.publicwork.org.

24. Yang quoted in Harry Boyte, "Civic Education as a Craft, Not a Program," in Sheilah Mann and John Patrick, eds., *Education for Civic Engagement in Democracy* (Bloomington, Ind.: ERIC Clearinghouse, 2000), p. 61.

25. For descriptions of Public Achievement, see Robert Hildreth, "Theorizing Citizenship and Evaluating Public Achievement," *PS: Political Science and Politics*, vol. 33, no. 3 (2000), pp. 627–34; and Boyte, "Civic Education as a Craft," pp. 61–72. For views on politics from participants, see the Mankato Public Achievement website (http://krypton.mankato.msus.edu/%7Ejak3/pa/welcome.html [January 2003]).

26. Nan Skelton quoted in "Creating a Culture of Learning: The West Side Neighborhood Learning Community," *University of Minnesota Research Review*, vol. 31, Winter/Spring (2002), p. 7. See also Harry Boyte and others, *Creating the Commonwealth* (Dayton, Ohio: Kettering Foundation, 2000); and "Program Spotlight," *FINE Forum e-Newsletter*, no. 5 (Fall), 2002 (www.gse.harvard.edu/hfrp/projects/fine/fineforum/forum5/spotlight.html [January 2003]). The CDC's public work approach is also one of the main resources for the large-scale civic engagement effort of the University of Minnesota, which explicitly builds on strengthening the public dimensions of the research and the teaching of faculty, disciplines, and colleges, as well as the University of Minnesota as a whole (see www.umn.edu/civic [January 2003]). For more detailed discussion of how the CDC political, public work approach has informed, in part, the university's civic engagement efforts through emphasis on building a broad alliance and tapping the diverse self-interests of faculty, disciplines, departments, and colleges, see Harry Boyte, "The Politics of Civic Engagement," *Academic Workplace*, New England Resource Center for Higher Education (www.nerche.org/index.html [February 2003]). For examples of more political, public work professional practice, see "Intellectual Workbench," Center for Democracy and Citizenship (www.publicwork.org/2_4_cmp.html#int [January 2003]). See also the Putting Families First website for the family-based movements that are emerging from CDC's partnerships (www.familylife1st.org [January 2003]).

27. See Boyte and Hollander, *Wingspread Declaration*, and Ehrlich and Hollander, *The Presidents' Declaration*.

28. For examples, see www.compact.org and www.umn.edu/civic.

29. Sommers quote paraphrased from Thomas Friedman, "There Is Hope," *New York Times*, October 27, 2002, Week in Review, p. 13.

Notes to Michael Schudson

1. Richard Flathman, "Liberal versus Civic, Republican, Democratic, and Other Vocational Educations," *Political Theory,* vol. 24 (February 1996) pp. 4–32 at 26.

2. See, for instance, Frederick Kempe, *Father/Land: A Personal Search for the New Germany* (Putnam, 1999) p. 148.

3. Sarah Vowell, *Take the Cannoli: Stories from the New World* (Simon and Schuster, 2000).

4. On this point and the subsequent paragraphs on American political history, I draw directly on my book *The Good Citizen: A History of American Civic Life* (New York: Free Press, 1998).

5. John F. Reynolds, *Testing Democracy: Electoral Behavior and Progressive Reform in New Jersey, 1880–1910* (University of North Carolina Press, 1988) p. 54. See also Schudson, *The Good Citizen,* pp. 144–187.

6. Stephen Elkin, "Citizen Competence and the Design of Democratic Institutions" in Stephen L. Elkin and Karol Edward Soltan, eds., *Citizen Competence and Democratic Institutions* (Pennsylvania State University Press, 1999) p. 394.

7. George W. Bush, inaugural address, January 2001 (www.whitehouse.gov/news/inaugural-address.html [January 2003]).

8. Cited in Douglas Cater, *The Fourth Branch of Government* (Boston: Houghton Mifflin, 1959) p. 169.

9. George W. Bush, prime time news conference, October 11, 2002 (www.whitehouse.gov/news/releases/2001/10/20011011-7.html#Sacrifices-by-Americans [January 2003]).

10. Tom Brokaw, *The Greatest Generation* (Random House, 1998) p. xxx.

11. Robert D. Putnam, *Bowling Alone* (Simon and Schuster, 2000).

12. See Stephen Holmes and Cass Sunstein, *The Cost of Rights: Why Liberty Depends on Taxes* (W. W. Norton, 1999).

13. Paul Lichterman, *The Search for Political Community* (Cambridge University Press, 1996).

Contributors

Daniel S. Blumenthal is professor and chair of the Department of Community Health and Preventive Medicine, as well as associate dean for community programs at Morehouse School of Medicine. Blumenthal has served with the Medical Committee for Human Rights, the Centers for Disease Control and Prevention in Atlanta, and the World Health Organization. He has been associated with the Emory University School of Medicine, and in 1969 he served as a VISTA (Volunteers in Service to America) volunteer in Lee County, Arkansas.

Harry C. Boyte is both senior fellow and codirector of the Center for Democracy and Citizenship in the Humphrey Institute at the University of Minnesota. Boyte was national coordinator for the New Citizenship, a bipartisan effort to bridge the citizen-government gap. He served as senior adviser to the National Commission for Civic Renewal, headed by former senator Sam Nunn and former education secretary William Bennett. In the 1960s, Boyte worked for Martin Luther King Jr. and the Southern Christian Leadership Conference. He has written seven books on community organizing, citizen action, and citizenship.

John M. Bridgeland serves as assistant to the president and director of the USA Freedom Corps. Most recently, Bridgeland served as the director of the Domestic Policy Council at the White House. He was also deputy policy director for the Bush-Cheney 2000 presidential campaign. Previously, Bridgeland served as chief of staff to Representative Rob Portman and founded Civic Solutions, a company working with nonprofits, foundations, faith-based institutions, and corporations on public policy issues.

Mario A. Brossard is a senior analyst at Peter D. Hart Research Associates. Brossard was formerly with the *Washington Post* as a writer and assistant director of polling. He also served as vice president and managing director of Knowledge Networks' political practice in Washington, D.C. His work has been published in *Why People Don't Trust Government*, edited by Joseph Nye, Philip D. Zelikow, and David C. King.

Louis Caldera is a former secretary of the army, chief operating officer of the Corporation for National and Community Service, and California assemblyman. He is currently the vice chancellor for university advancement for the California State University system. A graduate of West Point, Caldera became the seventeenth secretary of the army on July 2, 1998, after nomination to that post by President Clinton and confirmation by the U.S. Senate. In 2002 he was honored by the Congressional Hispanic Caucus Institute for his work developing leadership among Hispanic students.

Bruce Chapman is president and founder of the Discovery Institute. A former director of the Census Bureau (1981–83), Chapman also served as deputy assistant to President Ronald Reagan from 1983 to 1985 and simultaneously held the position of director of the White House Office of Planning and Evaluation. He was a fellow at the Hudson Institute for two years and has served on the Seattle City Council and as secretary of state for Washington State. In 1966 Chapman wrote *The Wrong Man in Uniform*, one of the earliest calls for a volunteer military, and he has also written, with George Gilder, *The Party That Lost Its Head*.

William Jefferson Clinton was the forty-second president of the United States, serving from 1993 to 2001. President Clinton played an integral role in the movement toward national service and signed the National and Community Service Trust Act of 1993, creating AmeriCorps and the Corporation for National and Community Service to expand opportunities for Americans to serve their communities. Prior to his presidency, Clinton served as both Arkansas attorney general and governor. Together with City Year, a division of AmeriCorps, he created the Clinton Democracy Fellowship to enable emerging leaders from South Africa to collaborate on citizen service ideas and policies through intensive study of American national service opportunities. Clinton's memoirs will be published in the fall of 2003.

Charles Cobb Jr. is senior writer and diplomatic correspondent for allAfrica.com and was a former Mississippi field secretary for the Student Nonviolent Coordinating Committee. His published work includes *Radical Equations—Civil Rights from Mississippi to the Algebra Project*, written with Robert P. Moses. Cobb previously worked for the U.S. House of Representatives Subcommittee on Africa and spent eleven years as a writer for *National Geographic*.

E.J. Dionne Jr. is a senior fellow at the Brookings Institution, where he focuses on American politics, civil society, and faith and public life. He is a syndicated columnist with the *Washington Post* Writers Group and cochair, with Jean Bethke Elshtain, of the Pew Forum on Religion and Public Life. He is also an editor of the upcoming *Pew Forum Dialogues on Religion and Public Life*. Dionne is the author of *Why Americans Hate Politics* and *They Only Look Dead*. He is editor or coeditor of several Brookings volumes: *Community Works: The Revival of Civil Society in America; What's God Got to Do with the American Experiment?* with John DiIulio; *Bush v. Gore* with William Kristol; and *Sacred Places, Civic Purposes: Should Government Help Faith-Based Charity?* with Ming Hsu Chen. He is a regular commentator on politics for national television and National Public Radio.

Kayla Meltzer Drogosz is a senior research analyst for the religion and civil society project at the Brookings Institution, where her research interests include ethics, political philosophy, civil society, and the public purposes of religion. Drogosz is the series coordinator for the *Pew Forum Dialogues on Religion and Public Life*, a project supported by a grant from the Pew Charitable Trusts. She received her degree from New College, Oxford University, continued her graduate studies in religion at Hebrew University, and received an MPA from the Maxwell School of Citizenship and Public Affairs at Syracuse University. Previously she served as public affairs associate with the policy offices of United Jewish Communities, and she has worked in the political section of the U.S. Mission to the United Nations. Her articles have also appeared in the *Brookings Review*.

Jane Eisner is currently a columnist for the *Philadelphia Inquirer*, having served that paper for two decades as a reporter, city hall bureau chief, foreign correspondent, and in many editing positions. During her tenure as editor of the editorial page, from 1994 to 1999, the editorial board initiated such features as Young Voices, Community Voices, and the award-winning Citizen Voices projects. Her column, "American Rhythms," is syndicated nationally.

Jean Bethke Elshtain is the Laura Spelman Rockefeller Professor of Social and Political Ethics at the University of Chicago. She is a member of the National Commission for Civic Renewal and currently serves as chair of both the Council on Families in America and the Council on Civil Society, as well as cochair, with E.J. Dionne Jr., of the Pew Forum on Religion and Public Life. Elshtain is the author of several books, including *The Jane Addams Reader* and *Jane Addams and the Dream of American Democracy; Who Are We? Critical Reflections and Hopeful Possibilities; Augustine and the Limits of Politics; Democracy on Trial;* and *Public Man, Private Woman: Women in Social and Political Thought.*

William Galston is the Saul I. Stern Professor of Civic Engagement and director of the Institute for Philosophy and Public Policy at the University of Maryland. He serves as director for the Center for Information and Research on Civic Learning and Engagement (CIRCLE), which conducts and funds research on the political and civic involvement of young people. Galston was deputy assistant to the president for domestic policy during the first Clinton administration and was executive director of the National Commission on Civic Renewal. He served as chief speechwriter for John Anderson's National Unity campaign, as issues director for Walter Mondale's presidential campaign, and as senior adviser to Albert Gore Jr. He has written several books, most recently, *Liberal Pluralism: The Implications of Value Pluralism for Political Theory and Practice*.

Stephen Goldsmith is the chairman of the Corporation for National and Community Service and serves as special adviser to President George W. Bush on faith-based and not-for-profit initiatives. He served as mayor of Indianapolis from 1992 until 1999. In addition to his roles as chair of the Center for Civic Innovation and senior fellow at the Manhattan Institute, Goldsmith is a professor of the practice of public management and faculty director of the Innovations in American Government Program at Harvard University's Kennedy School of Government. He also served as domestic policy adviser to Governor George W. Bush's presidential campaign and has published several books, most recently, *Putting Faith in Neighborhoods: Making Cities Work through Grassroots Citizenship*.

Robert D. Haas is the chairman of Levi Strauss. He served in the Peace Corps in the Ivory Coast from 1964 to 1966 and was a White House fellow from 1968 to 1969. Haas is a member of the North American Executive Committee of the Trilateral Commission, the Conference Board, the Council on Foreign Relations, and the California Business Roundtable. He also serves on the advisory board of governors of the Partnership for Public Service. Haas is president of the Levi Strauss Foundation and honorary director of the San Francisco AIDS Foundation.

Peter D. Hart founded and directs Peter D. Hart Research Associates and appears frequently on *Meet the Press,* the *Today Show,* and the *NewsHour with Jim Lehrer.* In 1989, along with Robert Teeter, Hart was selected by NBC News and the *Wall Street Journal* to conduct all public opinion polling for these institutions. He is a Woodrow Wilson visiting fellow and a visiting professor at the Sanford Institute of Public Policy at Duke University.

Stephen Hess is a senior fellow in the Governance Studies program at the Brookings Institution. Previously, he served as consultant to the president on executive office reorganization (1977); U.S. representative to the UN General Assembly (1976); editor in chief of the Republican Party Platform (1976); chairman of the White House Committee on Children and Youth (1970–71); presidential adviser on urban affairs (1969); and presidential speechwriter (1959–61). In 1957–58 he served in the Third Armored Division of the army, rising to the rank of private first class. Hess is the author or editor of more than fifteen books, most recently, *The Media and the War on Terrorism,* coedited with Marvin Kalb.

Alan Khazei is cofounder and chief executive officer of City Year, an "action tank" for national service that enlists hundreds of young adults from all backgrounds for one year of full-time community service and leadership development. Previously, Khazei served as field coordinator in the New Hampshire and national offices for Senator Gary Hart's presidential campaign. He is a member of the board of directors for the Commission on National and Community Service, and until 1993 he was vice chair of that commission.

John Lehman is currently a member of the 9/11 Commission and has served twenty-five years as a naval aviator in the Selected Reserve. He served as secretary of the navy from 1981 to 1987, under President Reagan. Prior to this he served as special counsel and senior staff member to Henry Kissinger on the National Security Council and was a delegate to the Mutual Balanced Force Reduction Negotiations in Vienna. He became deputy director of the U.S. Arms Control and Disarmament Agency in 1975 and was its chief operating officer until 1977. Lehman has written numerous books, including *Command of the Seas, Making War,* and *On Seas of Glory.*

Leslie Lenkowsky is chief executive officer of the Corporation for National and Community Service, the federal agency that oversees the Senior Corps, AmeriCorps, and Learn and Serve America programs. Appointed to that post by President George W. Bush in October 2001,

Lenkowsky had been a member of the corporation's board of directors since it was created in 1993. Before joining the Bush administration, Lenkowsky was professor of philanthropic studies and public policy at Indiana University/Purdue University at Indianapolis. He also served as president of the Hudson Institute. Lenkowsky has served as president of the Institute for Educational Affairs and deputy director of the United States Information Agency.

Paul C. Light is Douglas Dillon Senior Fellow at the Brookings Institution. He is the Paulette Goddard Professor of Public Service at New York University, the founding director of the Brookings Center for Public Service, and senior adviser to the National Commission on the Public Service, as well as the senior adviser to the Brookings Presidential Appointee Initiative. Previous positions include director of Governmental Studies at Brookings, director of the Public Policy Program for the Pew Charitable Trusts, senior adviser to the National Commission on the State and Local Public Service, senior adviser to the National Commission on the Public Service, and senior staff member of the Senate Governmental Affairs Committee. He is the author of numerous books on public service and management, most recently, *Government's Greatest Achievements: From Civil Rights to Homeland Security* and *Pathways to Nonprofit Excellence*.

Michael Lind is the Whitehead senior fellow at the New America Foundation. Lind has been editor or staff writer for the *New Yorker, Harper's Magazine,* and the *National Interest.* His articles have appeared in the *New York Times Magazine, Atlantic Monthly,* the *Washington Post,* and the *Los Angeles Times.* He has also appeared on CNN's *Crossfire,* C-SPAN, National Public Radio, and the *NewsHour with Jim Lehrer.* His books on political journalism and history include *The Next American Nation, Up from Conservatism,* and *Vietnam.* Lind's most recent books are *The Radical Center,* coauthored with Ted Halstead; and *Made in Texas: George W. Bush and the Southern Takeover of American Politics.*

Tod Lindberg is editor of *Policy Review* and a research fellow at the Hoover Institution at Stanford University. He writes a weekly column about politics for the *Washington Times* and has served as editor of its editorial page. Lindberg is also a contributing editor to the *Weekly Standard* and has been executive editor of the *National Interest* and managing editor of the *Public Interest*. In 1978 he was elected to a three-year term on a local board of education in suburban Chicago. He is currently a member of the board of visitors of the Institute on Political Journalism at Georgetown University.

Robert Litan is vice president and director of the Economic Studies program at the Brookings Institution, where he also holds the Cabot Family Chair in Economics. Previously, he was associate director of the Office of Management and Budget (1995–96); deputy assistant attorney general in the Antitrust Division, U.S. Department of Justice (1993–95); staff member of the President's Council of Economic Advisers (1977–79); member of the Presidential-Congressional Commission on the Causes of the Savings and Loan Crisis; and consultant to the Treasury Department. His most recent books include *Financial Sector Governance: The Roles of the Public and Private Sectors* and, with Yaakov Kop, *Sticking Together: The Israeli Experiment in Pluralism.*

Mark Magee is the creator and director of the Center for Civic Enterprise at the Progressive Policy Institute (PPI) in Washington, D.C. Magee served as fellow for citizenship and national service at PPI, producing policy reports on the efforts to expand national service and the connection between service and homeland security. He has also composed several reports on various methods of increasing citizen participation in both civilian and military service.

Will Marshall is president and a founder of the Progressive Policy Institute and served as policy director of the Democratic Leadership Council from the organization's inception in 1985. Marshall is coeditor of *Mandate for Change* and director of the Progressive Foundation. He has participated in the drafting of several pieces of national legislation, including a demonstration project for voluntary national service passed as part of the National and Community Service Act of 1990. His previous campaign and political experiences include serving as press secretary, spokesman, and speechwriter for the 1984 U.S. Senate campaign of former governor Jim Hunt; speechwriter and policy analyst for the late U.S. Representative Gillis Long; and spokesman and speechwriter for the 1982 U.S. Senate campaign of Dick Davis, a former lieutenant governor of Virginia.

John McCain was elected to the U.S. Senate in 1985 and has been involved in the national service debate, introducing the Call to Service Act of 2001 with Senator Evan Bayh. McCain is chairman of the Senate Committee on Commerce, Science, and Transportation. He was first elected to represent the state of Arizona in the U.S. House of Representatives in 1982, after a twenty-two-year career as a naval aviator. He recently wrote *Worth the Fighting For: A Memoir,* with Mark Salter.

Charles Moskos is professor of sociology at Northwestern University and chairman of the Inter-University Seminar on Armed Forces and Society. He is the architect of the National Service and Citizenship Act of 1989, developed by the Democratic Leadership Council. He has been a fellow at the Woodrow Wilson International Center for Scholars, a Rockefeller Humanities fellow, and a Guggenheim fellow. He holds the Distinguished Service Medal, the U.S. Army's highest decoration for a civilian. His books include *A Call to Civic Service, The New Conscientious Objection, All That We Can Be: Black Leadership and Racial Integration the Army Way* (with John Butler), and the *Postmodern Military.*

Robert Putnam is the Peter and Isabel Malkin Professor of Public Policy at Harvard University. He teaches undergraduate and graduate courses in American politics, international relations, comparative politics, and public policy. He is the founder of the Saguaro Seminar: Civic Engagement in America, a program that brings together leading practitioners and thinkers for a multiyear discussion to develop broad, actionable ideas to fortify the nation's civic connectedness. Putnam has authored or edited ten books and more than thirty scholarly works, including *Bowling Alone: The Collapse and Revival of American Community* and *Democracies in Flux: The Evolution of Social Capital in Contemporary Society.*

Charles B. Rangel is serving his seventeenth term as U.S. representative from New York. He served in the U.S. Army in Korea, 1948–52, and was awarded the Purple Heart and the Bronze Star. He is currently the ranking member of the House Committee on Ways and Means, deputy Democratic whip of the House of Representatives, a cochair of the Democratic Congressional Campaign Committee, and dean of the New York State congressional delegation. Representative Rangel is a founding member and former chairman of the Congressional Black Caucus.

Alice Rivlin is a senior fellow in the Economic Studies program at the Brookings Institution, directs the Brookings Greater Washington Research Program, and is a professor at the Milano Graduate School of the New School University. Before her current term at Brookings, Rivlin was vice chair of the Federal Reserve Board. She was founding director of the Congressional Budget Office, director of the White House Office of Management and Budget, chair of the District of Columbia Financial Management Assistance Authority, and assistant secretary for planning and evaluation at the Department of Health, Education, and Welfare. Rivlin has written numerous books, most recently *Beyond the Dot.coms* (with Robert Litan) and *Reviving the American Dream: The Economy, the States, and the Federal Government.*

Michael Schudson is professor of communication and adjunct professor of sociology at the University of California, San Diego (UCSD). He is the author of five books and editor of two others concerning the history and sociology of the American news media, advertising, popular culture, and cultural memory. Schudson is codirector of the UCSD Civic Collaborative, linking UCSD faculty and students to the broader San Diego community through research and teaching. Schudson's works include *The Good Citizen: A History of American Civic Life.*

Mark Shields is a syndicated columnist and moderator of CNN's *The Capital Gang.* In 1987 the political analysis team of Shields and David Gergen became a regular feature of the *MacNeil/Lehrer NewsHour.* Shields was originally paired with Paul Gigot, of the *Wall Street Journal,* and currently serves with David Brooks as the analysis team regularly featured on the Friday night *NewsHour with Jim Lehrer* during primaries, national conventions, and elections. Shields has written a book about the 1984 presidential campaign, *On the Campaign Trail*, and he has taught courses on American politics and the press at Harvard University and the Wharton School of the University of Pennsylvania.

Carmen Sirianni is professor of sociology and public policy, with a joint appointment at the Heller Graduate School for Social Policy and Management and the Center for Youth and Communities at Brandeis University. He is director of the Youth Civic Engagement Project and serves on the advisory board of the Center for Information and Research for Civic Learning and Engagement at the University of Maryland, as well as on the evaluation advisory board of the Youth Leadership Development Initiative. Sirianni was research director for the Reinventing Citizenship Project, convened in conjunction with the Domestic Policy Council at the White House and the Ford Foundation in 1994. He is founder and editor in chief of the Civic Practices Network. His most recent books are *Working in the Service Society* and *Civic Innovation in America: Community Empowerment, Public Policy, and the Movement for Civic Renewal*, coauthored with Lewis Friedland.

Theda Skocpol is the Victor S. Thomas Professor of Government and Sociology and director of the Center for American Political Studies at Harvard University. Skocpol's most recent book is *Diminished Democracy: From Membership to Management in American Civic Life*. She has written several others, including *Bringing the State Back In*, coedited with Peter B. Evans and Dietrich Rueschemeyer, and *Civic Engagement in American Democracy*, coedited with Morris P. Fiorina. Skocpol participated in policy discussions with former president Bill Clinton and in 2002 was named president of the American Political Science Association.

Andrew Stern was elected president of the Service Employees International Union (SEIU), the largest union of health care workers in North America, in April 1996, succeeding John J. Sweeney, who heads the AFL-CIO. Stern began his union career in 1973 as a state social service worker and activist member of SEIU Local 668, the Pennsylvania Social Services

Union, and he rose through the ranks to become its first elected full-time president. In 1980 Stern was named to the SEIU International Executive Board and in 1984 was chosen by Sweeney to oversee SEIU's organizing and field services programs. Stern is cochair of the Council of Institutional Investors and a member of the boards of the National Coordinating Committee for Multi-Employer Plans, the AFL-CIO Housing Investment Trust, and the Aspen Institute.

Jeff Swartz is the president and chief executive officer of Timberland. Swartz developed a social enterprise department at Timberland, creating a program where all employees receive forty hours of paid leave annually to perform community service. This innovative program has served as a model for other corporations that wish to promote service initiatives. Swartz is also chair of the National Board of Trustees for City Year, and in 2002 he became one of the first members of Business Strengthening America, a White House initiative to encourage contributions to community service by the business community.

Steven Waldman is a contributing editor for the *Washington Monthly* and the founder of Beliefnet.com, a website where individuals of all religious denominations are invited to explore spiritual matters online. Waldman is a former editor at *U.S. News & World Report,* and he was a senior adviser at the Corporation for National and Community Service. He is the author of *The Bill: How Legislation Really Becomes Law: A Case Study of the National Service Bill* (1995), a study of the legislation that created AmeriCorps.

Caspar W. Weinberger served as a defense secretary during the Reagan administration. He entered the U.S. Army as a private in 1941, was commissioned, and served in the Pacific theater. At the end of the war, he was a captain on General Douglas MacArthur's intelligence staff. He served three terms in the California State Assembly, becoming chairman of the California Republican Party in 1962. In 1970 he became chairman of the Federal Trade Commission, subsequently serving as deputy director and director of the Office of Management and Budget and as secretary of health, education, and welfare. After he left the Pentagon, he became publisher and chairman of *Forbes Magazine*, where over the next decade he wrote frequently on defense and national security issues. His books include *Fighting for Peace* and *The Next War*.

David Winston is the president of the Winston Group, a polling and survey research firm. He has served as director of planning for the Speaker of the House and also as senior vice president of Fabrizio McLaughlin and Associates. In the late 1990s, Winston also served on the Web-based Education Commission, established by Congress to address the future impact of the Internet on education. He is an outside analyst for Voter News Service and was polling editor for *PollTrack* of *PoliticsNow*, the former political website of *ABC News*, the *Washington Post*, and *National Journal*.

Harris Wofford is the chairman of America's Promise—the Alliance for Youth. Formerly, he was a U.S. senator from Pennsylvania and served as chief executive officer of the Corporation for National and Community Service. Under President Eisenhower, he was counsel to the Reverend Theodore Hesburgh of Notre Dame on the first U.S. Commission on Civil Rights. In the Kennedy years, he was a special assistant to the president and chaired the subcabinet group on civil rights. While on the White House staff, Wofford helped Sargent Shriver plan and organize the Peace Corps, and he became its associate director during the Johnson administration. Wofford has been a law professor and president of both the State University of New York at Old Westbury and Bryn Mawr College.

Robert Wuthnow is the Gerhard R. Andlinger '52 Professor of Sociology and director of the Center for the Study of Religion at Princeton University. He has written and edited numerous publications, including *"I Come Away Stronger": How Small Groups Are Shaping American Religion, Acts of Compassion,* and *Faith and Philanthropy in America: Exploring the Role of Religion in America's Voluntary Sector.* His current research projects focus on religion and the arts, contemporary spiritual practices, faith-based nonprofit service organizations, social capital, and the public role of American Protestantism.

Index

₿ THE BROOKINGS INSTITUTION

The Brookings Institution is an independent organization devoted to nonpartisan research, education, and publication in economics, government, foreign policy, and the social sciences generally. Its principal purposes are to aid in the development of sound public policies and to promote public understanding of issues of national importance. The Institution was founded on December 8, 1927, to merge the activities of the Institute for Government Research, founded in 1916, the Institute of Economics, founded in 1922, and the Robert Brookings Graduate School of Economics and Government, founded in 1924. The Institution maintains a position of neutrality on issues of public policy to safeguard the intellectual freedom of the staff. Interpretations or conclusions in Brookings publications should be understood to be solely those of the authors.

Board of Trustees

James A. Johnson	David Friend	Frank H. Pearl
Chairman	Ann M. Fudge	John Edward Porter
Strobe Talbott	Jeffrey W. Greenberg	Steven Rattner
President	Brian L. Greenspun	Rozanne L. Ridgway
Elizabeth E. Bailey	Lee H. Hamilton	Judith Rodin
Zoï Baird	William A. Haseltine	Warren B. Rudman
Alan R. Batkin	Teresa Heinz	Haim Saban
James W. Cicconi	Samuel Hellman	Leonard D. Schaeffer
Arthur B. Culvahouse Jr.	Joel Z. Hyatt	Joan E. Spero
Alan M. Dachs	Shirley Ann Jackson	Lawrence H. Summers
Robert A. Day	Robert L. Johnson	John L. Thornton
Kenneth M. Duberstein	Ann Dibble Jordan	Vincent J. Trosino
Lawrence K. Fish	Michael H. Jordan	Beatrice W. Welters
Richard W. Fisher	Marie L. Knowles	Stephen M. Wolf
Cyrus F. Freidheim Jr.	Mario M. Morino	Daniel Yergin
Bart Friedman	William A. Owens	

Honorary Trustees

Leonard Abramson	Andrew Heiskell	Constance Berry Newman
Rex J. Bates	F. Warren Hellman	Maconda Brown O'Connor
Louis W. Cabot	Robert A. Helman	Samuel Pisar
A. W. Clausen	Roy M. Huffington	J. Woodward Redmond
William T. Coleman Jr.	Vernon E. Jordan Jr.	Charles W. Robinson
Lloyd N. Cutler	Breene M. Kerr	James D. Robinson III
D. Ronald Daniel	James T. Lynn	B. Francis Saul II
Bruce B. Dayton	Jessica Tuchman Mathews	Ralph S. Saul
Charles W. Duncan Jr.	David O. Maxwell	Henry B. Schacht
Walter Y. Elisha	Donald F. McHenry	Michael P. Schulhof
Robert F. Erburu	Robert S. McNamara	John C. Whitehead
Henry Louis Gates Jr.	Mary Patterson McPherson	James D. Wolfensohn
Robert D. Haas	Arjay Miller	Ezra K. Zilkha